The Classical Association has a worldwide membership and is open to all who value the study of the languages, literature, and civilizations of ancient Greece and Rome. It creates opportunities for friendly exchange and cooperation among classicists, encourages scholarship through its journals and other publications, and supports classics in schools and universities. Every year it holds an annual conference, and it sponsors branches all over the country which put on programs of lectures and other activities.

The Classical Association has about 3,500 members. The annual sub-scription is £10. Members receive The *Presidential Address* once a year and a newsletter, *CA News,* twice a year. They may also subscribe at substantially reduced cost to the Classical Association's journals *Classical Quarterly, Classical Review* and *Greece & Rome.*

Membership application forms and more information can be found on the Association's website (www.classicalassociation.org) or contact the Secretary: The Classical Association, Senate House, Malet Street, London WC1E 7HU, tel: +44 (0)20 7862 8706, e-mail: office@classicalassociation.org.

Greece & Rome

NEW SURVEYS IN THE CLASSICS No. 28

VIRGIL

BY

PHILIP HARDIE

Published for the Classical Association
1998

CAMBRIDGE UNIVERSITY PRESS
Cambridge, New York, Melbourne, Madrid, Cape Town, Singapore,
São Paulo, Delhi, Dubai, Tokyo

Cambridge University Press
The Edinburgh Building, Cambridge CB2 8RU, UK

Published in the United States of America by Cambridge University Press, New York

www.cambridge.org
Information on this title: http://www.cambridge.org/series/sSeries.asp?code=NSY

First published for the Classical Association by Oxford University Press 1998
Transferred to digital printing by Cambridge University Press 2010

A catalogue record for this publication is available from the British Library

ISBN 978-0-19-922342-8 Paperback

PREFACE

It is thirty years since the publication of the first of the *Greece &
Rome* New Surveys in the Classics, Deryck Williams' elegant and
humane overview of Virgil's poetry and of the state of Virgil studies
at that time, reissued in 1986 with Addenda on new work between
1968–1984. By 1967 some of the main lines of modern Virgil
criticism had already emerged in forms still recognizable today: the
works of Klingner, Pöschl, Otis, and Putnam remain as starting-
points. But since then the terrain has been very considerably reshaped
by the undiminishing flood of new critical studies, particularly in the
areas of poetics, allusion, narrative, and politics and ideology.[1] The
poems of Virgil have shown themselves very fertile ground for
successive waves of critical theory, as the New Critical orthodoxy
of the sixties has been overtaken by narratology, post-structuralist
approaches of various stripes, and New Historicism. But our picture
of the texts has been altered no less by a renewed campaign of minute
scholarship, attentive to the allusive detail and verbal fretwork of the
poems. Our appreciation of Virgil the scholar-poet has, paradoxically
perhaps, advanced *pari passu* with the appearance of a post-modernist
Virgil.

My aim can be described in Deryck Williams' own words, 'to try to
give in modern terms a general survey of the nature and importance of
Virgil's poetry, based on a broad and selective consideration of recent
important work of a critical kind'. The bibliography on Virgil is vast, and
I cannot pretend to have read nearly all of it: I have attempted to provide
in the notes a fairly generous selection of works that I regard as
important or thought-provoking. Neither here, nor in the main text,
have I consistently sought to conceal my own views as to what matters
when reading Virgil, in the belief that no value-free interpretation is
possible, or indeed desirable; but I have at the same time tried to give
something approaching a representative account of Virgil at the end of
the twentieth century.

---

[1] For a good essay on the movements in twentieth-century Virgil criticism see S. J. Harrison's
'Introduction' to Harrison (1990). The appearance of an English translation of Richard Heinze's
Virgils epische Technik, nearly a hundred years after its first publication, has also provided the
occasion to reflect on continuity and discontinuity in the practices of Virgilian criticism: see P. R.
Hardie, 'Virgil's epic techniques: Heinze ninety years on', *CP* 90 (1995), 267–76.

For acute comments on drafts of various parts of this survey I am indebted to Alessandro Barchiesi, Ray Clare, Monica Gale, Richard Hunter, and Llewelyn Morgan. As editor Ian McAuslan has been a model of patience and of gentle but firm guidance.

October 1997   Philip Hardie

Acknowledgement: the author and editors are grateful to David West for permission to quote from his translation of the *Aeneid* (Penguin Classics, Harmondsworth, 1990).

CONTENTS

I Introduction   1
   Historical and Biographical Contexts. Reception   1

II The *Eclogues*   5
   The Limits of Pastoral. Virgil and Theocritus   5
   The Latin Poetic Tradition. Lucretius, Philosophy, and
      Love. The Neoterics and Catullus   10
   Poetry on Poetry   13
   History and Politics   18
   Structure and Unity. Composition and Chronology   22
   The Pastoral Experience   25

III The *Georgics*   28
   The Teacher and his Pupils. The Didactic Tradition   28
   The Romans and the Natural World. Farming.
      Ethnography and Cosmology   33
   History and Politics. Anthropomorphism. The Bees.
      Cultural Histories   35
   Poetics and Allusion. Etymology and Allusive Play. Genre
      (Pastoral and Epic)   39
   Myth. The Aristaeus Epyllion   44
   Structure. 'Digressions'   48
   Interpretation and Meaning. Philosophy and Religion.
      Sacrifice. Allusive Pluralism. A World of Art?   50

IV The *Aeneid*   53
   Epic Genealogies. The Homeric Models   53
   Roman Alexandrianism. Generic Polyphony   57
   Past to Present. History and Antiquarianism. Aetiology,
      Genealogy, Etymology. Cities and Sons. Cultural
      Histories   63
   Plot and Narrative. Points of View. Ecphrasis   71
   Character. Defining the Hero. The Godlike (Herculean)
      Hero. Epic Women   80
   Structure   86
   Imagery, Allegory, Symbolism   90

Meaning. Two (and More) Voices. Sources of Authority:
    Gods and Fate, Rhetoric and Philosophy   94

V Style, Language, Metre   102

Bibliographical Note   115

Select Bibliography   117

About the Author   123

Index   124

Index of Chief Passages Discussed   126

I. INTRODUCTION

Historical and Biographical Contexts. Reception.

In hindsight the three major works of Virgil appear to trace out a predetermined poetic career, beginning with the humble fictional world of the shepherds of the *Eclogues*, passing through the practical concerns of the *Georgics*, aimed at countryfolk living in the real contemporary world, and culminating in the epic *Aeneid*, addressing the widest concerns of Roman history and politics.[1] At the same time all three works, which between them range from the bottom to the top of the hierarchy of genres, constitute a strongly unified *œuvre*; more perhaps than most poets, Virgil alludes to his own earlier works in his later poems.[2] In all three there is a strong sense of being located at a critical point in history, and (particularly in the *Eclogues* and *Aeneid*) an equally strong sense of the exposed position of the individual subject within the historical process.

According to the ancient Lives Virgil himself was very much caught up in the great historical events of his time, which he experienced both from the side of the losers, when (so it is said) his father's farm was confiscated in the land-confiscations after the Battle of Philippi in 42 B.C., and from the side of the winners, when his poetic talent brought him the patronage of Octavian/Augustus and Maecenas.[3] The story that Virgil recited the *Georgics* to Octavian at Atella during his return to Rome in 29 B.C. after the Battle of Actium (*Vita Donati* 27)

[1] On Virgil's construction and enactment of a poetic teleology within his three major works see C. Hardie, *The Georgics: A Transitional Poem* (Abingdon, 1971); R. F. Thomas, 'From *recusatio* to commitment: the evolution of the Virgilian programme', *PLLS* 5 (1986), 61–73; E. Theodorakopoulos in Martindale (1997), 155–65. The sense of an overarching unity in the Virgilian *œuvre* finds schematic expression in the medieval *Rota Virgilii*, a diagram showing the hierarchical sequence in the three works of style (plain, middle, grand) and subject-matter (pastoral, agricultural, martial): see Wilkinson (1969), 274; E. R. Curtius, *European Literature and the Latin Middle Ages*, tr. W. R. Trask (London, Henley, and New York, 1953), 201 n. 35, 232. For the influence of the Virgilian sequence on the careers of later poets (e.g. Spenser and Milton) see L. Lipking, *The Life of the Poet: Beginning and Ending Poetic Careers* (Chicago and London, 1981), p. xi.

[2] F. Klingner, 'Die Einheit des virgilischen Lebenswerkes', *MDAI(R)* 45 (1930), 43–58 [= *Römische Geisteswelt* (Munich, 1961⁴), 274–92]; Theodorakopoulos (n. 1).

[3] Wilkinson (1969), ch. 2 is still an excellent account of the facts and traditions about the life and times of Virgil; for a detailed up-to-date survey of the subject see Horsfall (1995), ch. 1. A translation of Donatus' *Life of Virgil* is conveniently accessible in Camps (1969), Appendix 1.

gives a sense of his closeness to the centre of worldshaking events in the making. Although almost none of Virgil's poetry is in the first person, it is not surprising that Virgilian scholarship and criticism has from the first been marked by a strong biographical interest. This makes for good novels (Hermann Broch's *The Death of Virgil* is a landmark in the history of the modern novel),[4] but bad criticism. Despite the demise of the kind of biographical criticism that used literary texts as sources for reconstructing the life of the poet, this biographical interest survives in the form of the obsession, still burning for some critics, to determine Virgil's personal attitude towards Augustus. This concern is implicit in much of the debate between the so-called 'Harvard' (anti-Augustan) and 'European' (pro-Augustan) schools of critics (see p. 94 below).

More sophisticated approaches look to the institutional, social, and cultural contexts for Virgil's works. Patronage is central to the production of Augustan poetry: Peter White's discussion tends to suggest that poets like Virgil did not write to order in the way that propaganda is directed by modern centralized totalitarian states, the model implied in Ronald Syme's chapter on 'The organization of opinion' in the *Roman Revolution* (a classic that may still be recommended as background reading for students of Virgil).[5] The notion of propaganda itself, the applicability of the term to the output of the Augustan poets, and the adequacy of a simple distinction between 'Augustan' and 'anti-Augustan', have also been subjected to useful reexamination in recent years.[6] It is now possible to see Virgil's poems not as comments, whether of support or protest, from the sidelines of Roman history, but as themselves an important element in the various discourses and cultural practices that were central to the making of Augustan Rome. Augustus effected a cultural, no less than a political, revolution; or it would be truer to say that the political revolution was simultaneously a cultural revolution.[7] Virgil draws attention to the inseparability of the political and the cultural at those points in his works, such as the proem of *Georgics* 3 or the Speech of Anchises in *Aeneid* 6, where he constructs an

---

[4] On which see F. Cox, in Martindale (1997), 327–36.

[5] White (1993); Syme (1939).

[6] D. Kennedy, rev. Woodman and West (1984), in *LCM* 9.10 (1984), 157–60; id., '"Augustan" and "anti-Augustan": reflections on terms of reference', in A. Powell (ed.), *Roman Poetry and Propaganda in the Age of Augustus* (London, 1992), 26–58; A. Wallace-Hadrill, 'Time for Augustus: Ovid, Augustus and the *Fasti*', in Whitby, Hardie, and Whitby (1987), 221–30.

[7] To use the title of the important collection of essays edited by T. Habinek and A. Schiesaro, *The Roman Cultural Revolution* (Cambridge, 1997); the phrase had already been used by A. Wallace-Hadrill in his review of Zanker (1988), in *JRS* 79 (1989), 157–64.

analogy between the achievements of Rome's military and political heroes and those of the poet (see pp. 40-1, 53–4 below).

A landmark for our awareness of the importance of the visual arts in the image-making of the Augustan period was Paul Zanker's *The Power of Images in the Age of Augustus* (Ann Arbor, 1988), a book which has little to say directly on the literary texts, but which suggests many parallels with the themes and imagery of Virgil's poems. The many ecphrases in the *Aeneid* (see pp. 75–7 below) reveal Virgil's interest in the communicative power of visual images; monumental complexes of architecture and sculpture like the Palatine Temple of Apollo, the Ara Pacis, the Sundial of Augustus, and the Forum of Augustus engage in a message-bearing activity comparable to that of Augustan poetry.[8] Very recently Karl Galinsky has produced an important synoptic study of the history, literature, and art of the Augustan period (*Augustan Culture. An Interpretive Introduction* [Princeton, 1996]).

One measure of Virgil's success in grasping his historical moment and in producing poems that both express and give form to the critical political and cultural revolution of the late Republican and early Augustan period is the classic status that his works immediately achieved, and which has survived, more or less unassailed, down to the present day (what the future may hold is another matter). European pastoral and epic, two of the central genres in the Western tradition, define themselves primarily with reference to the *Eclogues* and the *Aeneid*. The many revivals over the last two thousand years of an Augustan imperial ideal have usually been accompanied by a renewed exploitation of the Virgilian texts. Nor are twentieth-century liberals the first to respond to the more private and melancholy interiority of Virgil's poetry; one need look no further than the immense popularity of Virgil's telling of the Orpheus story in *Georgics* 4. An attention to the psychological and spiritual aspects of Virgil's poems was also boosted by the widespread belief that he was an *anima naturaliter Christiana,* or even that the fourth *Eclogue* was a prophecy of the birth of Christ (see p. 21 below).

In recent years the study of the influence or *Nachleben* of Virgil has been given fresh vigour by the introduction of new approaches to

---

[8] Recently some scholars have applied to the visual monuments interpretative techniques traditionally at home in literary studies, looking for polysemy and ambiguity: see the (methodologically very different) approaches of G. K. Galinsky, 'Venus, polysemy, and the Ara Pacis Augustae', *AJA* 96 (1992), 457–75, and J. Elsner, 'Cult and sculpture: sacrifice in the Ara Pacis Augustae', *JRS* 81 (1991), 50–61. Hardie (1986) also looks for analogies between visual and textual iconographies (e.g. 120–43, 366–9, 379).

allusion and intertextuality and to the reception of texts. These have had the twofold effect of transforming our understanding of how later poets make use of earlier poets, and of undermining our previous confidence that new readings of ancient texts supersede older readings. Can we say with certainty that Milton's reading of Virgil, accessible to us through his own creative imitation of Virgil, is inferior or out of date compared to that of a Pöschl or Putnam? The reception of Virgil is a vast topic, and my note gives only a few titles that may introduce the interested reader to the field.[9]

[9] In general see C. A. Martindale (ed.), *Virgil and his Influence* (Bristol, 1984); the new *Cambridge Companion to Virgil* (Martindale [1997]) contains a number of essays on the reception of Virgil. Still unreplaced for the earlier period is Comparetti (1895); on the reception of the *Aeneid* by first-century A.D. Latin epic poets see Hardie (1993); on the later middle ages see C. Baswell, *Virgil in Medieval England. Figuring the Aeneid from the Twelfth Century to Chaucer* (Cambridge, 1995). For the Renaissance: C. Kallendorf, *In Praise of Aeneas. Virgil and Epideictic Rhetoric in the Early Italian Renaissance* (Hanover and London, 1989); id., *Virgil and the Myth of Venice: The Materiality and Ideology of Reading* (Oxford, 1999); C. Martindale, *John Milton and the Transformation of the Ancient Epic* (London and Sydney, 1986), ch. 3, 'Virgil'. For the modern period: T. Ziolkowski, *Virgil and the Moderns* (Princeton, 1993).

II. THE *ECLOGUES*[1]

The Limits of Pastoral. Virgil and Theocritus.

Pastoral as a kind of poetry is a paradoxical combination of apparent
naïveté and sophistication; William Empson refers to 'the pastoral
process of putting the complex into the simple'.[2] The pastoral landscape
in its more ideal moments is the stage for simple country folk who lead
an easy and uncomplicated life. But landscape and shepherds appear in
poems written by sophisticated poets, whose self-consciousness weighs
heavily on the figures who speak in their poems. The picture of an idyllic
world often conjured up by the words 'pastoral' or 'bucolic' is a
trivializing and selective simplification of the full reading experience
offered by the *Eclogues*. That simple image is presented to the reader in
the first five lines of *Eclogue* 1 in Meliboeus' description of his friend
Tityrus' happy situation: Tityrus reclines at ease in the shadow of a tree,
composing 'woodland music' on his rustic pipe and teaching the
sympathetic woods to echo the name of his girlfriend Amaryllis. But
this description frames Meliboeus' statement of his own plight: in
contrast to his settled friend he is in motion, away from the boundaries
of the idyllic Never Never Land, which in line 3 is already redefined with
the very Roman word *patria*. *Eclogue* 1 quickly bursts the limits of a
simple and timeless bucolicism to encompass the historical and social
realities of the city of Rome, in the course of a brief exchange of
experiences past and anticipated in which the humble herdsman Tityrus
meets a man-god, and the smallholder Meliboeus foresees an exile as far
distant as Britain (1.66), the limit of Julius Caesar's imperialist adventur-
ing a decade and a half before the time of composition. The first *Eclogue*
is typical of the collection as a whole in this testing of limits and in the
recurrent thwarting of the desire for fulfilment in an enclosed *locus
amoenus* or 'green cabinet'.[3] Much of the energy and interest of the

---

[1] *Bucolica* is the older title of the collection; *ecloga* 'chosen piece' denotes an individual poem
regarded as an independent piece. On the title see N. M. Horsfall, *BICS* 28 (1981), 108–9;
M. Geymonat, *BICS* 29 (1982), 17–18.

[2] W. Empson, *Some Versions of Pastoral* (Harmondsworth, 1966 [1935]), 25.

[3] Michael Putnam uses the phrase 'poetics of enclosure': 'Virgil's first *Eclogue*: poetics of
enclosure', in Boyle (1975), 81–104. On *Eclogue* 1 see also C. P. Segal, '*Tamen cantabitis, Arcades*:
exile and Arcadia in *Eclogues* 1 and 9', in Segal (1981), 271–300; B. F. Dick, 'Vergil's pastoral
poetic: a reading of the first *Eclogue*', *AJP* 91 (1970), 277–93; DuQuesnay (1981); Wright (1983).

Eclogues derives from the constant tension between the limiting case of a static pastoral 'idyll' and the forces that threaten to destabilize the idyll.

In literary terms a Roman poet defines the boundaries of his work with reference to the first or major exponent of the *genre* within which he writes, in the case of bucolic poetry the Hellenistic poet Theocritus, a native of Syracuse. Virgil explicitly signposts his model in the first line of each of the two poems in the middle of the book, 4 and 6, that most overtly challenge the limits of the *genre* (4.1 <u>Sicelides</u> *Musae* 'Sicilian Muses'; 6.1–2 *prima <u>Syracosio</u> dignata est ludere uersu | nostra . . . Thalea* 'my Muse first saw fit to sport in Syracusan verse'). More subtly the first lines of *Eclogue* 1 both echo the sound patterns of the opening words of the poem that stands first in our, and probably Virgil's, edition of Theocritus and also place Tityrus in the posture of the legendary singer Comatas addressed longingly in an untypically wistful passage of Theocritus (*Idyll* 7.88–9).[4] But to define the *Eclogues* in terms of the Greek model Theocritus is to push the question of definition a stage further back. The Theocritean corpus contains a wide variety of hexameter poems, by no means all of them about herdsmen, and there is an ongoing debate as to the definition of Theocritean 'bucolic'.[5]

Some of the certainly non-Theocritean poems in the corpus, notably 8 and 9, suggest that Theocritus' successors did narrow the range of his subject-matter to the sentimental encounters of sweet-natured herdsmen which we still tend to think of as typically 'pastoral'.[6] [Theocritus] 8 and 9 are among the models used by Virgil, whose verbal imitations of Theocritus otherwise concentrate on Theocritus 1, 3, 4, 5, 7, and 11 and the framing sections of 6,[7] that is, those poems which use what became the standard bucolic repertory of rustic banter, song-contests between

---

[4] See Coleman on *Ecl.* 1.1; Wright (1983), 108. On the question of editions of Theocritus in Virgil's day see DuQuesnay (1979), 38; J. W. Vaughn, 'Theocritus Vergilianus and Liber Bucolicon', *Aevum* 55 (1981), 47–68; K. Gutzwiller, 'The evidence for Theocritean poetry books', in M. A. Harder, R. F. Regtuit, and G. C. Wakker (eds.), *Theocritus* (Hellenistica Groningana 2) (Groningen, 1996), 119–48.

[5] See esp. D. Halperin, *Before Pastoral: Theocritus and the Ancient Tradition of Bucolic Poetry* (New Haven and London, 1983). Important works on the definition of pastoral poetry ancient and modern include Rosenmeyer (1969); R. Poggioli, 'The oaten flute', *Harvard Library Bulletin* 11 (1957), 147–84; L. Marx, *The Machine in the Garden: Technology and the Pastoral Ideal in America* (Oxford, 1964); P. J. Alpers, *What is Pastoral?* (Chicago, 1996).

[6] On the post-Theocritean development of bucolic see L. E. Rossi, 'Mondo pastorale e poesia bucolica di maniera: l'idillio ottavo del *corpus* teocriteo', *SIFC* 43 (1971), 5–25; J. van Sickle, 'Theocritus and the development of the conception of bucolic genre', *Ramus* 5 (1976), 18–44.

[7] DuQuesnay (1979), 38. On Virgil's imitation of Theocritus in general see S. Posch, *Beobachtungen zur Theokritnachwirkung bei Vergil* (Innsbruck and Munich, 1969); R. W. Garson, 'Theocritean elements in Virgil's *Eclogues*', *CQ* 21 (1971), 188–203. Detailed studies of Virgil's imitation of Theocritus in individual *Eclogues*: DuQuesnay (1977), 52–68 (*Ecl.* 4); id. (1976/77), 18–29 (*Ecl.* 5); id. (1979), 37–43 (*Ecl.* 2); id. (1981), 36–53 (*Ecl.* 1).

herdsmen, serenades to a reluctant beloved, wagers of precious art-
objects, and the gift or exchange of musical instruments or staffs in
recognition of musical excellence. The names of the fictional characters
in the *Eclogues* largely overlap with those of Theocritean herdsmen.[8]

Two Theocritean poems are of especial importance for Virgil, both
of them crucial for Theocritus' definition of his own bucolic world but
both also operating partly outside the limits of that world as under-
stood in a narrow sense, *Idyll* 1 containing Thrysis' song about the
dying Daphnis, the pastoral 'hero', mortal but privileged to visits from
the gods, and *Idyll* 7 in which Simichidas, in whom it is tempting to
see a mask for Theocritus, tells of a journey with friends from town to
a harvest festival in the country, in the course of which he meets and
has an exchange of songs with the mysterious goatherd Lycidas. Both
Idylls are substantial models for more than one *Eclogue*: the first lines
of *Idyll* 1 are echoed in the first lines of *Eclogue* 1; the elaborate
ecphrasis (description) of the cup offered by the goatherd to Thyrsis
in exchange for his song (*Id.* 1.27–61) is the model for the description
of the cups wagered in the song contest of *Eclogue* 3 (35–47), while
the death of Daphnis is the major model for the poems that end each
half of the *Eclogues* book, *Eclogue* 5 with the songs of Mopsus and
Menalcas on, respectively, the death and deification of Daphnis, and
Eclogue 10 in which Virgil's friend the poet Gallus plays the part of
Daphnis, figuratively dying of love in a version of the pastoral
landscape. But while the content of the two songs in *Eclogue* 5 is
drawn from *Idyll* 1, it is *Idyll* 7 that provides the model for the overall
shape of *Eclogue* 5, a courteous exchange of songs in which the junior
singer (Simichidas in *Idyll* 7, Mopsus in *Eclogue* 5) nevertheless fails to
conceal his ambition;[9] Mopsus' final gift of a crook to Menalcas recalls
Lycidas' presentation of his staff to Simichidas as a 'guest-friendship
gift of the Muses' at *Idyll* 7.128–9. The lush description of the *locus
amoenus* at the harvest festival at the end of *Idyll* 7 (131–47) has
already been a model for Meliboeus' wistfully idealizing description of
the landscape in which Tityrus is privileged to remain at *Ecl.* 1.51–8,
but the most sustained imitation of *Idyll* 7 is reserved for *Eclogue* 9, the
pendant to *Eclogue* 1, in which the Theocritean model of a journey
into the country that is also a journey of initiation into bucolic song is
inverted as two countrymen (one of whom is named Lycidas) pass the

---

[8] Names: A. Perutelli in Horsfall (1995), 42–3.
[9] On the personal dynamics of *Ecl.* 5 see G. Lee, 'A reading of Virgil's fifth *Eclogue*', *PCPS* 23 (1977), 62–70.

time as they walk reluctantly from the country to the city by
exchanging fragments of half-remembered songs.

From these examples it will be clear that Virgil's imitation of
Theocritus is complex, detailed, pointed, and playful. A single *Eclogue*
may combine imitation of two or more Theocritean *Idylls*;[10] alternatively
imitation of a single *Idyll* may be distributed over two or more *Eclogues*.
A Theocritean pattern or theme may be reworked in inverted form
(*oppositio in imitando*): for example at *Ecl.* 10.21–3 Apollo tells Gallus
that the girl he pines for, Lycoris, has followed another man into the
anti-pastoral landscape of a military campaign in the frozen north,
where in the Theocritean model (*Id.* 1.81–5) Priapus tells Daphnis
that the girl whom he shuns is searching for him through the pastoral
springs and glades. In this example imitation extends to the sounds of
the Greek model: the line-ending *tua cura, Lycoris* 'the object of your
erotic care, Lycoris' (*Ecl.* 10.22) echoes the line-ending at *Id.* 1.82 ἁ δέ
τε κώρα 'the girl'.[11] This kind of elaborate and self-conscious allusion is a
hallmark of the Alexandrian poets and their Latin imitators, and is a
constant in all of Virgil's three major works.[12]

By focusing on Virgil's imitation of Theocritean poems about herds-
men I have colluded with Virgil's overall tendency to conform to the
post-Theocritean narrower definition of bucolic poetry. But other
Eclogues are open to the wider range of Theocritean subject-matter.
Eclogue 4 is the least pastoral of the *Eclogues*, but it has an important
Theocritean model in *Idyll* 17, a hexameter encomium of Ptolemy II.[13]
Eclogue 4 opens with an explicit discussion of its place within a pastoral
book that may retroactively prompt the reader to think about the place
of *Idyll* 17 in Theocritus' bucolic book: how important is it that at 9–10
Theocritus prefaces his hesitation about where to start in his praises of
the king with the rustic image of a *woodcutter* embarrassed for choice in
the forests of Ida? The use, as model for the funerary rituals of Daphnis
at *Ecl.* 5.40–4, of the cult institutions for the divinized Helen prescribed
in *Idyll* 18, the Epithalamium for Helen, allusively anticipates Virgil's
reversal through deification of the Theocritean death of Daphnis; while
the Virgilian context alerts the reader to the possibility that the 'pastoral

[10] As in the combination of *Idylls* 3 and 11 as models for *Eclogue* 2: DuQuesnay (1979), 43–63.
[11] Ross (1975), 69.
[12] For a good survey of work on Virgilian allusion and intertextuality see Farrell (1991), 4–25;
see also Farrell in Martindale (1997), 222–38. Important recent theoretical studies of allusion in
Latin poetry: Conte (1986); S. Hinds, *Allusion and Intertext: Dynamics of Appropriation in Roman
Poetry* (Cambridge, 1998).
[13] DuQuesnay (1977), 52–68, analysing the components of the βασιλικόν; see also DuQuesnay
(1981), 41–2 on the parallels between *Id.* 14, an urban mime, and *Ecl.* 1.

analogy' at *Id.* 18.28–31 (one of the Theocritean models for *Ecl.* 5.32–4 *uitis ut arboribus decori est, ut uitibus uuae,* | *ut gregibus tauri, segetes ut pinguibus aruis,* | *tu decus omne tuis* 'as the vine adorns the trees, as the grapes the vine, as bulls the herds, as crops the rich fields, so you are the sole ornament of your people') serves to draw that non-pastoral poem into a tighter unity with the pastoral poems in the Theocritean collection.[14] The song of Alphesiboeus in *Eclogue* 8 is modelled on the song of Simaetha in one of Theocritus' urban idylls, *Idyll* 2, but the preparation of the love-magic is pointedly transferred to a countryside setting.[15] For all that pastoral poetry is often viewed as the expression of the city-dweller's nostalgic longing for an idyllic life in the countryside, there is in fact a marked family resemblance between Theocritus' dramatizations of the loves and musical activities of simple folk in both town and country, a resemblance that in literary terms reflects Theocritus' dependence on the mime. Virgil, who was to show his dramatic powers again in the construction of tragic episodes within the *Aeneid*, is fully alive to the dramatic qualities of pastoral poetry; the *Life of Donatus* (26) records that the *Eclogues* were indeed performed on stage.[16] The close affiliation between the Theocritean idyll and the Hellenistic mime is paralleled in Virgil's use of Roman comedy in the *Eclogues*.[17] There may be a certain paradox in the fact that pastoral is both an idealizing and a realistic genre.[18]

A Roman poet's claim to follow in the footsteps of the Greek inventor of a genre does not imply that that is his only model. The loss of much Hellenistic poetry and of much post-Theocritean pastoral poetry hinders a precise assessment of Virgil's use of the whole range of the Greek pastoral tradition. The opening lines of the first *Eclogue*, a seemingly innocent passage, but one which we have already seen to

[14] On the echoes of *Id.* 18 in *Ecl.* 5 see DuQuesnay (1976/77), 20.

[15] C. P. Segal, 'Alphesiboeus' song and Simaetha's magic: Virgil's eighth *Eclogue* and Theocritus's second *Idyll*', *GB* 14 (1987), 167–85. On *Eclogue* 8 see also A. Richter, *Virgile. La huitième bucolique* (Paris, 1970).

[16] See G. Highet, 'Performances of Vergil's *Bucolics*', *Vergilius* 20 (1974), 24–5; Horsfall (1995), 17; Coleiro (1979), 66–70. On the dramatic quality of the *Eclogues* see P. Steinmetz, 'Eclogen Vergils als dramatische Dichtungen', *A&A* 14 (1968), 115–25.

[17] Most prominently in the first words of *Ecl.* 3, *dic mihi, Damoeta, cuium pecus?*: see Clausen ad loc.; H. MacL. Currie, 'The third *Eclogue* and the Roman comic spirit', *Mnemos.* 29 (1976), 411–20. J. Wills, 'Virgil's *cuium*', *Vergilius* 39 (1993), 3–11 points out that *cuium* is also an attempt to catch the flavour of Theocritus' dialectal ψε (*Id.* 4.3); the use of dialects is a rich poetic resource for Theocritus, but one not available to a Latin poet; Virgil makes do with a liberal use of colloquialisms.

[18] On Theocritean realism see G. Zanker, *Realism in Alexandrian Poetry: A Literature and its Audience* (London, etc., 1987), index s.v. 'Theocritus'; on Virgilian realism see J. Hubaux, *Le Réalisme dans les Bucoliques de Virgile* (Liège and Paris, 1927).

contain programmatic allusion to Theocritus, offer other clues. The
pastoral singer reclining under the shade of a tree and the echoing of the
name 'Amaryllis' may both allude to a lost work of Philitas, an
important Hellenistic poet of the generation before Theocritus and
whose poetry may have been a significant ingredient in the compound
that we know as Theocritean bucolic.[19] Theocritus' first *Idyll* on the
death of Daphnis is the model for a line of pastoral laments of which
Milton's *Lycidas* is the most familiar specimen to an English readership;
Eclogue 5 and 10 contain echoes of Bion's *Lament for Adonis* and the
anonymous *Lament for Bion*.[20] This last work is one of the Greek
precedents for the introduction of real-life characters into the pastoral
world, which was to become so striking a feature of Virgilian and post-
Virgilian pastoral.

The Latin Poetic Tradition.
Lucretius, Philosophy, and Love. The Neoterics
and Catullus.

Virgil is the first Roman pastoral poet, but the world of the *Eclogues* is
constructed out of a Roman, as well as a Greek, poetic tradition. In this
his first major work Virgil is very conscious of his roots in the so-called
neoteric school of poets like Catullus, Calvus, and Cinna.[21] The choice
of Theocritus as a model in itself marks the young Virgil as an
'Alexandrian' poet. Praise of the Latin poems of Pollio and Varius
and Cinna is jarringly placed in the mouths of pastoral characters at *Ecl.*
3.84–9 and 9.35–6. Pollio, politician, poet, and patron of the young
Virgil, had been an intimate of the new poets of the 50s B.C., of whom
Cinna was one of the leaders, while Varius was Virgil's contemporary
and a future editor of the *Aeneid*. For Virgil, however, the most
important poet of the generation immediately after the neoterics of the
50s was Gallus, whom I discuss in the next section.

Another poet of the 50s B.C. whose influence on all of Virgil's works
it is difficult to overestimate is Lucretius.[22] The phrase *siluestris Musa*

---

[19] See E. L. Bowie, 'Theocritus' seventh Idyll, Philetas and Longus', *CQ* 35 (1985), 67–91, at
80–3.
[20] DuQuesnay (1976/77), 23–9; Schmidt (1972), 69–92 'Die hellenistische Bukolik (Bionepi-
taph)'. See also M. Paschalis, 'Virgil's sixth *Eclogue* and the *Lament for Bion*', *AJP* 116 (1995), 617–
21.
[21] Virgil and the neoterics: Otis (1964), 99–105; Farrell (1991), 278–314.
[22] *Eclogues* and Lucretius: G. Castelli, 'Echi lucreziani nelle *Ecloghe* virgiliane', *RSC* 14 (1966),
313–42; (1967), 14–39, 176–216; G. K. Galinsky, 'Vergil's second *Eclogue*: its theme and relation

used virtually as a definition of pastoral poetry at *Ecl.* 1.2 (*siluestrem tenui Musam meditaris auena* 'you practise the woodland Muse on your slender oaten straw') is Lucretian (*De rerum natura* 4.589), as too is the variant *agrestis Musa* 'rustic Muse' (*De rerum natura* 5.1398) in the programmatic 'second proem' at *Ecl.* 6.8. Lucretius uses images of pastoral and rustic life in a number of contexts which Virgil exploits to lend depth to the Theocritean tradition. At *De rerum natura* 4.589 the 'woodland muse' denotes the music ascribed to the piping Pan by credulous rustics, gulled into believing in the existence of supernatural musicians by the phenomenon of echo, which Lucretius demythologizes with a materialistic scientific explanation. In the *Eclogues* Virgil strives to reenchant the landscape, where echo is the sign of nature's sympathy with man[23] and where supernatural and legendary singers, a Silenus, an Orpheus, a Hesiod, have magical powers; at the same time the reader is made aware that the magic of pastoral song may be such stuff as dreams are made on. If the personified woods reecho to Tityrus singing of Amaryllis in *Ecl.* 1.4–5, Corydon's love-song in the next poem is a futile outpouring to the unresponsive mountains and woods (*Ecl.* 2.4–5).

The *agrestis Musa* of *De rerum natura* 5.1398 occurs in the course of a history of civilization, as Lucretius describes the simple pleasures and pastoral music-making of an earlier age before the corruptions of advanced city-life; this passage has a parallel in the prologue to *De rerum natura* 2 which contrasts the discontents of the life of luxury and military pomp with the simple contentment of countryfolk, 'lying on the soft grass by a stream of water under the branches of a tall tree' (2.29–30). In Virgil the timeless pastoral world is intermittently situated within the largest processes of time, history, and the development of civilization, most notably in the central triad of *Eclogue* 4–6, in which the interplay of pastoral miniaturism and cosmic grandeur is also worked out in spatial terms.[24] The moralizing town/country contrast as used by Lucretius is reflected in Virgil's occasional use of his pastoral landscape as a moralized image of the life to be preferred to the anxieties and disturbances that emanate from the city. To the forces leading to

to the *Eclogue* book', *C&M* 26 (1965), 161–91, at 165–8; van Sickle (1978), 88–9; S. M. Mizera, 'Lucretian elements in Menalcas' song, *Eclogue* 5', *Hermes* 110 (1982), 367–71.

[23] Echo: Desport (1952), 63–91; A. J. Boyle, 'Virgil's pastoral echo', *Ramus* 6 (1977), 121–31.
[24] Note especially the Lucretian language in the descriptions of the universe at *Ecl.* 4.51–2; 5.56–7; 6.31–40. Cosmic themes are already adumbrated in *Ecl.* 3.40–2, 104–5; on the 'interplay of opposites' in *Ecl.* 3 see C. P. Segal, 'Vergil's *caelatum opus*: an interpretation of the third *Eclogue*', in Segal (1981), 235–64.

deterioration in the human and natural worlds Virgil opposes the figure of a divine man: the young man hailed as a god by Tityrus in *Eclogue* 1 for preserving his country life-style, the mysterious child of *Eclogue* 4, and the deified Daphnis of *Eclogue* 5.[25] This saviour-figure, endowed with the power that Theocritus' pastoral hero Daphnis tragically lacks, has a Lucretian model in the 'divine man' Epicurus, whose praises are sung in the prologues of the *De rerum natura*.[26] The craving for a saviour-figure will be strongly felt in the *Georgics* and *Aeneid*.[27]

In the moralizing use of the country/city opposition the 'neoteric' *Eclogues* anticipate a central theme of Augustan poetry. Lucretian allusion raises the question of whether the moralizing has a specifically philosophical, Epicurean, underpinning.[28] There is no real reason to doubt the biographical tradition that in his youth Virgil was an Epicurean, the pupil of Siro. Furthermore there is a seductive analogy between the idealized pastoral life, lived in seclusion from the city in a state of relaxed leisure (*otium*: *Ecl.* 1.6; 5.61), where the social bonds are those of friendship between a small circle of herdsmen, and the Epicurean advocacy of the cultivation of friendship inside the 'Garden', abstention from political life, and the maximization of pleasure through the attainment of a state of calm contentment (*ataraxia*).[29] Like all of Virgil's works the *Eclogues* are touched by the ideas of Hellenistic philosophy, and even occasionally by technical philosophical language,[30] but it would be wrong to see the world of the *Eclogues* as a blueprint for an achieved state of Epicurean calm. For Lucretius one of the major threats to happiness is the insatiability of sexual desire; the destructiveness of love is a major theme in the *Eclogues*, as also in the *Georgics* and *Aeneid*. Corydon asks (*Ecl.* 2.68) *quis enim modus adsit amori?* ('for what limit can there be to love?') and the question is asked again of Gallus by Pan at *Ecl.* 10.28. Some critics[31] attempt to establish a

[25] On the 'pastoral hero' in the *Eclogues* see Berg (1974), tracing the way in which the 'pastoral hero' turns into the 'Roman hero', and is also paralleled in the figure of the *diuinus poeta* (*Ecl.* 5.45; 10.17; cf. 6.67 *Linus . . . diuino carmine pastor*).

[26] Cf. esp. *De rerum natura* 5.8 *deus ille fuit, deus, inclute Memmi* with *Ecl.* 5.64 *deus, deus ille, Menalca!* (and cf. *Ecl.* 1.6–7).

[27] The 'Heilsproblematik' is central to F. Klingner's interpretation of Virgil: see his 'Virgils erste Ekloge', *Hermes* 62 (1927), 129–53.

[28] Virgil and Epicureanism: N. de Witt, 'Vergil and Epicureanism', *CW* 25 (1932), 89–96; Wilkinson (1969), 20–4; Coleiro (1979), 37–9.

[29] The analogy is developed at length in Rosenmeyer (1969).

[30] E.g. *Ecl.* 2.27 *si numquam fallit imago*, alluding to the Epicurean doctrine of the infallibility of the senses: see A. Traina, '*Si numquam fallit imago*. Riflessioni sulle Bucoliche e l'epicureismo', *A&R* 10 (1965), 72–8.

[31] Notably Putnam (1970), e.g. 345. L. Alfonsi, 'Dalla II alla X ecloga', *Aevum* 35 (1961), 193–8

boundary between a pastoral kind of fulfilled and contented love, and a non-pastoral, disruptive kind, but the latter seems just as much at home in the pastoral landscape, as in Corydon's song in *Eclogue* 2, or in that of the unnamed lover impersonated in Damon's song in *Eclogue* 8, or in Pasiphae's hopeless wandering in the countryside in search of her beloved bull at *Ecl.* 6.45–60. There is no pastoral immunity to the kind of tortured erotic longings found in the poetry of the neoterics. Catullus' poignant juxtapositions of thoughts of erstwhile or fantasized erotic happiness with the harsh reality of the beloved's unfaithfulness or unconcern made as much impression on Virgil as did Lucretius' disdainful tirades against the folly of love. The love-crossed Corydon's self-rebuke at the end of *Ecl.* 2 is modelled immediately on the corresponding moment in the song of Polyphemus at Theocritus 11.72–9, but one may also compare Catullus' self-admonition in poem 8, and the short diatribe against *otium* at Cat. 51.13–16: the pastoral *otium* praised by Tityrus at *Ecl.* 1.6 turns out to be the precondition for Corydon's infatuation as it had been for Catullus' (if the *otium* stanza is an integral part of poem 51).[32]

Poetry on Poetry

The impulse to establish a clear demarcation between pastoral and non-pastoral kinds of love is encouraged by the appearance in *Eclogues* 6 and 10 of Virgil's friend Gallus, the first in the line of Roman love elegists. In *Eclogue* 10 Gallus plays the role of the dying Daphnis in Theocritus 1, with the consequence that Gallus' poetry becomes the theme of the poem; when a Roman poet writes about another poet it is that other poet's writing, not his real life, that is usually the true subject. *Eclogue* 10 is the fitting conclusion to a book that many modern critics read as a collection of poems about poetry.[33] The late antique commentator Servius notes on *Ecl.* 10.46 that 'these lines are all taken from Gallus'; it is clear that *Eclogue* 10 is largely made up of a patchwork of allusions to Gallus' own verse, and the publication in 1979 of a new nine-line

argues that *Ecl.* 2 takes an Epicurean perspective on destructive love. In general on love in the *Eclogues* see C. Fantazzi, 'Virgilian pastoral and Roman love poetry', *AJP* 87 (1966), 171–91.

[32] On the extensive reworking of Catullus 64 in *Ecl.* 4 see below.

[33] 'Dichtung der Dichtung' in the phrase of Schmidt (1972), 107. The poems of the second half of the book are more explicitly about poetry, but Wright (1983) argues that Tityrus' encounter with the young 'god' in *Ecl.* 1 already conceals an account of poetic initiation; Galinsky (n. 22) focuses on the *Eclogues*' thematization of poetry and its functions.

fragment of Gallus allowed us to see a number of allusions that had not hitherto been suspected. The game of reconstructing lost Gallus through literary detective work based on explicit or suspected allusion in the *Eclogues* and later Augustan poetry is at once irresistible and hazardous, given that Virgil's allusions are never straightforward, so that in using them to reconstruct Gallus we may arrive only at 'a semifictional hero-poet, embodying Virgil's own view of poetry'.[34] If the details may be irrecoverable until the sands of Egypt yield more papyrus fragments, more certain is the general interpretation of *Eclogue* 10 as some kind of dialogue between the different genres of pastoral and love elegy, at the end of which the love-elegist Gallus, enslaved to *Amor*, admits that his erotic woes cannot be contained and assuaged within the bounds of the pastoral landscape (for which read 'the genre of pastoral'), a realization that is also the occasion for the pastoral singer Virgil's decision to conclude his singing. This self-conscious play with generic distinctions was to become a central feature of Augustan poetry.[35]

Still more vexed is the interpretation of the other poem to feature Gallus, *Eclogue* 6, where he is honoured in a scene of poetic initiation at the climax of the Song of Silenus, a catalogue of cosmological and mythological themes that is above all a catalogue of *poetic* subjects, some kind of 'poetic genealogy', as David Ross puts it,[36] culminating in the poetry of Gallus. There are clear echoes in lines 31–40 of Lucretius and

---

[34] J. E. G. Zetzel, rev. Ross (1975), *CP* 72 (1977), 249–60 at 259. The game of reconstructing Gallus was started in earnest by F. Skutsch, *Aus Vergils Frühzeit* i. (Leipzig, 1901); *Aus Vergils Frühzeit* ii. *Gallus und Vergil* (Leipzig, 1906), in the tradition of nineteenth-century *Quellenforschung*. The most ambitious recent attempt is Ross (1975), still very thought-provoking despite the unfortunate accident of its publication shortly before the discovery of the new Gallus (E. Courtney, *The Fragmentary Latin Poets* (Oxford, 1993), 259–68), which was first published with full discussion by R. D. Anderson, P. J. Parsons, and R. G. M. Nisbet, *JRS* 69 (1979), 125–55. See also D. F. Kennedy, '*Arcades ambo*. Virgil, Gallus and Arcadia', *Hermathena* 143 (1987), 47–59; R. M. Rosen and J. Farrell, 'Acontius, Milanion, and Gallus: Vergil, *Ecl.* 10.52–61', *TAPA* 116 (1986), 241–54; C. G. Perkell, 'The "dying Gallus" and the design of *Eclogue* 10', *CP* 91 (1996), 128–40. Gallan allusion is probably present in many other *Eclogues*: DuQuesnay (1981), 40 suspects it in the opening lines of *Ecl.* 1; DuQuesnay (1979), 60–3 in *Ecl.* 2 (on the elegiac quality of Corydon's passion see also E. J. Kenney, 'Virgil and the elegiac sensibility', *ICS* 8 (1983), 44–64, at 49–52; DuQuesnay (1976/77), 33–4 hypothesizes a poem by Gallus celebrating the triumph of Julius Caesar as one of the models for *Ecl.* 5.

[35] The attempt to disentangle pastoral and elegiac elements in *Ecl.* 10 is made by D. A. Kidd, 'Imitation in the tenth *Eclogue*', *BICS* 11 (1964), 54–64, but is complicated by the possibility that Gallus himself used the countryside as a setting in his elegy, still an open question despite the negative conclusion of R. Whitaker, 'Did Gallus write "pastoral" elegies?', *CQ* 38 (1988), 454–8. For a searching analysis of the generic play by a leading theorist of genre in Latin poetry see Conte (1986), 100–29; fundamental on generic manipulation in Augustan poetry is Hinds (1987).

[36] Ross (1975), ch. 2.

of the Song of Orpheus in Apollonius of Rhodes' *Argonautica* 1.496–504, and of the neoteric poet Calvus' epyllion the *Io* in line 52,[37] and we may suspect allusions to other poets, including Parthenius, Gallus' Greek poetic mentor,[38] and possibly the learned Hellenistic poet Euphorion. But at the same time the crumbs gleaned from other poets' tables are shaped by Virgil's controlling imagination into a version of a universal history, telling of the progress (or degeneration) of the human race from the perspective of the disruptive effects of love. The pattern was one that Ovid was to put to good use in the *Metamorphoses*.[39] And although *Eclogue* 6 (together with *Eclogue* 4) is the least pastoral of the book, Virgil cunningly so selects and slants the catalogue of subjects that the familiar mountains, woods, fountains, pastures, and animals of the pastoral world appear in unfamiliar guises.[40]

Through this poetic shaping and appropriation of disparate themes Virgil ensures that the Song of Silenus also functions as a 'poetic genealogy' for his own, as well as for Gallus', poetry. The verbal echoes between 8 *agrestem tenui meditabor harundine Musam* ('I will practise the rustic Muse on the slender reed') and 82 *Phoebo quondam meditante* ('while Apollo practised once upon a time'), and between 9 *non iniussa cano* ('I sing of things not unbidden') and 83 *audiit Eurotas iussitque ediscere lauros* ('the Eurotas heard and bade the laurels to learn the song') forge a link between the Song of Silenus and the prologue to the poem in which Virgil, wearing the mask of one of his own pastoral characters, Tityrus, reformulates his poetic goals in this 'proem in the middle' of the book.[41] Where the dramatic opening of the first *Eclogue* must be coaxed into revealing its programmatic content, here at the beginning of the second half the programme is explicitly presented in a dedicatory address to Varus in which Virgil closely adapts the Prologue

[37] See R. F. Thomas, 'Theocritus, Calvus, and *Eclogue* 6', *CP* 74 (1979), 337–9.
[38] On Parthenius and his importance for the 'neoterics' see Ross (1975), *passim*; Clausen (1964b), 181–96.
[39] P. E. Knox, *Ovid's Metamorphoses and the Traditions of Augustan Poetry* (Cambridge, 1986), 10–14.
[40] Interpretations of *Eclogue* 6: F. Skutsch (n. 34) (catalogue of subjects of Gallus' poetry); Z. Stewart, 'The Song of Silenus', *HSCP* 64 (1959), 179–205 (catalogue of Alexandrian themes); J. P. Elder, '*Non iniussa cano*: Virgil's sixth *Eclogue*', *HSCP* 65 (1961), 109–25 (a brief for Virgil's own brand of bucolic poetry). Attempts to discover what *Ecl.* 6 tells us about the actual or potential development of Gallus' poetic career are made by Ross (1975), ch. 2; E. Courtney, 'Vergil's sixth *Eclogue*', *QUCC* 34 (1990), 99–112. Attempts to read a plot or unified pattern into the Song of Silenus: Otis (1964), 130 (degeneration from age of Saturn, reversing the progress of *Ecl.* 4); C. P. Segal, 'Vergil's sixth *Eclogue* and the problem of evil', in Segal (1981), 301–29; E. W. Leach, 'The unity of *Eclogue* 6', *Latomus* 27 (1968), 13–32.
[41] G. B. Conte, 'Proems in the middle', *YCS* 29 (1992), 147–59.

to Callimachus' *Aitia* (fr. 1.21–4 Pfeiffer) in what is the first surviving example in Latin poetry of the *recusatio*.[42] Here the generic contrast is between elevated epic on Roman wars and humble Theocritean pastoral, a *deductum carmen* 'fine-spun song' performed on a *tenuis harundo* 'slender reed'. *tenuis*, already placed prominently in *Ecl.* 1.2, translates one of the central terms of the Callimachean poetics, λεπτός, λεπταλέος 'slender'; the slight, unpretentious and playful[43] subject-matter of pastoral reflects a serious artistic decision to adhere to an Alexandrian, neoteric poetics. Departures from this are marked by reference to a widening of the limits of the pastoral world that is simultaneously an expansion of poetic horizons, as at the beginning of *Eclogue* 4 where dissatisfaction with the 'humble tamarisks' and the wish to make the pastoral woods 'worthy of a consul' trigger a straying from the confines of slender Callimachean poetry into the larger concerns of epic and panegyric (4.1 *paulo maiora canamus* 'let us sing of things a little grander'). The reference at *Ecl.* 6.3 to a time when the poet 'was setting out to sing of kings and battles', for which Apollo rebukes him, might indeed be understood to refer to the poet's attempt at a loftier flight in *Eclogue* 4. If the integrity of the pastoral world has been threatened towards the end of the first half of the book, here at the beginning of the second half the poet is recalled to the straight and narrow.

Virgil's dramatization of the poetic choices open to himself and to Gallus is of a piece with the concerns of his fictional characters. It is scarcely an exaggeration to say that the business of these countryfolk is song. The typical activity of Theocritean and Virgilian herdsmen is the song contest: *Eclogues* 3 and 7 are straightforward examples of the 'amoebean' contest, in which a two- or four-line snatch of song by the first singer is answered or capped by the same number of lines from the second singer.[44] In *Eclogues* 5 and 8 two longer songs are matched

[42] Roman Callimacheanism: Clausen (1964b); id., '*Cynthius*', *AJP* 97 (1976), 245–7; G. Hutchinson, *Hellenistic Poetry* (Oxford, 1988), ch. 6. The revisionist reading of the *Aitia* prologue in A. Cameron, *Callimachus and his Critics* (Princeton, 1995), ch. 12 need not materially affect our understanding of the use of the Callimachean passage by Roman poets.

[43] *ludere* is often used in Callimachean and neoteric contexts of composing light or playful verse, programmatically at *Ecl.* 1.10 *ludere quae uellem calamo permisit agresti*; cf. e.g. Cat. 50.1–2 *hesterno, Licini, die otiosi | multum lusimus in meis tabellis* (*otium* is the precondition for Catullan versifying, as it is for the singing of Virgil's shepherds).

[44] The contest in *Ecl.* 3 is adjudged a draw by the umpire Palaemon; in *Ecl.* 7 Meliboeus recalls that Corydon defeated Thyrsis, inevitably provoking readers into their own attempt to judge the contest on points: see Clausen (1994), 210–13. The jury is still out. On *Ecl.* 3 see also Segal (n. 24); C. Monteleone, *Palaemon. L'ecloga III di Virgilio: lusus intertestuale ed esegesi* (Naples, 1994). On *Ecl.* 7 see B. D. Frischer, *At tu aureus esto. Eine Interpretation von Vergils 7. Ekloge* (Bonn, 1975).

against each other. The imitative emulation of such contests is a transparent reflection of the actual practice of Greek and Roman poets: for Corydon and Thyrsis read Virgil imitating and rivalling a Theocritus or a Gallus.[45] At *Eclogue* 4.55–9 the poet's eagerness to live long enough to sing of the future deeds of the wonderful child leads him to boast that he would win any poetic competition with Orpheus, Linus, or Pan himself; the divide between the fictional and extra-fictional worlds is similarly breached at *Ecl.* 9.35–6 when Lycidas judges himself an inferior poet not by the standards of a Menalcas or a Corydon, but of the historical poets Varius and Cinna. Fittingly for a poem which concludes the first half of the book and is immediately followed by the explicit programmatics of the prologue of *Eclogue* 6, the singers of *Eclogue* 5 are particularly self-conscious about the choice of subject-matter and about poetic tradition and succession. Menalcas' suggestion to Mopsus at 5.10–11 that he choose a typical pastoral theme (*si quos aut Phyllidis ignis | aut Alconis habes laudes aut iurgia Codri* 'if you have anything on the flames of love for Phyllis, or praise of Alcon, or invective against Codrus') is rejected in favour of the more ambitious subject of the death of the 'pastoral hero' Daphnis. At the end of the exchange of songs Menalcas gives Mopsus the pipe to which he has previously sung songs labelled by the first lines of the second and third *Eclogues*, as if to identify a corpus of Virgilian pastoral, and to indicate that the younger singer Mopsus has now proved himself worthy to take on the mantle of 'Virgilian pastoral', perhaps hinting also that Menalcas, as a figure of the pastoral poet himself, is moving on from the themes of the first half of the book to something a little different. Another hint that *Eclogue* 5 is concerned with the making of poetry in the real world is Mopsus' statement at 13–14 that he has written out his poem on the bark of a tree, for typically pastoral singers are oral poets and their song-contests are oral improvisations.[46]

Virgil's most innovative reworking of the amoebean contest is in *Eclogue* 9, in which Lycidas and Moeris engage in an apology for a song contest as, in the absence of the greater singer Menalcas (a kind of 'Waiting for Godot'), they painfully call to memory fragments of song

---

[45] On *imitatio* and *aemulatio* see D. A. Russell, 'De *imitatione*', in West and Woodman (1979), 1–16.

[46] Mopsus' song ends with another reference to writing, the inscription to be placed on Daphnis' tomb. At *Ecl.* 6.10–12 Virgil archly refers to his poems as both sung and written. The other instance of writing in the pastoral world is Gallus' resolve to write his *amores* (very possibly the title of his collection of love elegies) on trees at *Ecl.* 10.52–4, a motif derived from Callimachus' story of Acontius and Cydippe (*Ait.* fr. 73 Pfeiffer; on Virgil's use of this Callimachean episode see E. J. Kenney, *ICS* 8 (1983), 49–52. On writing in the pastoral world see Putnam (1970), 169–70, 372–4.

which nevertheless manage to fall into two pairs of artfully corresponsive and contrasting passages.[47] In this poem the threatened disintegration of pastoral song seems to result from the failure of Menalcas' poetry to save Moeris' land from confiscation. Lycidas and Moeris are disappointed in their belief that the power of song might transcend the limits of an autonomous world of poetry (where song's power is that of charming an audience or defeating a poetic rival), and achieve consequences in the world of political power; that Menalcas' song might have an effect on the landscape in its way no less drastic than the magical song of a Silenus or Orpheus (*Ecl.* 6.27–8, 70–1). *uates* is the word that triumviral and Augustan poets use of themselves to assert their claim to a serious and influential role in the conduct of society and politics;[48] *uates* is the label that Lycidas self-deprecatingly denies for himself at *Ecl.* 9.33–4. An oscillation between an exultant conviction of the power of poetry and a disillusioned realization of its futility and marginality seems to lie close to the heart of Virgil's self-awareness as a poet.[49]

History and Politics

We have already on a number of occasions observed an overstepping of the boundary between the closed fictional world of the pastoral 'green cabinet' and the historical world of the pastoral poet. The precise relationship between these two worlds is one of the most vexed issues in the interpretation of the *Eclogues*, and this may be no accident if it is true that 'they are deliberately riddling and mystificatory'.[50] The problems are immediately confronted in an acute form in the first *Eclogue*. Who is the divine young man who calls the shots in the (unambiguously real) city of Rome? Do the experiences of Tityrus

[47] *Ecl.* 9: Segal (n. 3); E. A. Schmidt, 'Poesia e politica nella nona ecloga di Virgilio', *Maia* 24 (1972), 99–119.

[48] J. K. Newman, *The Concept of Vates in Augustan Poetry* (Brussels, 1967); Hardie (1986), 16–22.

[49] The Orphic power of poetry is the subject of Desport (1952); the futility of poetry is stressed by Boyle (1986); Boyle's title 'The Chaonian dove' is a quotation from *Ecl.* 9.13. Leech (1974), ch. 5 explores the theme of unsuccessful song; see also J. B. Solodow, '*Poeta impotens*: the last three *Eclogues*', *Latomus* 36 (1977), 757–71.

[50] Wright (1983), 112, referring to Berg (1974), 114–6. In a departure from Theocritean practice Virgil introduces actual riddles into his shepherds' songs at *Ecl.* 3.104–7 (and cf. 3.40–2). No answers are given in the text, and for each riddle scholars have come up with more than one answer; see Clausen ad loc.; T. K. Dix, 'Vergil in the Grynean grove: two riddles in the third *Eclogue*', *CP* 90 (1995), 256–62 (citing earlier solutions at 260, n. 13).

and Meliboeus mirror the real-life experiences of land-owners in Cisalpine Gaul during the land confiscations after the battle of Philippi in 42 B.C.? Is the name 'Tityrus' a mask for the poet Virgil?

Answers to these riddling questions are determined partly by scholarly fashion. Just as Franz Skutsch's approach to the problem of the literary allusions in *Eclogues* 6 and 10 was governed by a nineteenth-century source-critical method that aimed to excavate the original models (in this case the lost poems of Gallus) beneath the surface of the Virgilian text, so nineteenth- and early twentieth-century critics proceeded in the conviction that a rigorous scholarship could reconstruct the biographical and historical realities lightly cloaked in the fictional doings of Virgil's shepherds. In this they were encouraged by the biographical and allegorical practice of the ancient *Lives* and commentaries.[51] Great ingenuity was expended in the construction of a narrative about the Cisalpine land commission and Virgil's farm from *Eclogues* 1 and 9, poems which obviously form a pair within the overall structure of the book, both being concerned with the loss or preservation of land and status as a result of military upheaval. Yet no consensus was reached even on the question of the chronological ordering of 1 and 9: does 9 reflect a later disappointment of hopes raised in an approach to Octavian in 1, or does 1 represent the successful resolution of the threat of dispossession in 9?[52] Scholars toured the countryside around Mantua in order to identify the exact site of Virgil's farm from the topographical indications in the poems; modern critics are more likely to interpret the apparently specific details of the landscape at *Ecl.* 9.7–10 as an example of the 'reality effect' than as a precise clue to the whereabouts of Virgil's family estate.[53]

The undoubted presence in the text of allusion to historical events

---

[51] The tradition that in *Ecl.* 2 Alexis conceals a slave-boy loved by Virgil = Corydon goes back to Martial (see Clausen on 2.1). See R. J. Starr, 'Vergil's seventh *Eclogue* and its readers: biographical allegory as an interpretative strategy in antiquity and late antiquity', *CP* 90 (1995), 129–38. On the impact of Servius' allegory on the later reception of the *Eclogues* see A. Patterson, *Pastoral and Ideology. Virgil to Valéry* (Berkeley and Los Angeles, 1987), 24–5. In general on allegory see Rose (1942), ch. 6.

[52] The biographical-historical approach (which had already been criticized by F. Leo, 'Vergils erste und neunte Ecloge', *Hermes* 38 (1903), 1–18) underlies the discussion of Rose (1942). L. P. Wilkinson, 'Virgil and the evictions', *Hermes* 94 (1966), 320–4 extracts 'an intelligible story' from *Eclogues* 1 and 9; for a clear-headed reexamination of the issues see M. Winterbottom, 'Virgil and the confiscations', in McAuslan and Walcot (1990), 65–8. For a recent example of an attempt to make historical sense of the riddles in the text see DuQuesnay (1981), 115–30, who rejects the biographical approach, but applies the utmost ingenuity to accommodate Tityrus' oblique answers to Meliboeus' questions in *Ecl.* 1 to the *Realien* of Roman slavery and manumission.

[53] The tourists: e.g. E. K. Rand, *In Quest of Vergil's Birthplace* (Cambridge, Mass., 1930).

increases the temptation for the reader to interpret the names of the
herdsmen as allegorical masks for real persons.[54] Already in Theocritus
Idyll 7 the pastoral poet dramatizes his own encounter in an exchange
of songs with a character, Lycidas, from the pastoral world itself. In the
envoi to his book at *Ecl.* 10.70–7 Virgil casts himself in the role of one of
his characters, weaving his basket of poetry and driving home his goats,
now that they have had their fill of grazing as we and the poet have had
our fill of pastoral poetry. At *Ecl.* 6.4–5 Apollo as god of poetry
addresses the pastoral Virgil as 'Tityrus'. Yet we cannot simply identify
Tityrus with Virgil; for example at *Ecl.* 9.23–5 Tityrus appears in
Lycidas' quotation of a snatch of a song by Menalcas, whom in this
poem, as the figure of the outstanding pastoral singer, we might be more
inclined to take as the mask of the poet, especially when we remember
that at the end of *Eclogue* 5 Menalcas gives Mopsus the pipe to which he
had sung *Eclogues* 2 and 3. Servius' comment (on 1.1) that 'in this place
we should understand Virgil in the person of Tityrus; not everywhere,
however, but only when reason requires it' is not a bad rule of thumb.[55]

The relationship between the pastoral characters of the *Eclogues* and
historical personages might be compared to the potential of the
legendary characters of the *Aeneid* intermittently to foreshadow persons
and deeds in Roman history. Neither in the *Aeneid* nor the *Eclogues*
should we deny a measure of autonomy to the fictional setting and the
words and actions performed therein; and equally the *Eclogues* are as
saturated in history as is the *Aeneid*. Particularly suggestive—and
elusive—in this respect are *Eclogues* 4 and 5, which each tell of a saviour
man-god. The start of the wonderful sequence of events in *Eclogue* 4 is
firmly anchored in the consulship of Virgil's patron Pollio in 40 B.C.,
but the prophecy of the future career of the mysterious child and of the
reversal of the Hesiodic sequence of races of mankind is a heady mixture
of oracular mystification, mythology and poetic allusion, with a dash of
the mysterious wisdom of the east. The preview of a Golden Age as a
kind of miraculous pastoral paradise is presented in forms of discourse
used to address the great and powerful of Rome, the *basilikos logos*

---

[54] The extreme approach is exemplified in L. Herrmann, *Les masques et les visages dans les
Bucoliques de Virgile* (Brussels, 1930), reading the *Eclogues* as 'poésies à clef', and in the articles by
J. J. H. Savage, e.g. *TAPA* 89 (1958), 142–58 (*Ecl.* 3): *TAPA* 91 (1960), 353–75 (*Ecl.* 2); 94
(1963), 248–67 (*Ecl.*7).

[55] A more attractive variant of the allegorical approach is the interpretation of the characters of
the *Eclogues* as 'figures for aspects of Virgil himself' in the Jungian reading of the 'inner
autobiography' of the poems by M. Owen Lee, *Death and Rebirth in Virgil's Arcadia* (Albany,
NY, 1989).

(speech in praise of a king), the *laudatio consulis*, the *epithalamium* (combining allusion to Catullus 61, an epithalamium for a real couple, with Catullus 64, the mythological epithalamium for Peleus and Thetis). The identity of the child has provoked endless speculation: if one has to vote for a single candidate, the expected son of Antony and Octavia, whose dynastic alliance sealed the Pact of Brundisium in the autumn of 40 B.C., has as good a claim as any. But we should remember that it is an oracle's privilege to be ambiguous, and perhaps take a hint from the apparent impossibility of deciding between the competing solutions to the riddles at the end of the previous poem. The *Eclogues* were written in the rapidly changing and unpredictable conditions of the second Triumvirate, and a poet with an eye to future fame but also with a desire to intervene in contemporary political debate could do worse than develop an allusive and polysemous manner. How well Virgil succeeded in catching hold of ideas in the air in the later first century B.C., and avoided hitching his wagon to briefly shining stars, is seen in the ease with which Christian readers were able to understand *Eclogue* 4, the 'Messianic Eclogue', as a prophecy of their own saviour, thus ensuring Virgil a fame of which he could not have dreamed.[56] The idea of the return of the Golden Age, reused by Virgil in the panegyric of Augustus at *Aen.* 6.791–4, was also to establish itself permanently in the political imagery of Europe.[57]

In *Eclogue* 4 the Hesiodic decline of man from a primitive Golden Age is reversed in parallel with the growth to maturity of a child who will enjoy the company of the gods; in *Eclogue* 5 the death of the Theocritean

---

[56] The bibliography on *Ecl.* 4 is vast. The candidates for the identity of the child are conveniently surveyed by Coleman (1977), 150–2; see e.g. D. A. Slater, *CR* 26 (1912), 114–19 (the son of Antony and Octavia, with a useful listing of the parallels with Cat. 64, on which see also Williams (1968), 281–3; DuQuesnay (1977), 68–75); W. W. Tarn, *JRS* 22 (1932), 135–60; Rose (1942), ch. 8. The question of Virgil's possible use of Eastern sources (a thesis argued with vast erudition by E. Norden, *Die Geburt des Kindes. Geschichte einer religiösen Idee* [Leipzig and Berlin, 1924]) is scrupulously weighed by R. G. M. Nisbet, 'Virgil's fourth *Eclogue*: easterners and westerners', *BICS* 25 (1978), 59–78. The 'generic' structures of the poem are discussed by DuQuesnay (1977) (who here and in his other writings on the *Eclogues* makes powerful use of the methodology of Cairns [1972]). There is further useful discussion of the Greco-Roman models in E. W. Leach, '*Eclogue* 4: symbolism and sources', *Arethusa* 4 (1971), 167–84. On the Christian reading see S. Benko, 'Virgil's fourth *Eclogue* in Christian interpretation', *ANRW* II 31.1 (1980), 646–705. On the issue of the relative priority of *Eclogue* 4 and Horace *Epode* 16 see recently Clausen (1994), 145–51 (although Clausen is in a minority in holding that Virgil imitates Horace).

[57] Golden Age: I. S. Ryberg, 'Vergil's Golden Age', *TAPA* 89 (1958), 112–31; B. Gatz, *Weltalter, goldene Zeit, und sinnverwandte Vorstellungen* (Hildesheim, 1967); C. Fantazzi, 'Golden age in Arcadia', *Latomus* 33 (1974), 280–305; Galinsky (1996), 91–121; for later returns of the Golden Age see F. A. Yates, *Astraea. The Imperial Theme in the Sixteenth Century* (London, 1975), index s.vv. 'Golden Age, symbol of imperial *renovatio*'; H. Levin, *The Myth of the Golden Age in the Renaissance* (London, 1969).

pastoral hero Daphnis is unexpectedly reversed through his deification, whereupon nature and shepherds enter a state of pleasure and peace reminiscent of the Golden Age. A clue to the full significance of Daphnis' death and apotheosis is given in the epitaph to be carved on his tomb (5.43) *Daphnis ego in siluis, hinc usque ad sidera notus* ('I am the Daphnis in the woods, known from here as far as the stars'), which alludes to Daphnis' dying self-definition at Theocr. *Id.* 1.120–1, but bursts the narrow limits of the pastoral world ('in the woods') through an elevation to the stars which is also an allusion to Odysseus' notorious boast at *Odyssey* 9.20 'and my fame reaches the heavens'. Here, as in *Eclogue* 4, reference to epic heroes also hints at the grander themes of Roman history. If the deification of Daphnis would have surprised a connoisseur of Theocritus, no less startling in the context of Roman religion of the first century B.C. would have been the apotheosis of a dead human statesman, Julius Caesar, officially deified on 1 January 42 B.C. No contemporary reader could have failed to make the connection, which is not to say that the range of meanings of the deified Daphnis should be restricted to an allegory for Julius Caesar.[58] As we have seen, one of the models for the deified Daphnis is Lucretius' 'god', the philosopher Epicurus, and the condition of *uoluptas* and *otium* produced in the pastoral world at *Ecl.* 5.58–61 is closer to an Epicurean *ataraxia* than to the actual state of Rome in the late 40s B.C. The Theocritean Daphnis is also a master of bucolic song, and Menalcas' kid-gloved apostrophe of Mopsus as *diuine poeta* (5.45) may hint at a comparability between the godlikeness of apotheosed statesman and of the supreme poet. A sign perhaps of Virgil's youthful boldness (*Geo.* 4.565), but a daring move that he was to repeat.[59]

Structure and Unity. Composition and Chronology.

Earlier sections of this chapter will have made it clear that it is impossible to talk adequately about the meaning of individual *Eclogues* without reference to connections between poems and to the placing of individual

---

[58] *Ecl.* 5 and Julius Caesar: Otis (1964), 133–5; DuQuesnay (1976/77), 30–4. J. Perret, 'Daphnis pâtre et héros: perspectives sur un âge d'or', *REL* 60 (1982), 216–33 attempts unsuccessfully to close off the historical allegory.

[59] In the equivalence of *Imperator Caesar* and the poet-as-*triumphator* at the beginning of the third *Georgic*. The ultimate example of this self-promotion is Ovid's assertion for himself of an immortality that outbids the divinity of Julius Caesar and Augustus at the end of the *Metamorphoses*. Berg (1974), ch. 4 takes the Daphnis of *Ecl.* 5 as a figure of the poet.

poems within the book. The art with which Virgil has arranged the ten poems in the book of *Eclogues* is another sign of the 'Alexandrianism' of the work;[60] Virgil's choice of the number ten was followed by Horace, Tibullus, and Ovid, who composed carefully arranged books of ten, or multiplies of five, poems.

Various schemes have been discerned in the organization of the book.[61] At a simple level variation or continuity within the linear sequence is to be watched for: for example Tityrus' harmonious and melodious relationship with his environment in *Ecl.* 1 is followed by a poem in which Corydon is out of tune with his surroundings; the riddles at the end of the song contest of *Ecl.* 3 prepare us for the oracular riddles of *Ecl.* 4; the song of Alphesiboeus in *Ecl.* 8 ends with the success of his female character's love magic in bringing Daphnis back from the city, but in the very next line of the book, the first line of *Ecl.* 9, we see a rustic going *to* the city. In formal terms there is an alternation between the odd-numbered 'mimetic' dialogues and the even-numbered 'diegematic' poems in which the poet sets a scene in his own person. Looking at the architecture of the book as a whole, we clearly see two halves marked by the 'proem in the middle' at *Ecl.* 6.1–12. The limits of the second half are marked by the appearance of Gallus in *Eclogues* 6 and 10; correspondingly the first and last poems of the first half, *Eclogues* 1 and 5, each contain praise of a pastoral 'god', the recipient of sacrifice (*Ecl.* 1.6–8, 40–3; 5.62–80). The two halves also reflect each other: thus the implicitly programmatic opening of the first *Eclogue* is mirrored in the explicit literary programme at the beginning of the sixth *Eclogue*, while *Eclogues* 5 and 10 are linked through their shared use as a model of the Song of Thyrsis on the death of Daphnis in Theocritus' first *Idyll*. But where in *Eclogue* 5 the dead Daphnis is miraculously restored to a higher form of life, in *Eclogue* 10 there is no cure for the erotic sickness of which Gallus is figuratively dying. More generally one may see a contrast between the first half of

[60] Although the belief that this is how Alexandrian poets operated is largely hypothetical given the fragmentary state of the evidence. For the arrangement of the one (certainly) surviving Alexandrian poetry book, Callimachus' *Hymns*, see N. Hopkinson, *Callimachus. Hymn to Demeter* (Cambridge, 1984), 13; in general see N. Krevans, *The Poet as Editor: The Poetic Collection from Callimachus to Ovid* (forthcoming). Much has been written on the organization of Catullus' poetry book(s), but the issue is bedevilled by uncertainty as to whether we have Catullus' own edition of his poems: see W. Clausen in Kenney and Clausen (1982), 193–7. On the structure of the Roman poetry book see M. S. Santirocco, *Unity and Design in Horace's Odes* (Chapel Hill and London, 1986), ch. 1.

[61] For a useful survey and critical discussion see N. Rudd, *Lines of Enquiry: Studies in Latin Poetry* (Cambridge, 1976), ch. 5; Clausen 1994, pp. xx–xxvi. Particularly elaborate are the patterns discerned by J. B. van Sickle in various works, e.g. van Sickle (1978).

the book, more forward-looking and conciliatory, moving towards the joyful visions of poems 4 and 5, and the more introverted second half which moves towards the bleak demonstration of the powerlessness of pastoral poetry in the closural sequence of poems 9 and 10.[62] These patterns are overlaid with others: *Eclogues* 4, 5, and 6 form a triad of poems which strain at the limits of the pastoral world, with explicit or implicit allusion to events and persons in Roman history, bridging the central division of the book, and framed by the most typical examples of bucolic musical performance (*Eclogues* 2, 3 and 7, 8). A concentric arrangement pairs 1 and 9 (dispossession and journeys to the city), 2 and 8 (love songs), 3 and 7 (amoebean contests), and 4 and 6 (universal histories, elevation of a chosen individual). Beyond this some have seen elaborate numerical structures and correspondences in the book.[63]

The evident care with which Virgil has set the individual *Eclogues* in relationship to each other seriously complicates any attempt to establish an absolute chronology for the composition of the poems, an exercise typical of an older fashion for a documentary historical approach to the poems.[64] The fixed historical dates to which the poems refer are 42 B.C., the date of the land-confiscations (*Eclogues* 1 and 9), 40 B.C., the consulship of Pollio (*Ecl.* 4), and 39 B.C. (if *Ecl.* 8.6–13 is taken to refer to Pollio's campaign against the Parthini, rather than Octavian's campaigns of 35 B.C.).[65] But these are not necessarily the dates of the final shaping of these poems. Nor can a chronology be securely founded on internal cross-references between the poems, or on the criterion of the degree of dependence on Theocritean models (on the debatable assumption that later poems will show greater independence). An impression of artistic development may be a part of the fiction of the collection itself, which has as one of its major themes poetic tradition and originality, as we have seen. *Eclogues* 2 and 3 are often taken to be early because of their close dependence on Theocritus, but it is as logical

---

[62] Otis (1964), 130–1, followed by Segal (n. 40).

[63] This line begins with P. Maury, 'Le secret de Virgile et l'architecture des Bucoliques', *Lettres d'Humanité* 3 (1944), 71–147 (whose analyses are conveniently accessible in J. Perret, *Virgile*, rev. edn. (Paris, 1965), 15–30), and continues with e.g. Brown (1963); O. Skutsch, 'Symmetry and sense in the *Eclogues*', *HSCP* 73 (1969), 153–68; cf. the clear-headed discussion in Wilkinson (1969), 316–22.

[64] A useful overview of the issues in Coleman (1977), 14–21. Coleiro (1979), 93 lists 20 different orderings. See also E. A. Schmidt, *Zur Chronologie der Eklogen Vergils* (Heidelberg, 1974).

[65] A continuing debate: see D. Mankin, 'The addressee of Virgil's eighth *Eclogue*: a reconsideration', *Hermes* 116 (1988), 63–76 (Octavian); J. Farrell, 'Asinius Pollio in Vergil *Eclogue* 8', *CP* 86 (1991), 204–11 (Pollio); Clausen (1994), 233–9 (Octavian).

to suppose that Virgil composed two narrowly Theocritean pieces to place near the beginning of the book as a baseline against which to measure his departures from the model, signalled so blatantly at the beginning of *Eclogue* 4.[66] The quotation of the first lines of *Eclogues* 2 and 3 at the end of *Eclogue* 5 establishes a priority whose only necessary validity is within the world of Menalcas and Mopsus.

The Pastoral Experience

For many readers pastoral poetry has seemed to offer the dream of an escape from the discontents of civilization into a more perfect world of the mind. The rustic idyll, the Golden Age, the contentment of the philosophical sage, the transcendence of time and mortality in a world of art, these are the shapes assumed by this dream, and models for all of them may be found in the *Eclogues*. The classic formulation this century of the escapist interpretation of the *Eclogues* is Bruno Snell's essay 'Arcadia. The discovery of a spiritual landscape',[67] arguing that Virgil transforms the realism of Theocritean bucolic into a romantic dream landscape, to which he gave the name 'Arcadia' that has ever since been associated with the pastoral world. Yet Arcadia is the setting only for the last *Eclogue*, and is mentioned incidentally in three others.[68] The landscape of the *Eclogues* in fact has no secure location, sometimes in Italy, sometimes in Theocritus' Sicily, sometimes nowhere in particular. Geographically the *Eclogues* are impossible to pin down.[69]

Other critics try to nail the poems to a political or moral set of meanings. Virgil is the supporter of Pollio and Octavian,[70] the advocate

---

[66] Cf. the comparable arrangement of Horace's first book of *Satires*, whose first three poems conform to an acerbic Lucilian manner, which is then subjected to examination and rethinking in the fourth and subsequent satires: see J. E. G. Zetzel, 'Horace's *Liber Sermonum*: the structure of ambiguity', *Arethusa* 13 (1980), 59–77, at 63–5. T. K. Hubbard, 'Allusive artistry and Vergil's revisionary program: *Eclogues* 1–3', *MD* 34 (1995), 37–67 reads *Eclogues* 1–3 'as the first act in an intertextual drama of Vergil's poetic self-emergence'.

[67] In *The Discovery of the Mind* (tr. T. G. Rosenmeyer, Oxford, 1953), ch. 13 (first published in German in 1945) = Commager (1966), 14–27.

[68] R. Jenkyns, 'Virgil and Arcadia', *JRS* 79 (1989), 26–39 may go too far in denying that Arcadia is in any sense one of Virgil's pastoral landscapes, but his scepticism is salutary (his criticism of Snell is anticipated by G. Jachmann, *Maia* 5 (1952), 161–74). See also Kennedy (n. 34). On the history of the Arcadian ideal see E. Panofsky, 'Et in Arcadia ego: Poussin and the elegiac tradition', in *Meaning in the Visual Arts* (Garden City, 1955), ch. 7; M. Beard and J. Henderson, *Classics. A Very Short Introduction* (Cambridge, 1995), 102–5, 113–19.

[69] On the landscapes of the *Eclogues* see E. Flintoff, 'The setting of Virgil's *Eclogues*', *Latomus* 33 (1974), 814–46; Clausen (1994), pp. xxvi–xxx.

[70] E.g. the various articles by DuQuesnay; Berg (1974).

of the possibility of the reconstruction of Roman society out of the chaos of civil war. Or, more commonly these days, his is a bleakly pessimistic message about the possibility of success and order, whether in the political sphere or in the private sphere.[71]

Yet the dramatic form of most of the *Eclogues* is an obstacle to any simple access to the poet's meaning, world-view, or dreams. 'The desire to escape from reality . . . is a theme belonging to Vergil's Corydon and Damon, not to the Eclogue Poet or to Vergil himself.'[72] The most powerful expressions of the pastoral dream are put in the mouths of those characters most acutely aware of their own loss or distress, Meliboeus at the beginning of the first *Eclogue* and Gallus in the tenth. Another formal feature of the poems that acts to foil the immediacy of the message is the constant use of framing devices: the songs the shepherds sing are either framed by the pastoral poet's own scene-setting (in the even-numbered poems), or they are presented within the artificial convention of the song-contest. In some cases pastoral song comes as it were in quotation marks, as in the snatches of song remembered by Lycidas and Moeris in *Eclogue* 9, or in the exchange of prefabricated songs in *Eclogue* 5. A particularly complex chain of reception is outlined at *Ecl.* 6.82–4 where (if *omnia* in line 82 is taken to refer to the total contents of the Song of Silenus) Silenus sings a song that had been composed by Apollo, whose performance was heard by the river Eurotas, which bade the laurel trees to learn it; Silenus' performance, in turn, is relayed by the echoing vales to the stars. Virgil has the Song of Silenus from the Muses (13), and we have it from the lips of Virgil, or rather from the written page on which Virgil's song is deposited (10–12). Pastoral song is thus rarely if ever the unpremeditated expression of inner feelings and desires; devices of game-playing, framing and quotation ensure that irony, mediation and polyphony are an integral part of the reading experience.[73]

Although the *Eclogues* are largely dramatic in form, theirs is a drama characterized more by balance and suspension than by the resolution of debate or difference, a drama largely without plot. The first *Eclogue*

---

[71] The pessimists include Putnam and Boyle.

[72] Leach (1974), 24; C. G. Perkell, *CP* 91 (1996), 136 'The relationship between the poet of the whole poem and individual speakers is one of difference or distance, and therefore of irony.'

[73] For an excellent account of the importance of framing in pastoral poetics see Goldhill (1991), ch. 4 'Framing, polyphony and desire: Theocritus and Hellenistic poetics'. The notion of the frame is central to the penetrating study of Virgil's definition of his poetic self and of the relationship between poetry and reality by L. Rumpf, *Extremus labor. Vergils 10. Ekloge und die Poetik der Bucolica* (Göttingen, 1996).

opens with two balanced five-line utterances by Meliboeus and Tityrus, although unusually this meeting between two herdsmen does *not* develop into the formally balanced exchange of song that is almost *de rigueur* in their world. In this first poem modern readers' sympathies are torn between the two characters. At the end of the poem there is a suspension in Tityrus' invitation to Meliboeus to spend the night with him before moving on: the politely tentative form *poteras* leaves it unclear whether Meliboeus will or will not accept; is it also a tentative invitation to the reader to become a very temporary resident in the pastoral world? The balance of the song contest may be disturbed by the adjudication of victory to one of the two singers (as in *Ecl.* 7, although the grounds for the judgement seem undecidable to modern critics), but the umpire may find a decision impossible, as in *Ecl.* 3. Within the overall structure of the book poems with clear resolutions in one direction are balanced against others with a different conclusion, as the successful resurrection of Daphnis in *Ecl.* 5 is balanced against Gallus' failure to overcome his erotic fate in *Ecl.* 10. Rather than attempting to reach a definitive interpretation of the meaning of the *Eclogues* many critics prefer to operate with the model of a suspension or balancing of opposites. For Pöschl this balancing of opposites is evaluated aesthetically as the mark of a classical balance, as in the equilibrium between praise and lament in *Eclogue* 1.[74] Segal, talking about the end of the first *Eclogue*, speaks of an 'atmosphere of contraries . . . [which] sets the tone for the *Eclogues*', and, in a classic New Critical reading of the third *Eclogue*, of 'the creative suspension in which Virgil has framed the antitheses of the poem'. Paul Alpers, following Segal, states that 'The essence of Virgil's pastoral suspensions is the poet's capacity to render and acknowledge truths and relations, but not to claim the power to resolve them.'[75]

Virgil may have learnt the art of creating poems that frustrate simple readings through devices of suspension, framing, and distancing as a result of his choice of a genre, pastoral, that by its very forms encouraged such things, but the lesson was one that he was to carry with him into his exercises in the genres of didactic and epic.

[74] V. Pöschl, *Die Hirtendichtung Virgils* (Heidelberg, 1964), 29.
[75] Alpers (1979), 245; 96–103 for a survey of earlier essays in this kind of approach.

III. THE *GEORGICS*

The Teacher and his Pupils. The Didactic Tradition.

As evening falls at the end of the *Eclogues* we come out of the shade of the pastoral world, a shade harmful to crops (*Ecl.* 10.76) and 'rise' (*Ecl.* 10.75 *surgamus*) with the poet to the higher subject matter of a didactic poem; the reader, instead of eavesdropping on the self-enclosed world of fictional shepherds singing to each other, is now the addressee of instructions by the poet that aim at results in the world outside the poem.[1] We remain in the countryside, but now as the setting not for the leisurely pastimes of musical shepherds, but for the laborious annual round of the farmer. As in the *Eclogues* the countryside is at the mercy of individuals and events in the larger world; as in *Eclogue* 1 that dependence is soon focused on the great man in Rome, now named as (Octavian) Caesar, whose prospective divinity is framed in grandiosely cosmic terms, the reward for a heroism that far outreaches the simple benefaction for which the *iuuenis* of *Eclogue* 1 is magnified as a god by Tityrus. Octavian enters the *Georgics* from a world of epic journeying and struggle, to whose literal presence we are intermittently recalled from our work on the land, but which is also figuratively present within the world of the farmer, who has his own paths to follow and battles to fight. The poem's final image of Octavian 'thundering' in battle in the distant east (4.560–2) is a suitable advertisement of the full-dress epic on Octavian's legendary ancestor that is to follow.[2]

If the *Georgics* is tightly woven into Virgil's *œuvre* as a whole, it is probably true that for a modern audience it is the most difficult of the three poems with which to come to terms. We are still reasonably comfortable with pastoral and epic, but the genre of didactic has become strange: four books giving instruction on the cultivation of field crops, trees and vines, large animals, and bees, all rounded off with a mysterious mythological narrative, test our receptivity.[3] Gone are the

[1] On the *Georgics*' multi-levelled construction of its addressees see A. Schiesaro, 'Il destinatario discreto. Funzioni didascaliche e progetto culturale nelle Georgiche', in A. Schiesaro *et al.* (eds.), *Mega Nepios. The Addressee in Didactic Epic* (= *MD* 31 [1993] 129–47).

[2] At the end of the *Aeneid* Aeneas will also 'fulminate' (12.654, 922–3). On Virgil's sense of his own poetic career see ch. I n. 1. On Virgil's reuse of material from the *Georgics* in the *Aeneid* see Briggs (1980).

[3] In general see Toohey (1996); A. Dalzell, *The Criticism of Didactic Poetry: Essays on Lucretius,*

days when it could seriously be debated whether the *Georgics* was a practical farming manual for veterans settled on the land after the end of the civil wars (whatever our assessment of the poem's accuracy in technical detail, it is simply too incomplete as a systematic manual),[4] and emphasis is rightly put on the poem's place within the *literary* tradition of Greek and Roman didactic poetry.[5] The *Georgics* engages with the whole span of that long tradition, in which Virgil found models for the poet's pose as privileged mouthpiece for the most lofty and serious social, religious and philosophical instruction, above all in the poems of Hesiod, Empedocles, and Lucretius. This is the didacticism of the *uates*, the poet as portentous spokesman for his society (see p. 18 above). But in the Alexandrian didactic poems of Aratus and Nicander (whose *Georgika*, 'Farming Matters' may have supplied Virgil with his title),[6] and in the related aetiological poem in elegiacs by Callimachus, the *Aitia*,[7] Virgil found a more recherché didacticism, in which the poet displays a specialist learning for a narrower audience. In its combination of Alexandrian literary learning with a wider sense of a public mission the *Georgics* might also be seen as a poem transitional between the *Eclogues* and the *Aeneid*; however one should not forget that the 'Alexandrian' *Eclogues* are pervaded by a concern for wider historical and political issues, and that the public Roman epic, the *Aeneid*, is in many ways a very Alexandrian poem.

In choosing to write a didactic poem on farming, Virgil naturally takes for his model the founding text of the genre, Hesiod's *Works and Days*. At 2.176 he labels himself the Roman Hesiod: *Ascraeumque cano Romana per oppida carmen* ('I sing an Ascraean song through Roman towns'; Ascra is Hesiod's village).[8] As if to make the point that Hesiod's poem begins the tradition, imitation of Hesiod is most pronounced in the *first*

Virgil, and Ovid (Toronto, Buffalo and London, 1996); E. Pöhlmann, 'Charakteristika des römischen Lehrgedichts', *ANRW* 13 (1973), 813–901; B. Effe, *Dichtung und Lehre: Untersuchungen zur Typologie des antiken Lehrgedichts* (Munich, 1977).

[4] The position is clearly stated by Otis (1964), 144–8, although Wilkinson (1969), 3–4 still feels the need to refute the practical purpose. On Virgil's technical accuracy see M. S. Spurr, 'Agriculture and the *Georgics*', in McAuslan and Walcot (1990), 69–93; Wilkinson (1969), 329; on Roman farming in general see K. D. White, *Roman Farming* (London, 1970).

[5] For brief overviews see Wilkinson (1969), 56–65; G. Kromer, 'The didactic tradition in Vergil's *Georgics*', in Boyle (1979), 7–21; for full discussion of Virgil's use of the didactic models see Farrell (1991).

[6] Nicander's fragments do not encourage the idea that he was a major source for the *Georgics* (see Farrell [1991], 208 n. 5); book 4 may owe something to Nicander's lost *Melissourgika* on bee-keeping (Farrell [1991], 239 n. 67).

[7] The *Georgics* is full of *aitia*, mythological or other explanations of the origins of things: S. Schechter, 'The *aition* and Virgil's *Georgics*', *TAPA* 105 (1975), 347–91.

[8] On the implications of this claim see Farrell (1991), ch. 2.

Georgic, whose subject is defined in the first eight words as (1.1–2) 'What makes the crops fertile [= 'Works', the subject of 1.43–203], at what time of year to turn the land [= 'Days', the subject of 1.204–305]'.[9] Hesiod links his practical teaching with an urgent moral message to his wayward and indolent brother Perses, and to mankind in general, about the necessity of unremitting work in an Iron Age that has fallen from the primal ease of the Golden Age, and in which man's only hope lies in a compliance with the hard justice of Zeus. From Hesiod Virgil takes the location of the farmer's daily tasks within the longest view of human history; less than twenty lines into the didactic body of book 1 we are transported from the here and now of the start of the farmer's year to the creation of mankind by Deucalion (1.61–3), and at 1.118–59 Virgil presents his own version of the Hesiodic myth of ages in the so-called 'Theodicy', an explanation of Jupiter's decision to make hard work the law of the world.[10] Virgil, like Hesiod, sometimes speaks in the strains of an Old Testament prophet; for the Roman of the late 30s B.C. the general necessity for disciplined hard work was an even more urgent imperative after the social and moral disintegration of the Civil Wars.

To move from the beginning of the didactic tradition to one of Virgil's immediate predecessors, we find an equally important source for the committed didactic voice in Lucretius' poem on Epicurean physics, the *De rerum natura*. 'The influence, direct and indirect, exercised by Lucretius on the thought, the composition, and the style of the *Georgics* was perhaps stronger than that ever exercised, before or since, by one great poet on the work of another.'[11] Lucretius expounds the scientific teachings of a Hellenistic school of philosophy with the goal of converting a benighted audience to a state of enlightened bliss. His

[9] The concentration of Hesiodic material in the first book led J. Bayet to the hypothesis of a first, Hesiodic, version of the *Georgics*, later expanded: 'Les premières *Géorgiques* de Virgile (39–37 av. J.C.)', *Rev. Phil.* 4 (1930), 128–50, 227–47, an analytical approach now generally rejected. On Virgil's use of Hesiod see A. La Penna, 'Esiodo nella cultura e nella poesia di Virgilio', in *Hésiode et son influence* (*Entret. Hardt* 7) (Geneva, 1962), 213–70, at 225–47 on the *Georgics*.

[10] On the 'Theodicy' see Wilkinson (1969), 134–45; Putnam (1979), 32–6; Ross (1987), 79–82; H. Altevogt, *'Labor improbus': eine Vergilstudie* (Münster, 1952); H. Drexler, 'Zu Verg., *Georg.* 1.118–159', *RhM* 110 (1967), 165–74; E. M. Stehle, 'Virgil's *Georgics*: the threat of sloth', *TAPA* 104 (1974), 347–69.

[11] Sellar (1877), 199. Lucretius in the *Georgics*: Sellar (1877), ch. 6; C. Bailey, 'Virgil and Lucretius', *PCA* 28 (1931), 21–39; E. Paratore, 'Spunti lucreziani nelle *Georgiche*', *A&R* 20 (1939), 177–202; B. Farrington, 'Polemical allusions to the *De Rerum Natura* of Lucretius in the works of Vergil', in L. Varcl and R. F. Willetts (eds.), *Geras. Studies presented to G. Thomson* (Prague, 1963), 87–94; Klingner (1967), index s.v. 'Lucrez'; W. Liebeschuetz, 'The cycle of growth and decay in Lucretius and Virgil', *PVS* 7 (1967/68), 30–40; W. R. Nethercut, 'Vergil's *De rerum natura*', *Ramus* 2 (1973), 41–52; Hardie (1986), 158–67; Farrell (1991), ch. 5; K. Freudenburg, 'Lucretius, Vergil and the *causa morbi*', *Vergilius* 33 (1987), 59–74.

subject is the infinite universe itself, his target is the individual human soul; the use in a moral protreptic of an account of cosmic processes is inspired by another 'vatic' early Greek writer of didactic poetry, the Presocratic philosopher Empedocles.[12] Virgil's use of Lucretius is complex: he takes from him a sense of wonder at cosmic processes and at the abundant variety of the natural world, a feeling for the interconnectedness of things (one of the bases for the sustained anthropomorphism of the *Georgics*), and an eye for the elemental structures that underlie the complex variety of the phenomenal world.[13] The *De rerum natura* is a source both for positive images such as the springtime marriage of Heaven and Earth (*Geo.* 2.325–45: cf. Lucr. 1.250–61) or the happy life of the countrydweller contrasted with the discontents of urban luxury (*Geo.* 2.458–540: cf. Lucr. 2.20–36),[14] and for the negative images of plague (*Geo.* 3.478–566: cf. Lucr. 6.1138–1286)[15] and the destructive effects of love (*Geo.* 3.242–83).[16] This last passage draws not only on Lucretius' 'diatribe' on erotic infatuation at the end of *De rerum natura* 4, but also inverts the image of a constructive power of love in Lucretius' opening hymn to Venus, a passage which had already been reworked in Virgil's opening prayer to Octavian, a human saviour soon to enjoy a divinity that Lucretius accords only figuratively to his hero, Epicurus. Where Lucretius demythologizes remorselessly, Virgil, less dogmatically, remythologizes. The mixture of attraction and repulsion that Virgil feels for Lucretius surfaces in the passage on the poet's aspirations at *Geo.* 2.475–94.

Virgil found other models for the combination of the traditions of didactic poetry with Hellenistic philosophy and science in the Alexandrian scholar-scientist Eratosthenes' epic poem *Hermes*, the

[12] Virgil alludes to a piece of Empedoclean physiology in airing the possibility that he may be unable to aspire to the heights of scientific didactic at 2.483–4 (see comms. ad. loc.). On the possibility of Empedoclean allegory in the Song of Clymene at 4.345–7 see Farrell (1991), 260–1, 270–1.

[13] The scientific underpinning of the *Georgics* in a schematic opposition of elements is a central topic of Ross (1987), who however looks rather to Greek science than Lucretius for the sources.

[14] On the praise of country life see F. Klingner, 'Über das Lob des Landlebens in Virgils Georgica', *Hermes* 66 (1931), 159–89; id. (1967), 265–77; Williams (1968), 417–26 (comparison with Prop. 3.22); Buchheit (1972), 55–92; J. S. Clay, 'The argument of the end of Vergil's second Georgic', *Philol.* 120 (1976), 232–45.

[15] Plague: D. West, 'Two plagues. Virgil, *Georgics* 3.478–566 and Lucretius 6.1090–1286', in West and Woodman (1979), 71–88; E. L. Harrison, 'The Noric plague in Vergil's third *Georgic*', *PLLS* 2 (1979), 1–65; E. Flintoff, 'The Noric cattle plague', *QUCC* 13.1 (1983), 85–111; R. Clare, 'Chiron, Melampus and Tisiphone: myth and meaning in Vergil's plague of Noricum', *Hermathena* 158 (1995), 95–108; Freudenburg (n. 11); H. Klepl, *Lukrez und Vergil in ihren Lehrgedichten* (Darmstadt, 1967), 52–101.

[16] For an analysis of Virgil's use of Lucretius in this passage see Hardie (1986), 159–67.

model for the description of the five zones of the earth (*Geo.* 1.233–9), and in the Stoicizing Aratus' astronomical and meteorological *Phaeno-mena*, a didactic poem that enjoyed a remarkable vogue in Rome in the first centuries B.C. and A.D. and which was translated by, among others, the young Cicero and adapted by Virgil's older contemporary Varro of Atax.[17] Callimachus praised Aratus' poem for its Hesiodic manner (*Epigr.* 27 Pfeiffer); it is in recognition of this literary genealogy that Virgil's adaptation (1.351–463) of Aratus' 'Weather Signs' (*Phae-nomena* 733–1154), follows immediately on Virgil's rewriting of Hes-iod's 'Works' and 'Days'.[18]

Aratus' *Phaenomena* is a versification ('metaphrasis') of a prose treatise of the astronomer Eudoxus, a pupil of Plato; Lucretius makes poetry out of the prose treatises of Epicurus. Virgil also uses scientific and agricultural prose treatises, for example Aristotle's *Historia animal-ium* for the natural history of bees, and Aristotle's pupil Theophrastus' works on botany for much of the material on trees and bushes in *Georgics* 2. Of Roman treatises most important is the great scholar Varro's *Res rusticae*, published at 37/6 B.C. at just the time that Virgil was beginning the *Georgics*. Varro's opening invocation to twelve gods is the model for Virgil's invocation of twelve (only partly overlapping) gods at *Georgics* 1.5–20, and Varro is the source for many technical details in the last three books of the poem. For example at *Georgics* 3.322–38 Varro's instructions on the summer pasturing of sheep and goats are transmuted into a pastoral vision of the herdsman's daily routine.[19] But we should beware of assuming that Varro's prose treatise and Virgil's poem had completely different audiences or purposes; Columella certainly saw no contradiction in liberally quoting the *Georgics* in his later prose treatise *De re rustica*.[20]

---

[17] Varro's translation (fr. 14 Courtney) is imitated at *Geo.* 1.374–87.

[18] The relevant passages of Eratosthenes and Aratus are gathered at Mynors (1990), 325–30. On the Aratean adaptation see L. A. S. Jermyn, 'Weather-signs in Virgil', *G&R* 20 (1951), 26–37, 46–59; Farrell (1991), 157–68.

[19] On Virgil's use of his prose sources see L. A. S. Jermyn, 'Virgil's agricultural lore', *G&R* 18 (1949), 49–69 (use of Cato and Varro); R. F. Thomas, 'Prose into poetry: tradition and meaning in Virgil's *Georgics*', *HSCP* 91 (1987), 229–60 (232–5 on *Geo.* 3.322–38; see also Thomas (1988), i. 25–6; Wilkinson (1969), 11–13). E. W. Leach, '*Georgics* 2 and the poem', *Arethusa* 14 (1981), 35–48 argues that the *fortunatus* at 2.493 is Varro, and that he is a more important model for the conception of the poem than is usually allowed.

[20] Columella: Wilkinson (1969), 270–1. On the nature and intended audience of Varro's *Res rusticae* see E. Rawson, *Roman Culture and Society* (Oxford, 1991), 327–8; Miles (1980), 33–45; Horsfall (1995), 95.

The Romans and the Natural World. Farming.
Ethnography and Cosmology.

A modern reader whose attitudes towards man and the natural world are determined partly by Romantic ideas about nature and partly by late twentieth-century environmentalism may not find it easy to come to terms with the views of man's relation to the natural world expressed in the *Georgics*.[21] We will respond readily enough to the jaded city-dweller's dream of an idyllic life in the countryside at the end of *Georgics* 2, feel a thrill of sublime terror at the descriptions of storm (*Geo.* 1.322–34) and plague (3.478–566), and enjoy any number of local descriptive passages.[22] A nation of garden-lovers may regret that Virgil sails so briskly past the topic of horticulture (4.116–48);[23] we have to go back to eighteenth-century England, 'the great age of country-house life and agricultural interest',[24] to find a real sympathy for the *Georgics*' wealth of agricultural detail. An audience all too aware of the fragility of the ecosphere may wince at the recurrent image of farming as a war waged against the earth; for the ancient the ideal was a natural world tamed and disciplined by man.[25]

Here if anywhere it is crucial to recreate the 'period eye'. An interest in the possibility that Virgil writes from his personal experience of farming in northern Italy continues in some quarters,[26] but it is the expectations and interests of his readership that matter more. Many upper-class

---

[21] On Roman attitudes to nature, farming, and landscape see Miles (1980), ch. 1 'The Roman context' (a good survey); Ross (1987), 10–25; E. W. Leach, *The Rhetoric of Space. Literary and Artistic Representations of Landscape in Republican and Augustan Rome* (Princeton, 1988), esp. ch. 3 'Spatial patterns in Vergil's *Georgics*'.

[22] Wilkinson (1969), 3–14 seeks to define the poem as primarily descriptive; (11) 'The *Georgics* is ... the first poem in all literature in which description may be said to be the chief *raison d'être* and source of pleasure'. But note that Virgil seems to anticipate an aestheticism of this kind in his explanation of the reason for planting vines in regular formation (2.285–7) *non animum modo uti pascat prospectus inanem,* | *sed quia non aliter uiris dabit omnibus aequas* | *terra.*

[23] Columella took 4.148 literally and included a book in hexameters on gardening in his *De Re rustica*; the Renaissance produced many didactic poems on gardening.

[24] Wilkinson (1969), 300.

[25] Ross (1987), 22–4. Cf. the picture at Lucr. 5.1367–78 of the advance of cultivation up the previously afforested mountain-sides, combining productivity with a visual prospect of charming variety. On the relation of the ancients to their environment see J. D. Hughes, *Pan's Travail: Environmental Problems of the Ancient Greeks and Romans* (Baltimore and London, 1994).

[26] This wistful search for personal experience surfaces from time to time in Mynors' commentary (which is, however, fully alert to the literary sources); see Mynors (1990), p. vi. The reference to the land lost by Mantua, in the course of a detailed discussion of soil-types, at 2.198–9 seems deliberately to flaunt a literary allusivity rather than evoke Virgil's childhood memory (see Thomas ad loc.).

Romans did have estates in the country, in whose running they took an amateur interest;[27] the pleasure of such a Roman in the natural and technical details of the farm is vividly expressed in Cicero *De senectute* 51–60, a passage that may indeed be one of Virgil's sources.[28] Cicero's spokesman in this work, the elder Cato, whose *De agricultura* may be among Virgil's prose sources, was largely responsible for the construction of the myth of the origins of Roman moral and military superiority in the virtuous life of the Italian (typically Sabine) farmer,[29] a myth whose potency is exploited in the praise of country life at the end of book 2, and which provides one key to reading the *laudes Italiae* at 2.136–76, in which the natural and agricultural abundance of Italy appears as the indispensable precondition for the extension of Roman military might to the ends of the earth. But many modern critics sense that the terms in which Virgil here develops the stereotype reveal a fatal contradiction between the ideal of a peaceful life in the country and the violence of state militarism; at the very least we should allow the poet the freedom, should he wish it, to distance himself from prevailing value-systems and ideologies.[30] On the other hand we may press the contrast between the picture in the *laudes Italiae* of a successful military imperialism founded on the virtues of a race of Italian farmers and the suggestion at the end of book 1 of a close connection between the abandonment of the ancestral agrarian lifestyle and civil war (1.506–8), leading to a perversion of agricultural practice as the fields of Macedonia are manured with the blood of Roman citizens (1.491–2). The proper targets of Roman military might will then be foreign peoples in need of the benefits of Roman rule (4.561–2) and, figuratively, the earth with the plants and animals that grow on it, which must be 'conquered', 'disciplined', and 'civilized'.[31]

Hesiod's world revolves around his poverty-stricken village of Ascra; sailing for trade is a marginal and distinctly dangerous activity. Italy is at

[27] Like Horace in *Ep.* 1.14 and 1.16. See Horsfall (1995), 70–1; J. G. F. Powell on Cic. *De senect.* 51.
[28] E. de Saint-Denis, 'Une source de Virgile dans les *Géorgiques*', *REL* 16 (1938), 297–317, at 308–17; N. M. Horsfall, 'Cato, Cicero and the *Georgics*: a note', *Vergilius* 41 (1995), 55–6.
[29] Cato paints the stereotype of peasant farmers as good men and brave soldiers in the preface of his otherwise hardheadedly entrepreneurial *De agricultura*.
[30] *Laudes Italiae* as a lie: Thomas (1982), 36–51; Ross (1987), 116–28. On the passage see also A. G. McKay, 'Vergil's glorification of Italy (*Georgics* 2.136–74)', in J. R. C. Martyn (ed.), *Cicero and Virgil: Studies in Honour of H. Hunt* (Amsterdam, 1972), 149–68.
[31] Military imagery of farming: A. Betensky, 'The farmer's battles', in Boyle (1979), 108–19; R. F. Glei, *Der Vater der Dinge: Interpretationen zur poetischen, literarischen und kulturellen Dimension des Krieges bei Vergil* (Trier, 1991), 277–86. The relationship between literal warfare, against both foreign and civil opponents, and the figurative war on the earth is well discussed in Putnam (1979).

the centre of the world of the *Georgics*, but the reader is repeatedly reminded of the larger map: thus the *laudes Italiae* are introduced as the climax to a list of exotic lands and their produce (2.109–35). To map out the wider world Virgil draws on the ancient traditions of ethno-graphical writing, notably in the striking descriptions of the shepherd's life in the burning heat of Libya and the icebound cold of Scythia at 3.339–83, and in the account of the race of bees in book 4.[32] As often in antiquity, description of foreign peoples is a way of defining the nature of one's own society through comparison and contrast; for Virgil ethnography also provides a geographical context for Roman military activity: the Indians whose botanical wonders are described at 2.122–4 flee before the army of Octavian at 2.171–2. At one moment Virgil's eye dwells lovingly on familiar Italian localities, at another it conjures up the wonders of distant lands; his vision can also expand to encompass the world, even the universe itself (a trick already familiar from the *Eclogues*), as in the survey of the five zones of sky and earth, and the Antipodes, at 1.231–58 (after which the focus narrows dramatically to a picture of the farmer confined to his cottage by bad weather). Again Hellenistic astronomy and cosmology are put to work to specifically Roman ends, as in the apocalyptic description of the cosmic convulsions that followed the death of Julius Caesar at 1.466–514;[33] this connection between Roman history and religion, and the workings of the universe will continue as a central concern of the *Aeneid*.

History and Politics. Anthropomorphism. The Bees. Cultural Histories.

The discussion of Roman attitudes to farming, the countryside, and to man's place in the natural world has taken us deep into Roman history and politics. The *Georgics* were composed probably in the years 36–29 B.C.,[34] years that saw the final upheavals of the civil wars, Octavian's victory at Actium, and subsequent wars in the east prior to his triumphant return to Rome in 29 B.C. The poem's dedicatee and notional second-person didactic addressee is Octavian's right-hand man

---

[32] Thomas (1982) and (1988), and Ross (1987), index s.v. 'ethnography', offer extensive discussion; Dahlmann (1954) had demonstrated the ethnographical background to the description of the bees.

[33] See Buchheit (1972), 31–44; R. O. A. M. Lyne, '*Scilicet et tempus ueniet* . . . Virgil, *Georgics* 1.463–514', in Woodman and West (1974), 47–66.

[34] Date of *Georgics*: Wilkinson (1969), 69–70; Horsfall (1995), 63–5.

Maecenas;[35] at 1.40–2 pity of a distinctly Lucretian tinge for the unenlightened farmer prompts the poet into requesting the aid on the path of instruction of an Octavian whose prospective apotheosis in the preceding prayer casts him in the role of saviour man-god that Lucretius had ascribed to his philosophical hero Epicurus.[36] The opening invocation of Octavian is mirrored at the end of book 1 by the anxious prayer that Octavian should bring salvation to Rome and end the civil wars triggered by the murder of Julius Caesar (498–504); positive images of Octavian successfully pursuing the foreign wars that will ensure the settled peace at home necessary for the farmer's prosperity cap the *laudes Italiae* at 2.170–2 and conclude the whole poem at 4.560–2. At the centre of the poem Virgil alludes to the triple triumph of 29 B.C. that put the seal on Octavian's victory over foes civil and foreign, and to the Palatine temple of Apollo dedicated in the following year.[37]

The creation of order out of disorder on the political and military plane, in causal terms the necessary precondition for the farmer's success, is integrated thematically into the didactic concerns of the poem in two ways: firstly, through a sustained and developing anthropomorphism that allows not only the farmer, but also the soil, plants, and animals that are the object of his labour, to stand as figures for the human society in need of the Roman hero's salvific care; and secondly, through the intimation that Octavian comes as a culture hero to culminate a cultural history that reaches back to the origins of the world.

The anthropomorphism of the poem[38] is signalled in its third word, (1.1) *laetas* (*segetes*), both 'fertile' and 'happy' (crops), exploiting a countryman's turn of phrase to suggest a parallelism between vegetable or animal and human experience that is developed in the four books through an almost evolutionary progression. In book 1 the insistent image of farming as warfare or military training makes of the earth either a foreign enemy to be subdued or a recalcitrant conscript. The urge to animate the inanimate leads to a moment of surrealism in the hint that man fashions the components of the plough into a kind of monster with 'feet', 'ears', and 'teeth', in the reworking of the Hesiodic instructions on

---

[35] On the function of the poetic patron see White (1993).

[36] On the praise of Octavian as a 'thirteenth god', very much in the tradition of Hellenistic ruler-worship, see Mynors (1990), 1–3; G. Wissowa, 'Das Prooemium von Vergils *Georgica*', *Hermes* 52 (1917), 92–104.

[37] D. L. Drew, 'Virgil's marble temple (*Georg.* 3.10–39)', *CQ* 18 (1924), 195–202.

[38] See W. Liebeschuetz, 'Beast and man in the third book of Virgil's *Georgics*', *G&R* 12 (1965), 64–77; M. Gale, 'Man and beast in Lucretius and the *Georgics*', *CQ* 41 (1991), 414–26.

making a plough (1.169–75; cf. Hes. *Works and Days* 427–36).[39] The reader empathizes more readily with the nursery education and later training of the trees and vines in book 2, and their adolescent delight in new-found powers (2.363–4). An interest in propagation and the need to maintain the quality of the stock, first aired in a striking passage at 1.197–203 with reference to the degeneration of seed, expresses itself in book 2 in the language of maternity and paternity (2.18–19, 55–60). In book 3 the themes of education, training, and family bloodlines emerge as major topics in the rearing of horses and cattle. Emotions of horse and human charioteer are indistinguishable at 3.103–12; the defeated bull at 3.219–41 no longer needs human help to devise his own course of military training in preparation for a return to what is unsettlingly like human civil war.[40] The stud farmer's care over pedigree reflects the future epic poet's interest in tracing the Julian *gens* back to its Trojan ancestors (3.34–6); generational continuity will be a major theme of the *Aeneid*, an epic poem that might be read as an educational manual for future generations of Romans. The stability and continuity of animal and human societies alike are threatened by two natural forces, the figurative disease of love (3.242–83, concluding the first half of the book)[41] and literal disease, appearing in the most destructive form of the all-devouring plague (3.478–566, concluding the whole book), presented initially as a corruption of the air of heaven (3.478) but finally revealed as an eruption from the Underworld (3.551–3). Love, disease, and Hell make up a heady imagistic mix from which Virgil will draw deeply in the *Aeneid*.

Anthropomorphism reaches a climax with the bees in book 4, a species that antiquity regarded as having something divine about it.[42] Virgil's bees have a fully developed society, with a king, a city, division of labour, and a work ethic that Hesiod would have applauded. They indulge in that most typically human of activities, organized warfare (4.67–87), and they have an unsurpassed concern for the continuity of the race and society, even at the cost of individual survival (4.203–9). But we perceive the bee society with a kind of double vision: at times we view their society from within, as we would our own social structures, at other times we see them from the beekeeper's perspective as just another

[39] The plough: Putnam (1979), 36–7; W. W. De Grummond, 'The animated implement: a Catullan source for Virgil's plough', *Eranos* 91 (1993), 75–80.

[40] The battle of the bulls is reused in a simile applied to the duelling Aeneas and Turnus at *Aen.* 12.715–22; see Briggs (1980), 49–50.

[41] G. B. Miles, '*Georgics* 3.209–294: *amor* and civilization', *CSCA* 8 (1975), 177–97.

[42] Fundamental on the anthropomorphism of the bees is Dahlmann (1954); see also B. G. Whitfield, 'Virgil and the bees', *G&R* 3 (1956), 99–117; Buchheit (1972), 161–73.

farm animal to be provided for and kept under control. Their heroic
battles may in the end be calmed by a handful of dust from a human
hand (4.86–7). This double vision is also expressed through a para-
doxical contrast of large and small (4.3–4 *admiranda . . . leuium*
spectacula rerum | *magnanimosque duces* 'the marvellous spectacle of a
tiny world and great-hearted leaders'), notably in the simile comparing
the tiny honey-making labourers to the Cyclopes at their forge (4.170–
8). Another contrast is that between the strange and the familiar: at one
level the bee society is the culminating example of the poem's interest in
ethnographical marvels.[43] For example, they reproduce asexually
(4.197–209), and so are immune to the erotic fury that plagues other
animals and humans. Their devotion to their king outstrips that of the
peoples of Egypt, Lydia, Parthia, and Persia (4.210–2). Yet the parallel
with the *laudes Italiae* in book 2, where it is Italy that outdoes the
wonders of the east (2.136–9), may hint that it is in Italy and Rome that
such supreme devotion to a great leader is (or should be) found. The
continence, discipline, militarism, and willing self-sacrifice of the bees
irresistibly suggests an ideal image of a primitive Roman society that is
confirmed when the bees are startlingly referred to as *Quirites* (4.201), a
formal name for 'Romans'.[44]

Among their Roman virtues the bees also have a Roman vice: the use
of the word *discordia* to introduce the war of the bees at 4.68 hints at
'civil strife', and the description of the good and bad kings at 4.88–94
has suggested to some Octavian and Mark Antony.[45] Halfway through
book 4 Virgil raises the possibility that the hive may be destroyed by an
epidemic as total as the plague at the end of the previous book. The
remedy is the bizarre *bugonia*, the regeneration of bees from the carcass
of a brutally slaughtered ox, the most amazing of the paradoxical
wonders of this book, and one practised in Egypt, the land of wonders
par excellence for ancient ethnographers. At the same time the *bugonia*
may speak allegorically of a process close to home, the restoration of the
Roman state and society after the 'plague' of civil war; further discussion
will be deferred for a fuller consideration of the whole of the Aristaeus
epyllion that concludes the poem.

The experience of the bees touches on the most recent history of

---

[43] See Ross (1987), ch. 5; Thomas (1988), index s.vv. 'ethnography', θαῦμα. In general on
wonders of the east see J. S. Romm, *The Edges of the Earth in Ancient Thought: Geography,
Exploration, and Fiction* (Princeton, 1992), ch. 3.

[44] See J. Griffin, 'The fourth *Georgic*, Virgil and Rome', in Griffin (1985), 163–82.

[45] In an extreme version in Y. Nadeau, 'The lover and the statesman: a study in apiculture
(Virgil, *Georgics* 4.281–558)', in Woodman and West (1984), 59–82.

Rome, but they also have a cultural history that goes back to a mythological past, when Jupiter gave them their social 'nature' as reward for feeding the infant king of the gods (4.149–52).[46] It may be another of the paradoxes of bee society that it seems to be an Iron Age version of the Golden Age. In locating a present dispensation within the longest chronological perspective book 4, as in other respects, recapitulates a major concern of the whole poem (and a continuing preoccupation of the *Aeneid*; a precedent is provided by *Eclogue* 4); the account of Jupiter's endowment of bee nature in book 4 mirrors the less upbeat history of the onset of the Age of Jupiter in the Theodicy at 1.121–46. Virgil's version of cultural history is complex, and perhaps contradictory. He draws on Hesiod's myth of the declining races of man (*Works and Days* 106–201), on Aratus' variant of the Hesiodic myth (*Phaen.* 96–136), as well as on the mixture of progressivism and primitivism in Lucretius' account of cultural history at the end of *De rerum natura* 5.[47] Present-day life in the country, the end product of this historical evolution, is shown in images of both the 'soft primitivism' of the Golden Age and the hard dispensation of the Iron Age. Contemporary man is condemned to hard labour, but at times it is hinted that virtuous hard work may lead to a restoration of the Golden Age, if in less fantastic terms than the vision of *Eclogue* 4.[48] The juxtaposition of these divergent views on cultural progress and on the perfectibility of human society (and by implication of the new Roman order) is a major factor in the ongoing critical debate as to the overall message of the poem (see pp. 50–2 below).

Poetics and Allusion. Etymology and Allusive Play. Genre (Pastoral and Epic).

If the *Georgics* place recent Roman history and the coming of the saviour Octavian within the frame of a far larger cultural history, the poet of the *Georgics* also self-consciously locates his work within the traditions of

---

[46] Ross (1987), 191 stresses the coexistence in book 4 of a diachronic cultural history of the bees with a synchronic ethnographical description.

[47] Hesiod and Aratus: Farrell (1991), 142–8, 161–2; Lucretius: ibid. ch. 5.

[48] Golden Age: see ch. II n. 57, and add Johnston (1980) (arguing for Virgil's modification of the Hesiodic 'metallic' age into an 'agricultural' conception of the Golden Age); J. J. L. Smolenaars, 'Labour in the Golden Age. A unifying theme in Vergil's poems', *Mnemos.* 40 (1987), 391–405 ('optimistic'); Ross (1987) and Thomas (1988) offer 'pessimistic' readings. On primitivism see M. E. Taylor, 'Primitivism in Virgil', *AJP* 76 (1955), 261–78, and (in general) A. O. Lovejoy and G. Boas, *Primitivism and Related Ideas in Antiquity* (New York, 1965).

Greco-Roman poetry, constructing a literary genealogy for his poem. We have already looked at his use of the Roman poet's most basic way of defining his work, by reference to the Greek originator of the genre, at 2.176 *Ascraeumque cano Romana per oppida carmen;*[49] a more complex set of implicit acknowledgements had been provided by the allusions to Hesiod, Lucretius, and the prose writer Varro at the beginning of book 1.

The poetics of the *Georgics* are characterized by, firstly, an awareness of a range of choices available to the poet, and, secondly, by a sense of being in transition, of going on a poetic journey. Both aspects are highlighted in the major programmatic episode, which, as in the *Eclogues*, is placed not at the beginning of the work but in the 'proem in the middle'[50] at 3.1–48. This new beginning in fact continues a discussion of poetic choices and paths initiated in the central passage of the epilogue to book 2 (475–94),[51] which sets Virgil's chosen subject against a number of foils within the genre of didactic poetry proper, Aratus, Empedocles, and Lucretius.[52] In this passage Virgil bases his choice on the limits of personal ability, in a manner comparable to the typical *recusatio* of the love elegist; by contrast at 3.3–9 the proud assertion of his freedom to travel on untrodden poetic paths is (ironically) the poem's strongest statement of its indebtedness to a Callimachean poetics. The extent of the *Georgics'* debt to the *Aitia* has been clearer since the publication in 1975 of a new fragment that is a direct model for the proem of book 3, an epinician passage on the victory of Berenice that also stood at the beginning of the third book of a poem in four books.[53]

At 3.8–48, after the Callimachean rejection of outworn subjects, the poet envisages a path of poetry which will see him lead the Muses in triumph from mount Helicon to Italy, where, on the rural banks of the Mantuan river Mincius, he will erect a temple glorifying the achieve-

---

[49] Cf. Horace's definition of his lyric achievement at *Odes* 3.30.13–14 *princeps Aeolium carmen ad Italos | deduxisse modos*, where *Aeolium* refers to the poetry of Alcaeus and Sappho.

[50] G. B. Conte's term (see chapter II n. 41).

[51] On the fundamental unity of the epilogue of *Geo.* 2 and the proem of *Geo.* 3 see Buchheit (1972), 45–159; W. Wimmel, *Kallimachos in Rom* (Wiesbaden, 1960), 167–87; Hardie (1986), 33–51. The programmatic poetics of *Ecl.* 6 also continues an investigation into poetics entered on in the previous *Eclogue* (see p. 17 above).

[52] It should never have been doubted that the primary concern in 2.490–4 is the haunting of Virgil by his great Roman predecessor, Lucretius (as Mynors, but not Thomas, ad loc. allows).

[53] The fundamental discussion is by R. F. Thomas, 'Callimachus, the *Victoria Berenices*, and Roman poetry', *CQ* 33 (1983), 92–113. For Virgil's use elsewhere in the *Georgics* of the Callimachean opposition between grand and small-scale poetry see Thomas (1988), i. 2–3; the large/small contrast central to Virgil's treatment of the bees is related to his Callimacheanism (see Thomas on 4.6).

ments of Octavian and his ancestors, and celebrate athletic contests that will outdo the great games of Greece. Virgil here tests his wings for the epic flight that is to follow the *Georgics*; the fact that some scholars have taken the passage to refer to the poem in hand is a fruitful misunderstanding, pointing to the fact that the relationship between the *Georgics* and the future epic project is as much one of continuity as of an opposition between an Alexandrian, Callimachean, didactic poem and an 'anti-Callimachean' epic.[54] That the temple, monument to Octavian's military success, is to be built in the rustic Italian setting of the Mincius is in itself a further symbol of the community of interest between the didactic poet of the countryside and the 'epic' Roman hero. Virgil's own poetic 'triumph', audaciously claiming a figurative equivalence between poet and the *triumphator* of 29 B.C., is already in the process of being achieved in the *Georgics*' triumphant appropriation of Greek literary traditions (the leading of the Muses from the 'Boeotian' (*Aonio*) mount at 3.11 points back ultimately to Hesiod's meeting with the Muses on Helicon). The iconographic programme of the poetic temple traces a path backwards from the latest triumph of Octavian to his remotest Trojan ancestors; the whole of the proem is a dizzying ride through a long poetic genealogy which is still undergoing development. From Callimachus, by a 'double allusion',[55] we journey back both to Pindar's victory odes, the specific model for the *Victoria Berenices* (and a not inappropriate model to evoke at the beginning of a didactic book that gives instruction in the rearing of race-horses, 3.49–50)[56] and to the original didactic poet Hesiod, whose meeting with the Muses on Helicon Callimachus took as the model for his own poetic initiation at the beginning of the *Aitia*. The boast of future fame and the construction of a temple to mark Roman victories in the east draw on Ennian, epic, models (respectively Ennius' epitaph on himself, and the construction of the *templum Herculis Musarum* by Ennius' patron, M. Fulvius Nobilior, probably the climax of the first edition of the *Annals*),[57] but Ennius as mediated through Lucretius' engagement with Ennius at *De rerum natura* 1.102–26.[58]

---

[54] Wilkinson (1969), 323–4 gives a handy survey of interpretations of the proem to book 3; see also Buchheit (1972), 92–159; an excellent study of the allusive detail is provided by S. Lundström, 'Der Eingang des Proömiums zum dritten Buche der Georgica', *Hermes* 104 (1976), 163–91.

[55] On this kind of allusion see J. C. McKeown, *Ovid Amores* i. (Liverpool, 1987), 37–45.

[56] See L. P. Wilkinson, 'Pindar and the proem to the third *Georgic*', in W. Wimmel (ed.), *Forschungen zur römischen Literatur. Festschrift K. Büchner* (Wiesbaden, 1970), 286–90.

[57] See Mynors on 3.8–9, 13; Lundström (n. 54), 177.

[58] See Mynors on 3.10–11; the repeated *primus* at 3.10–12 also echoes *primum . . . primus* in Lucretius' account of the 'epic' flight of Epicurus at *De rer. nat.* 1.66–71 (see Hardie [1986], 48).

That a path through the didactic tradition should point in the direction of epic is not in itself surprising, given that the ancients sometimes classified didactic and epic under the same heading on the basis of their shared metre, the hexameter.[59] Nor should we forget that by the beginning of *Georgics* 3 we have already had ample evidence of this particular didactic poem's ability to accommodate epic moments, particularly in the military imagery that clusters in book 1 around the theme of waging war on the soil; epic becomes a more insistent presence in book 3 as we move up the chain of being to deal with race horses, war horses, and the feuding bulls who are described as if they were two great heroes duelling for a woman (3.219–41); at 4.3–5 the 'great-hearted leaders' and 'battles' of the bees are introduced in overtly epic terms.[60] Joseph Farrell notes the shift in the relative importance of poetic models, from Hesiod and Aratus in book 1, through a concentration of Lucretian allusion in books 2 and 3, to the greater epic colouring of book 4, culminating in the very Homeric Aristaeus narrative; he argues that this is not so much a development from a purely didactic kind of poetry towards the different, grander genre of epic, as intended 'to integrate Homer into the didactic branch of the epic tradition; . . . to show how even that branch of the tradition derives, ultimately, from Homer'.[61] Virgil achieves this integration not merely in line with the ancient belief that Homer was the fountainhead of all kinds of literature (including didactic),[62] but with reference to a tradition of allegorizing the epic narratives of Homer as containing philosophical and scientific teaching.[63]

The proem to book 3 explores the relationship between didactic and epic, and also that between pastoral (another hexameter genre) and epic: Virgil's didactic is generically aware both of its predecessor within the poet's *œuvre* and of its gestating successor. The subject-matter of book 3, the care of large animals, returns us to the pastoral world from which we had taken our leave at the end of the *Eclogues*, and it is therefore all the more striking that after the invocation to the pastoral

[59] Toohey (1996), 5–7. For a later Augustan poet's tendentious definition of the whole of the Latin hexameter tradition as didactic see P. R. Hardie, 'The Speech of Pythagoras in Ovid *Metamorphoses* 15: Empedoclean epos', *CQ* 45 (1995), 204–14.

[60] Compare the introduction of the peoples and wars of Italy in the invocation at *Aen.* 7.37–40.

[61] Farrell (1991), 238. Farrell's argument that the poem 'is informed by an allusive program that finds elements of unity among its diverse models' (133), develops the brief observations on the distribution of models within the poem by D. Wender, 'From Hesiod to Homer by way of Rome', in Boyle (1979), 59–64.

[62] Homer as the universal poet: Hardie (1986), 22–5.

[63] Farrell (1991), 256–72; Hardie (1986), index s.v. 'allegory'.

gods in 3.1–2 we plunge into a very epic world. In the body of the book there are further contrasts between passages of epic or epinician pretension, and scenes of pastoral tranquillity (3.143–5, 314–17 (in Arcadia), 322–38). The 'pastoral idea' appears briefly at other points in the poem (2.469–71; 4.23–4), and it should be noted that in the concluding mythological narrative both Aristaeus and Proteus are herdsmen (the latter of a flock of seals). Pastoral leisure (*otium*) is a foil to the hard labour of the farmer, offering a possibly delusive image of an innocent and easy life.[64]

Poetic self-consciousness in the *Georgics* manifests itself in many smaller instances of allusive play,[65] etymological puns,[66] overt or covert references to literary traditions,[67] and even a probable acrostic.[68] Even allowing for the bias of contemporary scholarly fashions, it is now hard to see how the *Georgics* could ever have been read as a working manual for the farmer. A further example of the shift in recent years from a historical or moralizing reading of the *Georgics* to a focus on the poem's concern with its own poetics and literary history is Richard Thomas' ingenious argument that the mysterious beekeeper and gardener, the Corycian old man at 4.116–48, is not so much an example of a successful policy of settling pirates or veterans on the land as a riddling allusion to the Hellenistic poet Philitas or to a character in his poetry.[69]

---

[64] See Ross (1987), 167–77 'The pastoral idea': id., 'The pastoral in the *Georgics*: *si numquam fallit imago*', *Arethusa* 23 (1990), 59–75, with D. M. Halperin's penetrating commentary, 'Pastoral violence in the *Georgics*', ibid. 77–93. On pastoral elements in the epic *Aeneid* see pp. 60–1.

[65] R. F. Thomas, 'Virgil's *Georgics* and the art of reference', *HSCP* 90 (1986), 171–98; F. Muecke, 'Poetic self-consciousness in *Georgics* 2', in Boyle (1979), 87–107; H. J. W. Wijsman, 'Ascanius, Gargara and female power (*Georgics* 3.269–270)', *HSCP* 95 (1993), 315–18. In general on allusion see ch. II n. 12.

[66] Ross (1987) has a keen eye for etymology; for a massive treatment by a pupil of Ross, see O'Hara (1996), with exhaustive bibliography.

[67] 2.380–96, origins of tragedy and Roman poetry (see Thomas ad loc.).

[68] 1.428–33 PV(BLIVS) VE(RGILIVS) MA(RO) backwards in alternate lines: see Brown (1963), ch. 6; M. Haslam, 'Hidden signs: Aratus *Diosemeiai* 46 ff., Vergil *Georgics* 1.424 ff.', *HSCP* 94 (1992), 199–204.

[69] R. F. Thomas, 'The Old Man revisited: memory, reference and genre in Virg., *Georg.* 4. 116–48', *MD* 29 (1992), 35–70. But the one reading need not exclude the other, and the episode does seem to owe something to Varro's story of the beekeeping Faliscan veterans (*Res rust.* 3.16.10). See also C. G. Perkell, 'On the Corycian farmer of Virgil's fourth *Georgic*', *TAPA* 111 (1981), 167–77; M. Leigh, 'Servius on Vergil's *Senex Corycius*: new evidence', *MD* 33 (1994), 181–95.

Myth. The Aristaeus Epyllion.

Another sign of the learned poet is the density of mythological material in the *Georgics*.[70] This is partly a consequence of the decision to follow Hesiod in placing agricultural precept within the context of a universal history of mankind; thus at 1.61–3 the necessity for the farmer to show himself a tough worker in his struggle with the hard earth is traced to the mythical creation of mankind from the stones cast by Deucalion. Myths can also occur in local *aitia*, as in the invention of charioteering and horse-riding by, respectively, Ericthonius and the Lapiths (3.113–17).[71] But mythology is not confined to such contexts; just as Virgil is in the habit of leaping from the small-scale to the large-scale, from the local to the universal in both spatial and temporal terms, so the reader is repeatedly transported from the quotidian to a world of art and fantasy, whether through short passages of mythological narrative and description, such as the Gigantomachy (1.278–83), Scylla and Nisus (1.404–9), Io and the gadfly (3.146–56), or Hero and Leander (3.258–63), or through briefer allusion, often to myths of metamorphosis.[72]

Lucretius' intensive engagement with mythology in the *De rerum natura* is another legitimating model for Virgil's use of myth in the *Georgics*,[73] but where Lucretius relentlessly strips the mythological out of his world-view, Virgil offers us myth as a way of making sense of the world. Lucretius' poem ends with the final destruction of illusion in the horrors of the plague; as we have seen, Virgil's rewriting of the Lucretian plague at the end of book 3 begins as scientific and medical observation, but ends as mythological apocalypse. But this is not the end of the poem; the reversal of the plague that destroys the bees in book 4 is presented in a story that is introduced as an *aition* for the pseudoscientific procedure of the *bugonia*, but develops into an apparently free-standing epyllion, the story of Aristaeus that in turn frames the story of Orpheus and Eurydice.

The history of the critical treatment of this mythological 'digression', that in length greatly exceeds mythological inserts in other ancient

---

[70] For a comprehensive treatment see W. Frentz, *Mythologisches in Vergils Georgica* (Meisenheim, 1967). Wilkinson (1969), 183–5 wrongly dismisses the mythology in the *Georgics* as mere ornament.

[71] On *aitia* see Schechter (n. 7).

[72] M. Gale, 'Virgil's metamorphoses: myth and allusion in the *Georgics*', *PCPS* 41 (1995), 36–61, esp. 49.

[73] M. Gale, *Myth and Poetry in Lucretius* (Cambridge, 1994).

didactic poems, is bound up with a notorious literary puzzle. Servius reports (on *Ecl.* 10.1 and *Geo.* 4.1) that the second half of *Georgics* 4 originally contained 'praises of Gallus', the famous poet, statesman, and friend of Virgil, but that after Augustus brought about the death of the disgraced Gallus Virgil replaced the *laudes Galli* with the story of Aristaeus (or of Orpheus). Current orthodoxy is inclined to disbelieve Servius, partly on grounds of external plausibility, and partly because of the development of powerful analyses of the relevance of the Aristaeus epyllion to the *Georgics* as a whole.[74] The modern reader is confronted with a bewildering array of more or less plausible interpretations of the epyllion, and the difficulty is no longer that of dragging a viable reading into the light but that of pinning down the meaning of the episode. But to insist on a single interpretation may be to do violence to this polymorphous and Protean text.

The components of the story are carefully assembled by Virgil:[75] there is no evidence of a prior connection of Aristaeus with *bugonia* (although he was credited with the invention of beekeeping, and is already at home in the *Georgics* as one of the twelve gods in the opening invocation at 1.14–15), nor of a prior connection between the stories of Aristaeus and Orpheus. A complex play of continuity and contrast relates the two parts of the story both to each other and to the rest of the poem. The structure of framing (Aristaeus) and framed (Orpheus and Eurydice) narratives is that of the neoteric 'epyllion';[76] in particular Virgil is much indebted to Catullus 64, in which the framing narrative of the wedding of Peleus and Thetis comments on and is commented on by the framed description of the unhappy tale of Theseus and Ariadne.[77] Aristaeus and Orpheus both

[74] For a detailed examination of the debate, with bibliographical notes, see H. Jacobson, 'Aristaeus, Orpheus, and the *laudes Galli*', *AJP* 105 (1984), 271–300; J. Hermes, *C. Cornelius Gallus und Vergil: Das Problem der Umarbeitung des vierten Georgica-Buches* (Münster, 1980). The decisive interventions against the credibility of Servius were W. B. Anderson, 'Gallus and the fourth *Georgic*', *CQ* 27 (1933), 36–45, 73; E. Norden, 'Orpheus und Eurydice', *Sitzungsberichte der preussischen Akad., phil.-hist. Klasse* (1934), 626–83 [= *Kleine Schriften* (Berlin, 1966), 468–532 at 469–74]. Recent defenders of Servius include Jacobson himself; E. Lefèvre, 'Die *laudes Galli* in Vergils Georgica', *WS* 99 (1986), 183–92; H. D. Jocelyn, 'Servius and the second edition of the *Georgics*', in *Atti del convegno mondiale scientifico di studi su Virgilio* (Milan, 1984), i. 431–48.
[75] Wilkinson (1969), ch. 5; Mynors on 4.281–314. In general see Lee (1996), ch. 1, a survey of earlier discussions; C. M. Bowra, 'Orpheus and Eurydice', *CQ* 2 (1952), 113–26; C. Segal, 'Orpheus and the fourth *Georgic*: Vergil on nature and civilization', *AJP* 87 (1966), 307–25 (repr. in id., *Orpheus: The Myth of the Poet* (Baltimore and London, 1989), 36–53); C. G. Perkell, 'A reading of Virgil's fourth *Georgic*', *Phoenix* 32 (1978), 211–21.
[76] On the epyllion see M. M. Crump, *The Epyllion from Theocritus to Ovid* (Oxford, 1931), ch. 9 on Aristaeus; K. J. Gutzwiller, *Studies in the Hellenistic Epyllion* (Meisenheim, 1981).
[77] A. M. Crabbe, '*Ignoscenda quidem* . . . Catullus 64 and the fourth *Georgic*', *CQ* 27 (1977), 342–51. Catullus 64 was a major model for *Ecl.* 4, and continues to be a presence in the *Aeneid*, especially in Dido's speeches in *Aen.* 4.

lose what is most precious to them (the bees, Eurydice); in their search
for what is lost they both approach subterranean deities (Cyrene, the
rulers of the Underworld). Aristaeus succeeds, showing himself to be a
model pupil (suitably enough in a didactic poem) when he faithfully
follows his mother's instructions, firstly to bind Proteus in order to
discover the cause of his loss, and secondly to perform the placatory
sacrifice which leads to the *bugonia*. By contrast Orpheus fails, through
his inability to follow Proserpina's instruction not to look back at
Eurydice. The contrast between the hero who sees his goal through to
the end, and the hero who fails because he gives in to emotion is
reflected in the very different narrative manners of the two parts. The
Aristaeus narrative closely follows Homeric models (Achilles' com-
plaints to his mother Thetis at *Iliad* 1.345–427 and 18.22–137;
Menelaus' consultation of Proteus at *Odyssey* 4.351–572).[78] The
Orpheus and Eurydice narrative uses a more subjective, neoteric,
manner;[79] its generic affinities are not so much with epic as with
tragedy[80] and elegy (the simile of the complaining nightingale at
4.511–15 hints at an *aition* of elegiac lament). There are pronounced
similarities between the predicaments of Orpheus and of Gallus in
Eclogue 10,[81] and extensive allusion to the lost poetry of Gallus is very
likely; it is not impossible that some awareness of this lies at the root of
Servius' story about the *laudes Galli*.[82]

Aristaeus and Orpheus thus appear as two contrasting types of
culture hero.[83] Aristaeus, whose farming activities cover all the branches
dealt with in the *Georgics* (see 4.326–32), is forced by a disaster in the
natural world to invent a technology, thus exemplifying the lesson of
the Theodicy in book 1 (with 4.315 compare the language of 1.133).
Orpheus in antiquity was often held to be the founder of society and
civilization,[84] and even agriculture, but in the fourth *Georgic* he is totally

[78] Otis (1964), 193–7; Farrell (1991), 104–13.
[79] Otis (1964), 197–208; Thomas on 4.453–527.
[80] Norden (n. 74), 509–18. For another possible example of tragic allusion see M. Dewar,
'Octavian and Orestes in the finale of the first *Georgic*', *CQ* 38 (1988), 563–5, suggesting an allusion
to Aesch. *Cho.* 1021–5 in the simile of the chariot out of control at 1.512–14.
[81] Thomas on 4.453–527.
[82] A hypothesis aired by R. G. Coleman, 'Gallus, the *Bucolics*, and the ending of the fourth
Georgic', *AJP* 83 (1962), 55–71.
[83] See A. Bradley, 'Augustan culture and a radical alternative: Vergil's *Georgics*', *Arion* 8 (1969),
347–58; G. B. Conte, 'Aristaeus, Orpheus, and the *Georgics*', in Conte (1986), 130–40, discerns an
opposition of ways of life, between Aristaeus the model farmer who learns and successfully acts on
instructions, and Orpheus the solipsistic love poet condemned to a purely contemplative mode.
[84] E.g. Hor. *Ars Poet.* 391–3; see W. K. C. Guthrie, *Orpheus and Greek Religion* (London, 1935),
40–1.

absorbed in his passion for Eurydice, wandering in a desolate landscape far from town or cultivation, ultimately to be punished for his rejection of the social institution of marriage by the Thracian Maenads who tear apart his body (4.516–22). His dismembered remains may fertilize the fields (4.522); his enduring legacy is a poetry without practical or social utility, an elegiac lament that his head continues to sing even after death, and which is echoed by nature in the manner of pastoral poetry (4.523–7).

A further set of oppositions binds together the Orpheus story and the first half of book 4.[85] The bees provide a model of social cohesion and discipline, to the point of effacing the individual; they are fortunate in lacking the sexual drive that in book 3 was seen to cause so much disruption among other animals and man (4.197–9). Somewhat surprisingly, given the frequent ancient use of the bee as a figure for the poet, they seem to lack music and any of the non-practical arts. By complete contrast Orpheus lives and dies for love and poetry. His fate may be a salutary warning, but would *we* settle for social stability and contentment at the cost of the possibility of finding personal fulfilment through love and art?—this is the question Virgil seems to ask.

This by no means exhausts the meanings that have been found in the Aristaeus epyllion. The expiation by sacrifice of the death of Eurydice is the last example of an interest in correct religious observance as a precondition for agricultural success that runs through the poem, beginning with the opening invocation to the gods of the countryside.[86] Some see in the descents to the cave of Cyrene and the Underworld, and the regeneration of life out of death in the *bugonia*, allusions to the mystery religions.[87]

Orpheus may in some way stand for the poet Gallus; it is hard not to see in Aristaeus' success in regenerating the hive, destroyed as a consequence of disastrous transgression and restored only through

[85] I follow J. Griffin, 'The fourth *Georgic*, Virgil and Rome', in Griffin (1985), 163–82.

[86] 1.338–50 (worship of Ceres); 2.192–4 (sacrifice to Bacchus); 2.380–96 (worship of Bacchus); 2.473, 527–31 (*sacra deum* and religious holidays in the ideal rustic life). But religious observance is futile in the plague (3.455–6, 486–93). See P. Boyancé, 'La religion des "Géorgiques" à la lumière des travaux récents', *ANRW* II 31.1 (1980), 549–73.

[87] J. Chomarat, 'L'initiation d'Aristée', *REL* 52 (1974), 185–207; cf. P. Scazzoso, 'Riflessi misterici nelle "Georgiche" di Virgilio', *Paideia* 11 (1956), 5–28. The Underworld scene is reused in Aeneas' *katabasis* in *Aen.* 6, which has also been argued to contain allusion to the mystery religions: G. Luck, 'Virgil and the mystery religions', *AJP* 94 (1973), 147–66. D. S. Wender, 'Resurrection in the fourth *Georgic*', *AJP* 90 (1969), 424–36 sees a contrast between the socially useful 'fertility rite' of the Thracian mothers who tear Orpheus apart, and the self-oriented and foreign mystical cults for which Orpheus himself stands.

further violence, some reflection of the role of Octavian/Augustus in restoring Rome after the sinfulness and violence of the plague of civil war.[88] This would conclude the poem's recurrent suggestion of an analogy between the world of the farm and the world of Roman politics and war; the use of legend to foreshadow recent history will be a central device of the *Aeneid*. And if Aristaeus and Orpheus can be opposed as figures of the statesman and the poet, it is an opposition that is repeated, in playful and perhaps conciliatory manner, in the contrast in the *sphragis* (4.559–66) between Caesar Octavian thundering in war in the remote east on his imperial mission, and the poet Virgil indulging himself in his poetic games in the sequestered leisure of the Greek city of Naples.[89]

Structure. 'Digressions'.

The meanings of the Aristaeus epyllion emerge from the relationships between its parts, and between this mythological 'digression' and the agricultural instruction of the rest of book 4 and of the poem as a whole. The *Georgics*, as all of Virgil's works, reveal the closest attention to the organization and structure of the component parts. As in all ancient didactic poems one may distinguish between more narrowly didactic sections and passages of description, narrative, or poetic self-reflection;[90] the latter tend to occupy structurally significant positions at the end of a book or of the first half of a book, but it is wrong to regard them as digressions or purple passages, designed to provide relief for the reader before the next lesson. Two books published in 1963 and 1964, those by Klingner and Otis, first brought out fully the importance of an understanding of the complex movement and structure of the poem.[91]

---

[88] E.g. Miles (1980), 291; Lee (1996); for a fully developed allegorization see Nadeau (n. 45); Llewelyn Morgan will present a searching study of these issues in a forthcoming book. Otis (1964), 213 thinks an identification with Augustus 'inept', and takes Aristaeus to stand for 'the sinful self-destruction, atonement and revival of the Roman people'.

[89] On the *sphragis*: Buchheit (1972), 174–82; M. Korenjak, 'Parthenope und Parthenias: zur Sphragis der Georgika', *Mnemos.* 48 (1995), 201–2 (*Parthenope*, a name for Naples, puns on Virgil's nickname *Parthenias*, 'the maidenly').

[90] The 'digressions': 1.118–59 the 'Theodicy' (see n. 10); 1.466–514 Omens on the death of Julius Caesar (see n. 33); 2.136–76 *Laudes Italiae* (see n. 30); 2.323–45 Praise of Spring; 2.458–540 Praise of country life (see n. 14); 3.1–48 Poet's triumph and temple (see nn. 53–7); 3.242–83 Power of love (see n. 16); 3.478–566 Plague (see n. 15); 4.116–48 Corycian old man (see n. 69).

[91] Klingner (1963); Otis (1964), esp. 148–54. The distinction between didactic and purple passages had been undermined by E. Burck, 'Die Komposition von Vergils Georgika', *Hermes* 64 (1929), 279–321. Another early essay in analysing the structural correspondences in the poem was

The four books, which together trace an upward progress from the earth
and the next to inanimate field crops to the bees and the concluding
narratives of human loss and recovery, may be divided into two halves
(vegetable v. animal), or grouped by alternate books, with the contrast
between 'the relative gaiety and lightness of Books II and IV' and 'the
sombre and heavy character of I and III'.[92] Books 1 and 3 both end
pessimistically (the omens after the death of Julius Caesar and civil war;
the plague). Books may also be linked by bridging movements (the
epilogue to book 2 and the proem to book 3 together forming a block
spanning the work's central division), and by recapitulation and con-
tinuation (at the middle of book 4 we reach the same point as at the end
of book 3, but the annihilating plague is now remediable). For this
architectural arrangement of books and blocks of books Virgil found
precedent in Lucretius[93] and Callimachus' *Aitia* (how much we can no
longer say).[94] The text repeatedly mirrors and comments on itself; for
example, the proem to book 3 reassuringly concludes its picture of
Roman control of the world with the image of Envy safely confined in
the Underworld (37–9), a political (and poetical) analogue to the
philosopher's triumph over the Underworld at 2.490–2, but book 3
closes with the image of a plague Fury released from Hell and
rampaging freely over the earth in despite of all human attempts at
control (551–3).[95] Structure may also be expressed in a precisely
numerical manner: thus Maecenas is addressed by name at four
symmetrically arranged points, 1.2; 2.41; 3.41; 4.2.[96]

D. L. Drew, 'The structure of Vergil's *Georgics*', *AJP* 50 (1929), 242–54 (though he concluded that the system of correspondence breaks down in the Aristaeus episode, which is therefore a make-weight for the excised *laudes Galli*).

[92] Otis (1964), 151.

[93] E. J. Kenney and M. R. Gale, *Lucretius* (*Greece & Rome* New Surveys 11, Oxford, 1995), 16–21.

[94] For some speculation see Y. Nadeau, 'Aristaeus: Augustus: Berenice: Aeneas', *Mnemos.* 42 (1989), 97–101; see also ch. II n. 60.

[95] Putnam (1979), 233.

[96] R. S. Scodel and R. F. Thomas, 'Virgil and the Euphrates', *AJP* 105 (1984), 339 point out that on its three occurrences the name *Euphrates* occurs six lines from the end of a book, and six lines from the end of Callim. *Hy.* 2 (a key passage of poetic programmatics). Some have looked for Pythagorean numerical schemes: G. Le Grelle, 'Le première livre des *Géorgiques*, poème pythagor-icien', *LEC* 17 (1949), 139–225, followed by Brown (1963); for judicious discussion see Wilkinson (1969), 316–22.

Interpretation and Meaning. Philosophy and Religion.
Sacrifice. Allusive Pluralism. A World of Art?

The delineation of formal correspondences and significant relationships
within the text of the *Georgics* does not of itself tell us what the
significance of the poem is, as the history of recent criticism makes
clear. This may be all the more puzzling in the case of a didactic poem, a
genre whose business it would seem to be to convey a truth about its
subject, to lead the reader on a path from ignorance to enlightenment.
Perhaps the one thing that modern critics are agreed about is that the
Georgics is not a manual for farmers. Instead it is read as a poem about
man and nature, in the widest senses, or about man and society, and
more specifically the Romans and the problems of their society in the
30s and early 20s B.C. The overall movement of the poem is
'determined by an emotional-symbolic and *not* by an agricultural-
didactic plan'.[97] 'What purports to offer a methodology to cope with
the external world is actually one grand trope for life itself.'[98] The
Georgics is '. . . a profoundly ambitious work of philosophical specu-
lation'.[99] The poem's habit of expanding from the local detail to the
grandest temporal and spatial perspective certainly encourages this kind
of global interpretative ambition; only recently has there developed a
corresponding appreciation of the miniaturist artistry of the work,
chiefly through an attention to literary allusion rather than to the
detail of the agricultural and natural-historical subject-matter.

The *Georgics* is marked by pronounced mood-swings, juxtaposing
images of unrelieved gloom with bright pictures of natural and human
prosperity. Progress and degeneration are, undeniably, major themes of
the poem, but critics are sharply divided as to the overall balance. The
debate between optimists and pessimists (often referred to as the
'Harvard school') exactly replicates the debate over the tendency of
the *Aeneid*,[100] and as in the case of the *Aeneid* the issue is often focused
on the ending, the Aristaeus epyllion. For Brooks Otis Orpheus, despite
his calls on our sympathy, 'lacks the strength of character, the control of
passion which are the indispensable conditions of victory', while
Aristaeus is able to work successfully with nature through 'exercising

---

[97] B. Otis, rev. Wilkinson (1969), *Phoenix* 26 (1972), 40–62, at 61.
[98] Putnam (1979), 15.
[99] Miles (1980), p. xiii.
[100] See p. 94 below.

his full moral powers of control, work, self-sacrifice and devotion to his *patria*.[101] But many more recent critics find that the disproportionate sufferings of Orpheus and Eurydice cancel out the value of the unsympathetic Aristaeus' success in regenerating his bees through a repugnant and violent process. 'Ambivalence' and 'paradox' are words commonly used of the poem's message, but more often than not with a conviction of the 'ultimate darkness of the Virgilian world'.[102] The phrase *labor omnia uicit | improbus* in the Theodicy at 1.145–6 has become a battlefield: does it mean 'unflinching, or grim, labour over-came all difficulties' (both optimistic), or 'insatiable toil occupied all areas of existence' (pessimistic)?[103] Other critics delight in the unre-solved nature of the poem, sublimating the imperfections and contra-dictions of the natural and historical world into a higher world of art.[104] 'An exquisite ambivalence surely prevails.'[105]

Others, sensing that didactic should have a stake in epistemology, present the matter in terms of truth and untruth, or of different levels of knowledge and belief. Ross (1987), commendably alive to the import-ance of Greco-Roman science for the *Georgics*' outlook on the world, sees a perhaps too easy distinction between the realistic—and true— pictures of hard labour and frequent disaster, and 'The Virgilian Lie' in the idealizing praises of Italy (2.136–76), Spring (2.323–45), and Country Life (2.495–540).[106] But in what sense is the description of the plague at the end of book 3 realistic? Virgil's concern with truth and the knowable is another aspect of his engagement with Lucretius, whose *De rerum natura* relentlessly destroys false idols in order to reveal the hard clarity of the simple principles that underlie all reality. At 2.475–94

---

[101] Otis (1964), 212–13. Otis later qualified his view, concluding (*Phoenix* 26 (1972), 59), 'The most marvellous achievements of poetry and agriculture . . . are tragically limited'. Other optimists include Klingner (1963), who perceives a synthesis of death in life and life out of death in the final triumph of book 4; Stehle (n. 10), for whom Aristaeus transcends the irresponsibility of the Golden Age.

[102] Thomas (1988), i. 24. Pessimists include Ross (1987), Thomas (1982) and (1988), and A. J. Boyle, who sees a failure in the poem to 'subsume' human tragedy and failure in the spiritual regeneration of Rome ('*In medio Caesar*: paradox and politics in Virgil's *Georgics*', in Boyle (1979), 65–86; see id. (1986), ch. 3.

[103] The translations are those offered by Thomas on 1.145–6, himself a committed pessimist, as is Altevogt (n. 10). For an optimistic ('progressive') interpretation see R. Jenkyns, '*Labor improbus*', *CQ* 43 (1993), 243–8.

[104] A. Parry, 'The idea of art in Virgil's *Georgics*', *Arethusa* 5 (1972), 35–52, concluding (52) 'The grief is elevated to the highest art, and in that art, the epitome of all human art and craft, lies the true immortality of the poem, the resolution of man's confrontation with the absolute of death.' For Putnam (1979), 315 art itself is 'poised between perfection and fragmentation, firm order and chaos, ethereal musings and cloddish reality'.

[105] Griffin (1985), 176.

[106] See p. 31 above.

Virgil, fearing a failure of intellect in a search for a Lucretian-type truth, takes refuge in a world of Greek myth and conventional religion (precisely the targets of Lucretius' rationalism). Perkell sees in the poem an opposition between a 'rational and material' path to knowledge, the farmer's way, and a more 'intuitive and imagistic' path, the poet's way, expressed above all through myth.[107] Although there may be a danger of anachronism in applying to the *Georgics* a contrast of Faith and Reason, the poem does seem to operate with a contrast between philosophico-scientific inquiry and religious practice. But philosophy and religion are not in themselves simple categories. At 1.415–23 we are offered a materialist and non-providential explanation, in the Lucretian manner, of ravens' ability to forecast the weather, while at 4.219–27 Virgil refers to a Stoic-Pythagorean doctrine about the divine and immortal souls of all living beings.[108] The poem ends with an instance of the central practice of ancient religion, sacrifice (leading to the *bugonia*), but this too may be ambivalent: is the violent act a reaffirmation of correct relations between the human and the divine,[109] or has such confidence already been destroyed by the futility of sacrifice in the plague at 3.486–93,[110] or is sacrifice a sign of man's fall from a Golden Age in which animals were not slaughtered (cf. 2.537)?[111]

Virgil seems to exploit a multiplicity of allusion and point of view[112] in order to suggest the complexity of issues in the world. The solution to Aristaeus' problem of the lost hive is ultimately a simple one, but many contemporary readers are left feeling that this is a text with more problems than answers. One concluding statement may stand for many: 'The poem privileges mystery, not solution; complexity and ambiguity, not certainty.'[113]

[107] Perkell (1989), ch. 3.

[108] Philosophy in the *Georgics*: Wilkinson (1969), ch. 6.

[109] So T. N. Habinek, 'Sacrifice, society, and Vergil's ox-born bees', in M. Griffith and D. J. Mastronarde (eds.), *Cabinet of the Muses: Essays on Classical and Comparative Literature in Honor of T. G. Rosenmeyer* (Atlanta, 1990), 209–23.

[110] R. F. Thomas, 'The "sacrifice" at the end of the *Georgics*, Aristaeus, and Vergilian closure', *CP* 86 (1991), 211–18, answering Habinek. Clare (n. 15) argues that Aristaeus' success reasserts the value of didacticism in the face of the ravages of disease.

[111] Thomas denies that 2.537 *impia . . . caesis gens est epulata iuuencis* need refer to a *sacrificial* feast, but the verbal echo at 3.23 *caesosque uidere iuuencos* (of sacrifice) strongly suggests a link.

[112] Gale (n. 72) argues that the poem's polyphony is a deliberate result of its allusive pluralism. W. W. Batstone, 'On the surface of the *Georgics*', *Arethusa* 21 (1988), 227–45 applies a reader-response approach to the shifting perspectives of the poem.

[113] Perkell (1989), 190.

IV. THE *AENEID*

Epic Genealogies. The Homeric Models.

At the heart of the *Aeneid* the hero descends to the world of the dead and in its innermost recess is reunited with his father. Anchises, Aeneas's link to his destroyed Trojan past, reveals to his son the future of his race in the form of a procession of the souls of Roman heroes as yet unborn. In this place where time past, present, and future is held together, the *Aeneid* also comes to a heightened consciousness of its own literary genealogy, as literary memory is overlaid on family and racial memory.[1] The whole of the Underworld episode is modelled on Odysseus' visit to the land of the dead in *Odyssey* 11: Aeneas' meeting with his father reworks Odysseus' meeting with his mother Anticleia (*Od.* 11.152–224), which is immediately followed by the Catalogue of Heroines (*Od.* 11.225–332), the formal model for Virgil's very masculine Parade of Heroes. But the tears and words with which Anchises greets his son (6.684–9) allude to the Roman epic of Ennius and specifically to the scene at the opening of the *Annals* in which Ennius established his own place within the epic tradition, by narrating a dream in which the phantom of Homer explained to the sleeping poet how, through a Pythagorean metempsychosis, the true soul of Homer was reincarnated in the breast of Ennius himself. In restaging this scene of succession in the dreamlike setting of the Underworld Virgil hints at his own relationship to the dead epic poets to whose company he seeks admittance. The encounter of Aeneas and Anchises occurs within a set-piece of Homeric imitation; Anchises' running commentary on the Parade of Heroes functions as a summary of the matter of Ennius' historical epic, which it 'completes' by extending the story to Augustus' achievement of world-empire and restoration of a Golden Age (6.791–800).[2] Ennian historical

---

[1] Hardie (1993), 101–5 'Poetic succession'; epic underworlds are a conventional place for the poet to explore his own traditions: G. Most, 'Il poeta nell'Ade: catabasi, epico e teoria dell"epos" tra Omero e Virgilio', *SIFC* 85 (1992), 1014–26. Memory is a central function of epic (the Muses are daughters of Mnemosyne 'Memory'); on the role of memory in the *Aeneid* see Henry (1989).

[2] Augustus occupies a central section in the Parade (6.791–805), the main part of which concludes with a famous quotation from Ennius, 6.846 *unus qui nobis cunctando restituis rem* (cf. Enn. *Ann.* 363 Skutsch). Ennius and Virgil: Norden (1976), 365–75; E. Norden, *Ennius und Vergilius. Kriegsbilder aus Roms grosser Zeit* (Leipzig and Berlin, 1915); Wigodsky (1972), 40–79. On earlier Latin epic see Goldberg (1995).

epic is thus framed in a Homeric mythological episode; in the first part
of his speech (6.724–51) Anchises encapsulates another branch of the
hexameter tradition, with a philosophico-theological account of the
nature of the world and of the soul that is indebted both to Anticleia's
explanation to Odysseus of what happens to humans after death (*Od.*
11.216–24) and to the Ennian Homer's more philosophical account of
these matters,[3] but couched in markedly Lucretian language: a minia-
ture didactic 'de rerum natura' to set beside the miniature *Annals* that is
to follow.[4]

The *Aeneid* is alive to the whole of the epic tradition, but it looks back
continuously to the origins of that tradition in the poems of Homer.[5]
The version of literary history inscribed in the *Aeneid* thus reflects
Virgil's momentous decision to replace Ennius' historical epic with a
narrative poem that tells of Roman history from the perspective of the
legendary ancestor of the current ruling family, Aeneas (who is himself a
significant hero in the *Iliad*). Writing in the 20s B.C. of Virgil's growing
epic, the elegist Propertius announces, perhaps not without a touch of
the facetious, 'give way, writers of Rome, give way, writers of Greece!
Something greater than the *Iliad* is coming to birth.' (2.34.65–6). The
pentameter, *nescio quid maius nascitur Iliade*, echoes Virgil's own
announcement, after the invocation that begins the second half of the
Aeneid, that 'a greater succession of events is coming to birth for me, I
am setting about a greater work' (7.44–5 *maior rerum mihi nascitur
ordo, | maius opus moueo*). Here the comparatives *maior* and *maius* point
(at least on the surface) not to the relative ranking of Homer and Virgil

[3] Skutsch (1985), 153–67.

[4] Austin on 6.724–51 'The manner is constantly and pointedly Lucretian; the matter would have
excited Lucretius' disdain.' On Virgil's use of the Ennian and Lucretian models in this passage see
Hardie (1986), 69–83; in general on Virgil's imitation in the *Aeneid* of Lucretius, at once reverential
and antagonistic, see ibid. ch.5. The *Georgics* had already explored the continuities between
hexameter didactic and heroic hexameter epic; see pp. 40–2 above. For other examples of the
miniature summary, a device that allows Virgil both to refer to the epic traditions on which he draws
and to advertise, by contrast, the novelty of his own epic project, see the Shield of Aeneas at *Aen.*
8.626–728, a visual version of an Ennian historical epic, and the scenes in the temple of Juno at *Aen.*
1.453–93, an encapsulation of the hackneyed matter of the Epic Cycle: see A. Barchiesi, *A&A* 40
(1994), 117–18; in general see E. C. Kopff, 'Virgil and the cyclic epics', *ANRW* II 31.2 (1981),
919–47. In a sense the whole of the *Aeneid*, a monumental twelve-book epic, is at the same time an
exquisite miniaturization of the whole of the Greco-Roman literary tradition.

[5] On Virgil's use of Homer Knauer (1964a) is indispensable, not least for his line-by-line tables
of correspondences between the Homeric and Virgilian epics; his general conclusions are
summarized in Knauer (1964b); Otis (1964) is still essential, if now somewhat dated, reading on
the literary-historical background to Virgil's audacious decision to confront Homer head-on, with
chapters on 'The Odyssean *Aeneid*' (ch. 6) and 'The Iliadic *Aeneid*' (ch. 7). See also Camps (1969),
ch. 8; for a sophisticated discussion of the literary effects of Virgil's Homeric imitation see Barchiesi
(1984).

but to Virgil's raising of his own epic pretensions as he moves from the Odyssean wanderings of the first six books to the Iliadic battles of the last six books.[6] The first two words of the poem, *arma uirumque*, signal (in reverse order) the two halves of the poem, dealing respectively with an Odyssean 'man' and Iliadic warfare.[7] This dichotomy has a general validity, but needs qualification; it is not just that some Iliadic episodes find a home in the 'Odyssean' half (notably the funeral games of *Iliad* 23, the model for the games in *Aen.* 5) and vice versa (Aeneas' visit to Evander in *Aen.* 8 is modelled on Telemachus' visits to Pylos and Sparta in *Od.* 3 and 4),[8] but that Iliadic and Odyssean models may be combined in one Virgilian episode,[9] on the large scale for example in the mapping on to the death of Turnus of both the Iliadic death of Achilles and the Odyssean slaughter of the suitors, or, on a smaller scale, in the combination in Numanus Remulus' violent invective against the Trojans (9.598–620) of Thersites' taunting of the Achaeans (*Il.* 2.235) with Alcinous' account of the Phaeacians' national characteristics (*Od.* 8.248–9).

Virgil's imitation of Homer is thoroughly Alexandrian both in its allusive density and erudition, and in its constant challenge to the reader to compare and contrast source and imitation, to use our knowledge of the Homeric texts as an interpretative filter in our reading of the *Aeneid*, and conversely to read the *Aeneid* as a commentary on the Homeric poems.[10] For example our response to the kind of heroism displayed by Aeneas (see below, pp. 80–2) is guided by our memory of the behaviour of the several Homeric characters of which he is a composite. The reader's task of assessing the Homeric affinities of the Virgilian characters mirrors a competitive use of exemplarity on the part of the fictional characters themselves: the outcome of the war in Latium will be decided by the result of a sometimes self-conscious competition between Turnus and Aeneas

---

[6] In antiquity the *Iliad* was regarded as the more sublime of the two Homeric epics: [Longinus] *De Sublimitate* 9.11–15 (with Russell ad loc.).

[7] On the proem of *Aen.* 1 see Anderson (1969), ch. 1; Buchheit (1963), 13–58.

[8] For a convenient overview of the situation see Knauer (1964a), folding chart 5; for an analysis of the compilation of Homeric episodes within a single book see Hardie (1994), 6–10. Cairns (1989), ch. 8 presents an interesting, if overstated, argument for the greater importance of the *Odyssey* than the *Iliad* as a model for the *Aeneid*. On Virgil's use of each Homeric epic see R. D. Williams, 'Virgil and the *Odyssey*', *Phoenix* 17 (1963), 266–74; Gransden (1984).

[9] A particular type of the more general use of what Knauer calls 'Kontamination', i.e. the combination of more than one Homeric model in a single Virgilian passage; inversely, by 'dédoublement' a single Homeric model may be divided between two Virgilian episodes: for example the person of Patroclus feeds into the characters and exploits of both Pallas and Camilla.

[10] The most influential work in modern studies of allusion is Conte (1986); for discussions of allusion see also ch. II n. 12.

as to who plays the roles of the Iliadic winner, Achilles, and the Iliadic loser, Hector. At the end Aeneas' outburst on seeing the swordbelt of Pallas finally sweeps away any doubt that it is *his* anger and grief that is to be identified with the fearful wrath of Achilles announced as the theme of the *Iliad* in that poem's first word.[11]

Virgil's allusive practice also forces us to ask *whose* Homer does he imitate? By the late first century B.C. the Homeric poems had been subjected to a great variety of reading practices, with consequences ranging from the basic establishment of the text to the widest issues of interpretation. For an example of choices at the level of textual variants take Apollo's prophecy to the Trojans at 3.97–8, *hic domus Aeneae cunctis dominabitur oris | et nati natorum et qui nascentur ab illis* ('here [in your former motherland] the house of Aeneas will rule over all lands, and his sons' sons and their children'). Apollo 'quotes' a prediction made by Poseidon at *Iliad* 20.307–8, but not in quite the form found in modern texts, which read 'But as it is the might of Aeneas will rule over the Trojans . . .' Virgil's Apollo chooses a variant, preserved in the scholia and Strabo, that reads 'But as it is the race of Aeneas will rule over all men . . .'; the variant presumably arose as the result of a desire to incorporate into the *Iliad* a reference to Rome's dominance in the Mediterranean, and it suited Virgil's purposes neatly.[12] The Homeric interpretation of Greek, especially Hellenistic, commentators, also leaves its traces: R. R. Schlunk demonstrated that in his tendency to omit absurd or indecorous details in his Homeric models Virgil conforms to the *decorum*-based criticism of the Alexandrian commentators, fragments of which survive in the Homeric scholia. For example the scholia complain that it is most implausible that at *Iliad* 23.857–8 Achilles should foresee that one of the contestants in the archery contest might cut the cord attaching the dove to the post; in the contest at *Aen.* 5.507–12 it comes as an unexpected accident when Mnestheus' shot severs the cord.[13] The fashion for the allegorical interpretation of the Homeric myths, associated in particular with the Hellenistic scholars of Pergamum, is also visible in the *Aeneid*, for example in the association of Juno with the lower air and storms, in line with the allegorization of Hera as *aer* 'air',[14] or in the natural-philosophical subject-matter of the song of

[11] See Anderson (1957); L. A. Mackay, 'Achilles as model for Aeneas', *TAPA* 88 (1957), 11–16; D. West, 'The deaths of Hector and Turnus', in McAuslan and Walcot (1990), 14–23; T. van Nortwick, 'Aeneas, Turnus, and Achilles', *TAPA* 110 (1980), 303–14.
[12] E. L. Harrison, 'Vergil and the Homeric tradition', *PLLS* 3 (1981), 209–25, at 215 with n. 10.
[13] Schlunk (1974), 15–17.
[14] Feeney (1991), 149–50.

Iopas at 1.742–6, reflecting an interpretation of the scandalous story of Ares and Aphrodite in the Homeric song of Demodocus (*Od.* 8.266–366) as in truth an allegory of cosmic principles.[15]

The audacity of embarking on a comprehensive imitation of Homer was compounded by the prevalent ancient view that Homer was not only the earliest poet writing in the grandest genre, but that he was a universal poet, the source of all later literature and wisdom, of almost god-like stature, and one who saw into the deepest mysteries of the universe.[16] It is a mark of the success of the *Aeneid*'s ambition that later centuries saw Virgil himself as a universal and almost divine poet.[17] This act of literary aggrandizement also makes the *Aeneid* a peculiarly apt complement to the ideology of the new *princeps* Augustus, buttressed as it is by a claim to the universal power of Rome; Virgil's poetic triumph, as vividly described at the beginning of the third *Georgic*,[18] makes of him the fitting poet for the *triumphator* Augustus; the literary imperialist rides by the side of the military imperialist.

Roman Alexandrianism. Generic Polyphony.

Paradoxically the epic universalism of the *Aeneid* allows the poem to include much that is not grandiosely epic. If Homer is the fountainhead of all later literature, to imitate the poet who contains multitudes will allow the admission of things that seem less than epic, or even non-epic.[19] Like

---

[15] Knauer (1964a), 168 n. 1; Hardie (1986), 62–3; Farrell (1991), 258–60. Hardie (1986), ch. 8 interprets the Shield of Aeneas in *Aen.* 8 as a symbol of the cosmic pretensions of Roman power, reflecting an allegorization of the Shield of Achilles in *Iliad* 18 as a symbol of the physical universe. On allegory in the *Aeneid* see also p. 94 below.

[16] For a statement by a later Latin epic poet, who himself almost literally worshipped Virgil, see Sil. Ital. *Pun.* 13.786–9 (the Sibyl on the ghost of Homer) '*meruit deus esse uideri,* | *et fuit in tanto non paruum pectore numen.* | *carmine complexus terram, mare, sidera, manes* | *et cantu Musas et Phoebum aequauit honore*'. Ptolemy IV erected a shrine to Homer, the Homereion, in Alexandria, with which the relief in the British Museum by Archelaus of Priene of the 'Apotheosis of Homer' may be connected. See C. O. Brink, 'Ennius and the Hellenistic worship of Homer', *AJP* 93 (1972), 547–67; Hardie (1986), 22–5. A representative account of the universal Homer is [Plutarch] *On the life and poetry of Homer*: see J. J. Keaney and R. Lamberton (eds.), *Essay on the Life and Poetry of Homer (Plutarch)* (Atlanta, 1996).

[17] On the late antique and medieval pictures of the divinely omniscient and wonder-working Virgil see Comparetti (1895). The tradition of the universal Virgil finds its latest apologists in T. S. Eliot, who elevated the *Aeneid* to the status of *the* European classic (*What is a Classic?* [London, 1945]), and in the once influential book by T. Haecker, *Vergil, Vater des Abendlandes* (Leipzig, 1931) (tr. A. W. Wheen, *Virgil, Father of the West* [London, 1934]).

[18] See p. 41 above.

[19] On the *Aeneid*'s receptivity to non-epic genres see Jackson Knight (1966), 159–78; later epic in the classical tradition is also self-conscious about its generic inclusivity: see B. K. Lewalski, *Paradise*

the *Eclogues* and the *Georgics*, the *Aeneid* is characterized by a generic mixture of the high and the low, the neoteric and the Augustan (in the sense of the more publicly committed poetry of Virgil and Horace). In this respect the *Aeneid* also looks forward to Ovid's long hexameter poem, the *Metamorphoses*, whose overtly paradoxical combination of a Calli-machean *deductum carmen* with a non-Callimachean *perpetuum carmen* lays bare a contradiction already present in the *Aeneid*.[20] The play of genres within the text is not simply an object for formalist analysis; a genre brings with it a way of looking at the world and a set of values, and to juxtapose different genres is at the same time to question the perspectives within which we judge moral and political issues.[21]

For an example of how epic and neoteric models are combined let us return to the speech with which Anchises welcomes his son in the Underworld and in which Virgil begins to outline a genealogy of his overarching genre, epic. At 6.692–3 Anchises exclaims *quas ego te terras et quanta per aequora uectum | accipio! quantis iactatum, nate, periclis!* ('I welcome you, my son, borne over what lands and over how many seas, tossed by how many dangers!') He defines his son's adventures as Odyssean, with obvious allusion to the first four lines of the *Odyssey*, while within the *Aeneid* the verb *iactare* has an almost technical applica-tion to the Odyssean sufferings of Aeneas (first used at 1.3 in the context of the narrator's own adaptation of the Odyssean opening). But Gian Biagio Conte points out that Anchises' verbal formulation more closely follows the first line of Catullus 101, *multas per gentes et multa per aequora uectus*, where allusion to the opening of the *Odyssey* lends a quality of epic suffering to Catullus' very personal journey to make an offering at the grave of his brother, who died near Troy.[22] By this allusion Virgil signals his recognition of Catullus' Homeric source, which he reinstates in an epic context; but at the same time he introduces into his epic an element of Catullan pathos, retaining the non-Homeric use of the expression in a conversation between two close relatives, one of whom is dead.

Lost and the Rhetoric of Literary Forms (Princeton, 1985), ch. 1 '*Paradise Lost* as an encyclopedic epic'.

[20] Hinds (1987), 19. Hinds' book is central for the study of the dynamics of generic play in Augustan poetry; see also G. B. Conte, *Genres and Readers: Lucretius, Love Elegy, Pliny's Encyclopedia* (Baltimore and London, 1994); J. Farrell, 'Dialogue of genres in Ovid's "Lovesong of Polyphemus" (*Metamorphoses* 13.719–897)', *AJP* 113 (1992), 235–68. On paradox as a constituent feature of Virgilian poetics see P. R. Hardie, 'Virgil: a paradoxical poet?', *PLLS* 9 (1996), 103–21.

[21] On the inseparability of generic analysis from the wider meaning and ideology of texts see S. Hinds, '*Arma* in Ovid's *Fasti*', *Arethusa* 25 (1992), 81–153.

[22] Conte (1986), 32–9.

Virgil's understanding that the Alexandrian and the epic (Homeric) are not mutually exclusive conforms with the demonstration by modern scholars that poets like Callimachus and Theocritus work out their poetics through a constructive engagement with, rather than hostility towards, Homer. (What *is* non-Callimachean about the *Aeneid* is its willingness to challenge the Homeric poems in their totality.) A larger example of Virgil's reincorporation into a full-scale epic of material from a Catullan poem constructed out of fragments of epic tradition is the massive diversion into the Dido episode in *Aeneid* 4 of elements of Catullus 64 (already an important model in the *Eclogues* and *Georgics*), in particular the reworking of Ariadne's lament in the speeches of Dido.[23]

Catullus' 'epyllion' has as one of its main, if somewhat disguised, models the single surviving Hellenistic epic, the *Argonautica* of Apollonius of Rhodes, a writer who is now seen to share the poetic goals of poets like Callimachus.[24] A major growth area in recent scholarship on the *Aeneid* has been the study of its debts to Hellenistic poetry,[25] and nowhere have the results been as spectacular as in the case of Apollonius' *Argonautica*, whose influence on the *Aeneid* was seen by Knauer in 1964 as a mere trickle amidst the flood of Homeric material, but which now emerges as a major presence throughout the poem.[26] The importance of the Medea and Jason narrative in *Argonautica* 3 for Virgil's Dido and Aeneas is obvious, but a further model is the Hypsipyle episode in *Argonautica* 1. Virgil, like Apollonius, begins the second half of his epic by invoking the Muse of love poetry, Erato (7.37; cf. *Argon.* 3.1), posing readers a puzzle as to why his Iliadic 'greater work' should be placed under the same Muse as Apollonius' story of the love of Medea and Jason.[27] The journey of Aeneas is constructed as an

---

[23] Catullus and Virgil (see also ch. III n. 77); E. K. Rand, 'Catullus and the Augustans', *HSCP* 17 (1906), 15–30; R. E. H. Westendorp Boerma, 'Vergil's debt to Catullus', *Acta Classica* 1 (1958), 51–63; E. L. Harrison, 'Cleverness in Virgilian imitation', in Harrison (1990), 445–8 [on Cat. 66.39 and *Aen.* 6.460]; J. Ferguson, 'Catullus and Virgil', *PVS* 11 (1971/72), 25–47; R. Drew Griffith, 'Catullus' *Coma Berenices* and Aeneas' farewell to Dido', *TAPA* 125 (1995), 47–59; M. C. J. Putnam, 'The lyric genius of the *Aeneid*', *Arion* 3.2 (1995), 81–101; Wills (1996), 26–30 [on Ariadne's lament and the speeches of Dido in *Aen.* 4]; Lyne (n. 197); Petrini (n. 71).

[24] R. L. Hunter, *Apollonius of Rhodes: Argonautica Book III* (Cambridge, 1989), 32–8. For an analysis of the use of Apollonius in Catullus 64 see R. J. Clare, 'Catullus 64 and the *Argonautica* of Apollonius Rhodius: allusion and exemplarity', *PCPS* 42 (1996), 60–88.

[25] There are many valuable observations in Clausen (1987), but it is far from being a comprehensive study of its subject. See also A. S. Hollis, 'Hellenistic colouring in Virgil's *Aeneid*', *HSCP* 94 (1992), 269–85.

[26] See the massive study by D. Nelis, *The Aeneid and the Argonautica of Apollonius Rhodius* (Leeds, 1998); D. C. Feeney, 'Following after Hercules, in Virgil and Apollonius', *PVS* 18 (1986), 47–85.

[27] S. Kyriakidis, '*Invocatio ad Musam* (*Aen.* 7.37)', *MD* 33 (1994), 197–206, with bibliography at 197 n. 2.

Argonautic quest, as well as an Odyssean wandering: the Harpies episode in *Aeneid* 3 is diverted from the Argo story into the legend of Aeneas. The simile at 8.622–3 comparing the gleam of the divine armour brought to Aeneas by Venus to a cloud lit up by the sun is taken from *Argonautica* 4.125–6, where it is applied to the Golden Fleece when Jason first sees it; allusion to the Argonauts' arrival at Colchis in Aeneas' journey up the Tiber at the beginning of *Aeneid* 8 foreshadows this hint at the end that Aeneas' new armour, with the Shield displaying scenes of the whole of Roman history, is *his* Golden Fleece.[28] More generally the *Aeneid* takes over from the *Argonautica* the Hellenistic epic's awareness of its belatedness in relation to Homer, and its interest in the aetiological traces left on the landscape by the adventures of its heroes.[29]

In these last respects Apollonius' *Argonautica* explores the same territory as Callimachus' poetry. In *Aeneid* 8 Aeneas takes a break from his Odyssean and Iliadic heroics to become a Callimachean collector of aetiological lore from Evander, his host on the future site of Rome.[30] The impoverished Arcadian king's reception of the hero in his humble dwelling falls into a pattern used more than once by Callimachus, in Molorchus' reception of Herakles in *Aitia* 3, and in Hekale's reception of Theseus in the epyllion *Hekale* (in each case on the eve of the hero's slaying of a monster).[31] In these episodes Callimachus, in typically 'Alexandrian' manner, engineers scenes of a less than epic elevation through a selective reading of Homer, for the original for such 'theoxenies' (receptions of a god or hero into a simple dwelling) is the swineherd Eumaeus' reception of Odysseus, disguised as a beggar, in *Odyssey* 14.

Callimachus' contemporary Theocritus created a new non-heroic, humble, genre of hexameter bucolic in part through a selective reading of Homer.[32] The Evander episode in *Aeneid* 8 is also one of the places where pastoral enters the Homeric epic world (the inverse of the introduction of epic themes into the bucolic world in *Eclogue* 4: see

[28] P. R. Hardie, 'Ships and ship-names in the *Aeneid*', in Whitby, Hardie, and Whitby (1987), 163–71, at 163, 170.
[29] R. L. Hunter, *The Argonautica of Apollonius* (Cambridge, 1993), ch. 7 '*Argonautica* and *Aeneid*'. On the *Argonautica*'s relationship to its literary past see Goldhill (1991), ch. 5.
[30] E. V. George, *Aeneid VIII and the Aitia of Callimachus* (Leiden, 1974).
[31] Gransden (1976), 26. For examples of detailed allusion to Callimachus in the *Aeneid* see S. J. Heyworth, 'Deceitful Crete: *Aeneid* 3.84 and the *Hymns* of Callimachus', *CQ* 43 (1993), 255–7; A. Barchiesi, 'Immovable Delos: *Aeneid* 3.73–98 and the *Hymns* of Callimachus', *CQ* 44 (1994), 438–43.
[32] On bucolic's epic origins see Halperin (ch. II n. 5).

p. 16 above). Cattle graze in what was to become the Roman Forum; the humble inhabitants of the site of Rome are, significantly, Arcadians;[33] even the extravagantly hyperbolical narrative of the fight between Hercules and Cacus is at heart a tale about cattle-rustlers. Aeneas spends one night in Evander's hut before he must return to the epic business of warfare, rather as Meliboeus is invited by Tityrus at the end of *Eclogue* 1 to rest with him for the night before continuing his journey into an exile forced on him by the effects of war. In the *Eclogues* the tranquil world of the shepherds is recurrently threatened by violent events in the historical world; the transition in *Aeneid* 7 from the peaceful state that preceded the Trojan arrival to all-out war is also figured as a generic transition, from pastoral to epic: Allecto's last intervention (7.475–539) causes Ascanius unwittingly to shoot the pet stag belonging to the royal herdsman's daughter Silvia ('girl of the woods');[34] Allecto, the 'plague lurking in the woods', 7.505, calls the vengeful farmers to arms with a blast on her trumpet, cruelly labelled a *pastorale signum* ('herdsmen's signal'), to which nature resounds in a parody of the pastoral echo (7.514–18). A little later ploughshares and sickles give way to swords (7.635–6; cf. *Geo.* 1.506–8), as that other kind of countryside poetry, georgic, yields to epic.[35] The Homeric king is 'shepherd of his people', and herdsmen appear regularly in Homeric similes; working from these precedents, Virgil weaves a pattern of pastoral imagery around Aeneas, that stretches from the simile comparing the stunned hero on the night of the sack of Troy to a shepherd listening passively to the sound of forest-fire or mountain torrent (2.304–8) to the simile comparing Aeneas' siege-assault on Latinus' city to a shepherd smoking out bees (12.587–92).[36]

Love elegy, like pastoral, is a genre that occupies a position at the bottom of the hierarchy of genres.[37] The Latin love elegist flaunts the inactive and unRoman nature of his lifestyle; one way of viewing the situation in *Aeneid* 4 is as the interference of the values of the world of

[33] *Pace* R. Jenkyns, 'Virgil and Arcadia', *JRS* 79 (1989), 26–39. See W. Wimmel, *'Hirtenkrieg' und arkadisches Rom: Reduktionsmedien in Vergils Aeneis* (Munich, 1973); D. M. Rosenberg, *Oaten Reeds and Trumpets: Pastoral and Epic in Virgil, Spenser, and Milton* (Lewisburg, 1981), 51–3 on Evander.

[34] Silvia's stag: E. Vance, 'Sylvia's pet stag: wildness and domesticity in Virgil's *Aeneid*', *Arethusa* 14 (1981), 127–38; M. C. J. Putnam, 'Silvia's stag and Virgilian ekphrasis', *MD* 34 (1995), 107–33.

[35] On allusion to the *Georgics* in the *Aeneid* see Briggs (1980).

[36] W. S. Anderson, *'Pastor Aeneas*: on pastoral themes in the *Aeneid'*, *TAPA* 99 (1968), 1–17.

[37] For this concept see A. Fowler, *Kinds of Literature: An Introduction to the Theory of Genres and Modes* (Oxford, 1982), ch. 12 'Hierarchy of genres and canons of literature'.

love elegy in the Roman (and epic) mission of Aeneas. The effect of her infatuation on Dido is to paralyse her city-building activity (4.86–9);[38] her speech to Aeneas at 4.305–30 is an example of the 'schetliastic propemptikon', like those addressed by the elegist to his *puella* on the point of her departure on a voyage.[39]

But tragedy is the genre that we most readily associate with Dido. Friedrich Leo went so far as to say that *Aeneid* 4 was 'the only Roman tragedy worthy of being put beside the Greek plays'. Dido fits the Aristotelian model of the tragic hero well enough, a superior being brought low by a tragic 'flaw';[40] her speeches and manner of death are in the tragic manner;[41] some critics even try to discern the outline of a five-act structure in *Aeneid* 4.[42] The 'tragedy of Dido' is introduced in *Aeneid* 1 in the speech in which Venus (as part of her—actor-like?—disguise wearing *coturni*, the boots of a hunter, but also the tragic 'buskins', 1.337) outlines to Aeneas the previous history of Dido, in the manner of the prologue delivered by a god in a Euripidean tragedy.[43] The influence of tragedy on the *Aeneid* is pervasive, and arguably the single most important factor in Virgil's successful revitalization of the genre of epic.[44] In order to set in motion the second, Iliadic, half of the poem Juno, a typically angry epic god, employs a character more at home in tragedy than in epic, the Fury Allecto.[45] Some readers see in

---

[38] See Pease on 4.86.

[39] On the schetliastic propemptikon see Cairns (1972), 7. Cairns (1989), ch. 6 takes the case for the influence of love elegy on the *Aeneid* as far as it can go.

[40] *culpa* at 4.19, 172 may be meant to put us in mind of the Aristotelian ἁμαρτία; see N. Rudd, 'Dido's *culpa*', in *Lines of Enquiry: Studies in Latin Poetry* (Cambridge, 1976), 32–53; J. L. Moles, 'Aristotle and Dido's *hamartia*', in McAuslan and Walcot (1990), 142–8; id., 'The tragedy and guilt of Dido', in Whitby, Hardie, and Whitby (1987), 153–61. In general see Pease (1935), 8–11; N. W. De Witt, 'The Dido episode as tragedy', *CJ* 2 (1907), 283–8; K. Quinn, 'Virgil's tragic queen', in *Latin Explorations: Critical Studies in Roman Literature* (London, 1963), 29–58; id. (1968), 323–49 'The contribution of tragedy'; F. Muecke, 'Foreshadowing and dramatic irony in the story of Dido', *AJP* 104 (1983), 134–55.

[41] I have already pointed to the models of Catullus' Ariadne and, possibly, love elegy for Dido's speeches. Virgil looks back to the tragic models that underlie the hexameter narratives of Catullus 64 and Apollonius *Argonautica* 3, producing a tissue of quite extraordinary complexity, even by Virgil's standards. Dido is one of the most densely allusive of all Virgilian characters: see recently the convincing demonstration that Penelope is another important model by G. C. Polk, 'Vergil's Penelope: the Diana simile in *Aeneid* 1.498–502', *Vergilius* 42 (1996), 38–49.

[42] E.g. A. Wlosok, 'Vergils Didotragödie. Ein Beitrag zum Problem des Tragischen in der Aeneis', in H. Görgemanns and E. A. Schmidt (eds.), *Studien zum antiken Epos* (Meisenheim, 1976), 228–50.

[43] See E. L. Harrison, 'Why did Venus wear boots? Some reflections on *Aeneid* 1.314 f.', *PVS* 12 (1972/73), 10–25.

[44] For the argument see Hardie in Martindale (1997), ch. 20.

[45] Note especially the infernal *Lyssa* ('madness') used by Hera to drive Herakles mad in Eur. *Herc. Fur.* 822 ff. On Allecto see Heinze (1993), 148–50; Pöschl (1962), 28–33; E. Fraenkel, 'Some aspects of the structure of *Aeneid* VII', in Harrison (1990), 253–76, at 258–65; Lyne (1987), 13–19,

Turnus, as much as in Dido, the pattern of a tragic career.[46] In the scene in the first book that corresponds to her evocation of Allecto Juno plays the part of the Odyssean Poseidon in raising a storm against her human enemy, but both in her opening monologue and in the ensuing storm description there are allusions to Roman tragedies on subjects from the Greek *Nostoi* from Troy.[47] The *furor* that rages through the poem owes as much to the madness and Maenadism of tragedy as it does to the anger and *thumos* ('battle-spirit') of epic.

Past to Present. History and Antiquarianism. Aetiology, Genealogy, Etymology. Cities and Sons. Cultural Histories.

The *Aeneid* contains implicit sketches of Greco-Roman literary history, but the poem's ostensible subject is the history of a nation, of a race, and of the leading families of that race. It quickly established itself as the national epic of the Romans, replacing Ennius' *Annals*. Whereas Ennius wrote a historical epic, recording Roman history sequentially from the Sack of Troy down to the most recent events of the second century B.C., the *Aeneid* may better be described as an aetiological epic, locating the origins of Roman history and culture in a legendary past. The decision to write about a Trojan hero allows Virgil to write a very Homeric kind of epic, but the concern to relate the Homeric past to a Roman present transforms the poem into a Hellenistic aetiological poem. The epic labours of the *Aeneid* have as their goal the foundation of a race (1.33 *tantae molis erat Romanam* <u>condere</u> *gentem* 'so great a struggle it was to found the Roman race'); from the time of leaving Troy the hero is programmed to found a city (in contrast to the 'city-sacking'

24–7. The generic change in *Aen.* 7 may thus be understood also as one from pastoral to tragedy: cf. Milton *Paradise Lost* 9.1–7 'No more of talk where God or angel guest | With man, as with his friend, familiar used | To sit indulgent, and with him partake | Rural repast, permitting him the while | Venial discourse unblamed: I now must change | Those notes to tragic; foul distrust, and breach | Disloyal on the part of man . . .'

[46] E.g. J. B. Garstang, 'The tragedy of Turnus', *Phoenix* 9 (1950), 47–58; M. von Albrecht, 'Zur Tragik von Vergils Turnusgestalt: Aristotelisches in der *Aeneis*', in M. von Albrecht and E. Heck (eds.), *Silvae: Festschrift für E. Zinn* (Tübingen, 1970), 1–5. Recent book-length studies of Turnus: P. Schenk, *Die Gestalt des Turnus in Vergils Aeneis* (Königstein, 1984); C. Renger, *Aeneas und Turnus: Analyse einer Feindschaft* (Frankfurt, 1985).

[47] See Austin on 1.44, 87, 88, 90, 102. Given the fragmentary state of the evidence, it is easy to overlook the importance of *Roman* tragic models for the *Aeneid*: see S. Stabryla, *Latin Tragedy in Virgil's Poetry* (Wroclaw, 1970); Wigodsky (1972), 18–21, 76–97. Mezentius has the features of an Accian stage tyrant: see A. La Penna, 'Mezenzio: una tragedia della tirannia e del titanismo antico', *Maia* 32 (1980), 3–30.

hero of the *Odyssey*); the foundation of the city of Rome lies far beyond
the chronological limit of the primary narrative, but is in an important
sense the *telos* or goal of the poem. The *Aeneid* is thus a specimen of the
'ktistic' (foundation) epic popular in the Hellenistic period as an
expression of national pride and antiquarian curiosity.[48]

The story of the Trojan origins of Rome was first developed by Greek
historians concerned to accommodate the history of the rising Medi-
terranean power within their own traditions, but by Virgil's time it had
been willingly adopted by Romans as a way of articulating their
relationship with the Greek East, and existed in many variants.[49]
Virgil works freely with the tradition to create his own pattern of plot,
introducing some stories into the Aeneas legend for the first time.[50] The
Aeneas legend gained in prominence in the first century B.C. through
the exploitation by Julius Caesar, and then by his adopted son Octavian
(Augustus), of the claim that the Julian *gens* was descended from
Aeneas' son Iulus (Ascanius);[51] the *Aeneid* thus becomes an epic on
the foundation of a dynasty as well as of a city. The wider craze among
upper-class Romans for tracing Trojan ancestors is reflected in the
Aeneid in the derivation of a number of other families from characters in
the poem; for example the names of three of the four competitors in the
ship-race are said to be the source of the names of Roman *gentes* (5.116–
23).[52]

The *Aeneid* delights in historical and antiquarian learning,[53] an aspect
of the *Aeneid* which appealed particularly to the Virgil-worshippers of
the 'pagan revival' of the late fourth- and early fifth-century A.D.,
anxious to maintain links with old Roman traditions in the face of a

[48] On the *Aeneid* as foundation-poem see N. M. Horsfall, 'Aeneas the colonist', *Vergilius* 35
(1989), 8–27; see also id., 'Virgil and the poetry of explanations', *G&R* 38 (1991), 203–11. The
first sentence of the poem, after the opening *arma uirumque cano*, outlines a journey between two
cities *Troiae . . . Romae*.
[49] See J. Perret, *Les Origines de la légende troyenne de Rome (281–31)* (Paris, 1942); G. K. Galinsky,
Aeneas, Sicily and Rome (Princeton, 1969); N. M. Horsfall, in J. N. Bremmer and N. M. Horsfall,
Roman Myth and Mythography (London, 1987), 12–24; T. J. Cornell, *The Beginnings of Rome, Italy
and Rome from the Bronze Age to the Punic Wars (c. 1000–264 B.C.)* (London and New York, 1995),
63–8; E. S. Gruen, *Culture and National Identity in Republican Rome* (London, 1992), 6–51.
[50] Particularly contentious is the question of whether Virgil invented the story of Dido's love for
Aeneas: for the evidence see Pease (1935), 14–21.
[51] 1.288 *Iulius, a magno demissum nomen Iulo*. See S. Weinstock, *Divus Julius* (Oxford, 1971), 5–
12.
[52] The scholar and antiquarian Varro, an important source for the *Aeneid*, wrote a work *De
familiis Troianis*; see T. P. Wiseman, 'Legendary genealogies in late-Republican Rome', *G&R* 21
(1974), 153–64.
[53] The keenest modern investigator of Virgil's expertise as scholar and antiquarian is N. M.
Horsfall in many articles and a book, *Virgilio: L'epopea in alambicco* (Naples, 1991).

triumphant Christianity.[54] Augustus' own stake in stressing the tradi-
tionalism of his régime was well served by the Alexandrian and late
Republican traditions of antiquarianism obviously so congenial to Virgil,
particularly in the field of religion (where Augustus invested so much of
his ideological energy). The definition of Aeneas' goal at 1.5–6 is
twofold: to found a city, and to bring the gods to Latium. As a priestly
hero Aeneas departs from the Homeric models, but fittingly foresha-
dows the priestly role of Augustus.[55] The *Aeneid* provides *aitia* or
models for various features of Roman religion, such as the distinction
between the *omen oblatiuum* and the *omen impetratiuum* (2.679–98),[56] or
the practice of sacrificing with veiled head (3.405–7).[57] The aetiological
book 8 is full of such things, most notably the *aition* of the worship of
Hercules at the Ara Maxima: Evander's protestation at 8.185–9 that the
cult of Hercules is not the product of 'an empty superstition, ignorant of
the ancient gods' further serves to root recent honours paid to the
godlike Augustus in the traditions of Rome's remotest antiquity.[58]

If *Aeneid* 8 is above all the book of Roman origins, the previous book
sketches a very varied picture of early Italy, culminating in the colourful
and often bizarre Catalogue of Italians at 7.641–817 (modelled on the
Catalogue of Ships in *Iliad* 2), which draws on Cato's *Origines* and
Varro's *De Gente Populi Romani*. The Catalogue gives antiquarian and
legendary depth to a gazetteer of Italy, catering for a pride in the
primitive traditions of old Italy at the same time as fostering a sense
that the past is a foreign country.[59] Augustus appealed as much to an
Italian as to a narrowly Roman nationalism; at *Res Gestae* 25.2 he boasts
that 'the whole of Italy of its own accord swore allegiance' to him in the
war against Antony, and at *Aeneid* 8.678–9 on the Shield of Aeneas
Augustus is depicted at Actium leading into battle the Italians together

---

[54] Comparetti (1895), ch. 5; R. A. Kaster, *Guardians of Language: The Grammarians and Society in Late Antiquity* (Berkeley, etc., 1988), ch. 5 'Servius'.

[55] See H. J. Rose, *Aeneas Pontifex* (London, 1948); the sacral mission of the Julian *gens* is stressed by E. Norden, 'Vergils *Aeneis* im Lichte ihrer Zeit', in *Kleine Schriften* (Berlin, 1966), 358–421, at 393–6; in general on religion in the *Aeneid* see Bailey (1935).

[56] Austin on 2.691; Heinze (1993), 32–4.

[57] Williams on 3.405.

[58] See Gransden on 8.187. On the historical and antiquarian allusions in *Aen.* 8 see Binder (1971).

[59] W. Warde Fowler, *Virgil's Gathering of the Clans*, 2nd edn. (Oxford, 1918); B. Rehm, *Das geographische Bild des alten Italiens in Vergils Aeneis* (*Philol.* Suppl. 24.2, 1932); Fordyce on 7.641 ff., with further bibliography; C. F. Saylor, 'The magnificent fifteen: Vergil's catalogues of the Latin and Etruscan forces', *CP* 69 (1974), 249–57; W. P. Basson, *Pivotal Catalogues in the Aeneid* (Amsterdam, 1975), 117–56. On the shorter Catalogue of Etruscans at 10.163–214 see Harrison (1991), 106–11.

with 'the senators and people' (i.e. the *Roman* SPQR). Sixty years earlier Rome had been at war with her Italian allies in the Social War (91–87 B.C.), a conflict arguably foreshadowed in the last half of the *Aeneid* in the war between an Italian confederation and the ancestor of the Romans. In the *Aeneid* Virgil's attachment to Italy, already displayed in the *Eclogues* and in the *Georgics*, engages with Augustus' policy of national unity.

In order to link the present with the past, aetiology and genealogy both exploit etymology. Names of peoples and places are linguistic bearers of historical or legendary origins; Virgil draws both on the Alexandrian poets' delight in etymologizing and on Roman linguistic scholarship, given encyclopedic treatment in Varro's *De Lingua Latina* (published in 45/4 B.C.). In the *Aeneid* etymologies cluster densely in lists or catalogues with historical or antiquarian content, such as the Parade of Heroes in book 6 or the Catalogue of Italians in book 7, but the etymologizing habit is ubiquitous in the poem and is applied to all kinds of words, not just proper names.[60]

Cities and Sons

The *Aeneid* is concerned not just to locate the origins of the present in the past, but also to narrate the processes of change, smooth or violent, by which the present develops from the past. In this epic of exile the hero and his people are in a state of transition, forced by circumstances into a journey towards a future that remains to be fashioned (whereas the wanderings of Odysseus are directed towards the recovery of a past stability).[61] One effect of writing a national epic from the perspective of a remote legendary past is to create a sense of the distance travelled between that past and the present. The Romans never tired of marvelling at what a mighty oak of a city had grown from so small an acorn: Virgil's key statement of this amazing growth is placed at the point where Aeneas first approaches the pastoral settlement of Evander on the

[60] Virgilian etymology is now treated exhaustively in O'Hara (1996), with an introduction placing Virgil's practice within the whole history of ancient etymology (see in particular 102–11 'The poetic function of Vergilian etymologizing'), and a comprehensive catalogue of individual Virgilian etymologies (erring deliberately on the side of caution as to what counts as an etymology); for a more speculative study of the etymological associations of proper names see M. Paschalis, *Virgil's Aeneid: Semantic Relations and Proper Names* (Oxford, 1997).

[61] The Roman sense of national identity seems bound up with myths of exile and outlawry (as in the case of the foundation story of Romulus; the first Romans are emphatically *not* autochthonous); see C. Edwards, *Writing Rome: Textual Approaches to the City* (Cambridge, 1996), ch. 5 'The city of exiles'.

site of the future world city, 8.98–100 *cum muros arcemque procul ac rara domorum | tecta uident, quae nunc Romana potentia caelo | aequauit, tum res inopes Euandrus habebat.* ('in the distance they see the walls, the citadel, and the scattered dwellings, which Roman power has now brought level with the heavens, but which then Evander ruled as his poor domain'). Evander's guided tour of his settlement is glossed by the narrator with references to the present-day appearance of Rome, so that, as in a double exposure, the reader sees the gilded temples of Augustan Rome superimposed on the rustic landscape.[62] Change and growth is the law for the new city-to-be of Rome, which as, in a sense, the true hero of the poem is subject to the imperative imposed on the epic hero to be the best and greatest.[63] An object lesson in how not to refound Troy is provided by the city of Helenus and Andromache at Buthrotum, an exact miniature replica of the destroyed city, but one trapped in a sterile obsession with a dead past (3.349–51).[64]

Before ever the wondrously mutating city of Rome is founded, the line from past to present is traced through a succession of different cities, Troy, the 'city' in the form of the camp thrown up by the Trojans on first landing at the mouth of the Tiber,[65] Lavinium, Alba Longa, and then Rome. Two of these cities are violently overthrown: Alba Longa (as later Carthage) is destroyed in the course of Rome's relentless expansion, while without the destruction of Troy there would have been no Trojan exile, and hence no Rome. Aeneas' task in book 2 is to detach himself from the horror of the Sack of Troy,[66] in order to ensure the survival of himself and his line. Cities are violently destroyed and must be replaced with new and better cities; the continuity of the bloodline must be preserved at all costs. The most hackneyed image of the *Aeneid* is that of Aeneas leaving Troy with his father on his shoulders and his son at his side, and it encapsulates the poem's central (and centrally

---

[62] Edwards (n. 61), 30–43, 52–63. For other examples of the contrast between humble past and mighty present see Prop. 4.1; Tib. 2.5; Ovid, *Fasti* 1.509–36.

[63] On this imperative see Hardie (1993), 3–10. The wrath of Juno at the beginning of the poem has as its correlate not a quarrel between human heroes, but one between the cities of Carthage and Rome for world-empire (1.12–22); within the narrative the *aition* for the Punic Wars is the wrath of the slighted Dido.

[64] See Quint (1993), ch. 2; Hardie (1993), 15–17; M. Bettini, 'Ghosts of exile: doubles and nostalgia in Vergil's *parva Troia* (*Aeneid* 3.294ff.)', *CSCA* 16 (1997), 8–33.

[65] Pointedly called an *urbs* on several occasions: Hardie (1994), 10–11. Jupiter foretells the sequence of foundations at 1.261–77. On the theme of cities in the *Aeneid* see J. Morwood, 'Aeneas, Augustus, and the theme of the city', *G&R* 38 (1991), 212–23.

[66] Modelled in part on Ennius' account of the sack of Alba Longa: see Austin on 2.313, 486ff. On the epic and historiographical set-piece of the sacking of a city see G. M. Paul, '*Urbs capta*: sketch of an ancient literary motif', *Phoenix* 36 (1982), 144–55.

epic) concern with fathers and sons.[67] This is another place where a Homeric theme intersects with a Roman, and specifically Augustan, obsession: the upper-class Roman families' cult of their ancestors, the desire of sons to live up to the virtuous deeds of their fathers and remoter ancestors, and the concern to perpetuate the male line become the expression of dynastic policy in Augustus' cult of the deified Julius and in his anxiety to ensure the succession.[68] In the *Aeneid* the generational cohesion of the Julian family with its past is represented through Aeneas' celebration of anniversary funeral games for his father in book 5, foreshadowing the games held in honour of Julius Caesar by Octavian in 44 B.C.,[69] and in Aeneas' otherwordly pilgrimage in book 6 to his dead past, where Anchises reassures his son of the success of future generations. Within the main narrative Ascanius/Iulus is the bearer of the family's hopes for the future: the divine guarantee of those hopes given by the omen of the flame around Ascanius' head at 2.679–86 is finally confirmed in Apollo's prophetic reaction to the boy's first success in war at 9.621–58.[70] On the human level Aeneas' last instruction to his son is to live up to the examples of courage offered by himself and Ascanius' uncle, Hector (12.432–40).[71]

Ascanius' success and survival mirrors that of Telemachus, who by the end of the *Odyssey* has proved himself as the worthy son of his father Odysseus, but Ascanius is the exception in the list of young men (and a woman, Camilla) in the *Aeneid* who die before their time and bring only grief to their fathers: Polites (cut down before the eyes of his father

---

[67] The subject of M. O. Lee's stimulating *Fathers and Sons in Virgil's Aeneid* (Albany, N.Y., 1979).

[68] On the importance of family traditions see J. Griffin, 'The creation of characters in the *Aeneid*', in Griffin (1985), 183–97. As *pater patriae* Augustus becomes the ideal father of all the Romans— and perhaps the ideal son of all the great Romans of the past, a relationship given visual expression both at the funeral of Augustus, accompanied by the *imagines* of all the Roman great men of the past, not just members of the Julian *gens* (Dio 56.34), and in the Forum of Augustus, with its galleries of statues both of members of the Julian *gens* and of other great Romans, with the statue of Augustus as *pater patriae* in the centre of the Forum. The statue galleries have often been compared with the Parade of Heroes in *Aen.* 6: e.g. H. T. Rowell, 'Vergil and the Forum of Augustus', *AJP* 62 (1941), 261–76; although a direct connection is questioned by A. De Grassi, 'Virgilio e il Foro di Augusto', *Epigraphica* 7 (1945), 88–103.

[69] The connection between the comet of 44 B.C., taken as a sign of Julius' apotheosis, and Acestes' flaming arrow (5.522–8) was denied by Heinze (1993), 133, but is convincingly defended by D. West, 'On serial narration and on the Julian star', *PVS* 21 (1993), 1–16; see also Drew (1927), ch. 2. For other contemporary resonances of the games in *Aen.* 5 see A. Feldherr, 'Ships of state: *Aeneid* 5 and Augustan circus spectacle', *CA* 14 (1995), 245–65.

[70] See Hardie on 9.621–71.

[71] This scene is given a more pessimistic reading by Lyne (1987), ch. 4 'The hero and his son'. On Ascanius see also N. Moseley, *Characters and Epithets. A Study of Vergil's Aeneid* (New Haven, 1926), 47–67. See also M. Petrini, *The Child and the Hero: Coming of Age in Catullus and Vergil* (Ann Arbor, 1997).

Priam, 2.526–32), Polydorus, Nisus and Euryalus,[72] Pallas, Lausus, and Turnus himself. The models for this series are Iliadic (Patroclus, Hector, Achilles) rather than Odyssean; the fragility of hopes vested in the coming generation was exemplified in a death that occurred as Virgil was writing the *Aeneid*, that of Marcellus in 23 B.C., with which Virgil chooses to conclude the first half of the poem (6.860–86).

From the point of view of Augustus this story of change and growth cuts in two ways: on the one hand through his restoration of stability in Rome Augustus is the preserver and guarantor of the structures of Roman tradition that have grown over the centuries; but on the other hand he is also in the position of an Aeneas, who must travel away from the wreckage of a previous order (Troy, Republican Rome) to a new dispensation.[73] The paradox of an irreversible 'Roman revolution'[74] that is based on an intensely conservative ideology of a return to the past is reflected in Apollo's riddling oracular instruction to the Trojans at 3.96 to 'search out your ancient mother' (the solution: the Trojan ancestor Dardanus came from Italy), so that Aeneas' journey is both an exile and a homecoming. Augustus seeks to disguise his unprecedented status as ruler by presenting himself as just another traditional Roman leader; in the *Aeneid*'s final *rapprochement* in heaven Jupiter reassures Juno that the Trojan newcomers in Italy will lose their name and merge into the traditional language and ways of the native Italians (12.833–7).

The *Aeneid* also places the story of the Trojans and their Roman descendants within the context of larger cultural histories, of a kind already used in the *Georgics* (see pp. 38–9 above). Jupiter's rapid survey for Venus' benefit of the whole of Roman history ends with a hint of the coming of a new Golden Age (1.291) that is made explicit in Anchises' prophecy of the career of Augustus at 6.792–4.[75] A more complex view of the development of human society is found in Evander's history of Latium at 8.314–36 that combines elements of a Hesiodic myth of ages with a Lucretian account of the evolution of civilization out of a state of 'hard primitivism', leaving it to the reader to fill in the dots and complete

---

[72] See Hardie (1994), 23–34 (with bibliography); Farron (1993), 155–64 'Recent interpretations of the Nisus-Euryalus episode'.

[73] For the Sack of Troy in *Aen.* 2 as an allegory of the downfall of the Republic (Priam as Pompey) see A. Bowie, 'The death of Priam: allegory and history in the *Aeneid*', *CQ* 40 (1990), 470–81. For further discussion of historical allegory in the *Aeneid* see pp. 92–3 below.

[74] To use the title of Syme's classic book (1939), still valuable background reading for the student of the *Aeneid*, even if ch. 30 on the 'Organization of opinion' is now dated.

[75] On the Golden Age see ch. II n. 57 and ch. III n. 48.

the story from the effects of Aeneas' arrival in Italy down to the present day.[76] At 9.598–620 the Italian Numanus Remulus attempts a character assassination of the Trojans by contrasting a stereotype of a hardy and virtuous primitive Italy with an equally clichéd picture of the decadent Oriental; in the heat of battle Numanus aims more at rhetorical effect than at the truth.[77]

The construction of a Roman cultural identity in the two centuries before Virgil's time is largely the history of the Romans' negotiation of their relationship to the kingdoms and civilization of the Greek East. It is possible that the war with Pyrrhus (280–75 B.C.), who claimed to be descended from Achilles, first made the Romans think of themselves as Trojans;[78] the *Aeneid* tells the surprising success story of a band of Trojan refugees from a city wiped out by a Greek expedition, whose descendants turn the tables by conquering the conqueror. This remoter history is foretold by Jupiter (1.283–5) and Anchises (6.836–40), and is figuratively foreshadowed in Aeneas' assumption of the role of the 'best of the Achaeans', Achilles, in his defeat of Turnus, who is doomed to reenact the death of the Trojan Hector. Already before that point a real Greek, Diomedes, has rather surprisingly acknowledged the superior military strength of the Trojan Aeneas, as an excuse for not allying himself with the Latin army (11.278–93). But the *Aeneid* does not simply tell of ultimate Roman military control of the Greek world; not least important of the stories of cultural transition told in the *Aeneid* is that of the 'Hellenization of Rome'.[79] As we read through the poem we find that a prejudiced hostility to all things Greek as expressed in the totally negative image of the dishonest and cunning Ulysses and his creature Sinon in book 2[80] and of the unscrupulous violence of Achilles' son Neoptolemus will be superseded by the piety and virtuous lifestyle of the Greek king who lives on the site of Rome itself, Evander ('good

---

[76] See Gransden (1976), 36–41; Thomas (1982), ch. 4. On Virgil's picture of Italy see also B. Tilly, *Vergil's Latium* (Oxford, 1947); H. J. Schweizer, *Vergil und Italien: Interpretationen zu den italischen Gestalten der Aeneis* (Aarau, 1967); A. G. McKay, *Vergil's Italy* (Greenwich, Conn., and Bath, 1970).

[77] See Hardie on 9.598–620, with further bibliography (esp. N. M. Horsfall, 'Numanus Remulus: ethnography and propaganda in *Aen.* 9.598 ff.', in Harrison (1990), 305–15). 'Harvard School' readers are tempted to take Numanus' speech at face value: Thomas (1982), 98-100.

[78] Cornell (n. 49), 65.

[79] See Gruen (n. 49); Galinsky (1996), 332–63 'Greek and Roman'.

[80] Drawing on a persistent strain in the post-Homeric reception of the figure of Odysseus: Stanford (1963), chs. 7, 8, 10. It is worth noting that we only hear of Ulysses in the *Aeneid* through the words of characters with a *parti pris* (cf. also 9.602 *fandi fictor Ulixes* [Numanus]). On the developing image of the Greeks see A. Rengakos, 'Zum Griechenbild in Vergils Aeneas', *A&A* 39 (1993), 112–24.

man'), a Greek from whom the Trojans are happy to receive gifts of horses (8.551–3). It is something of a shock in a poem of Roman origins to find that there were Greeks at Rome before it was Rome; Virgil perhaps hints that the Roman cultural identity was always defined through a relationship with Greece. Similarly in the Catalogue of Italians in book 7 many of the old towns and heroes of Italy turn out to have Greek origins.

The most famous definition of the Roman cultural mission is given by Anchises at 6.847–53 in an epilogue to the Parade of Heroes.[81] He tells the Roman to practise the arts of empire, just warfare, and law and order, and to leave excellence in sculpture, oratory, and astronomy to the Greeks (*alii*). This austere division between Greek and Roman arts is belied by its very context, the speech of a character in a Roman epic that challenges comparison with Homer himself. The *Aeneid* itself is the monument to the final naturalization on Roman soil of Greek cultural goods transported from the east, a journey parallel to that of its hero Aeneas, from east to west, from the world of Homer to the world of Augustus.

Plot and Narrative. Points of View. Ecphrasis.

In recent years increasing attention has been paid to the ways in which the narrative of the *Aeneid* works in giving shape to the raw material of its legendary and historical subject-matter, and to the ways in which it addresses the reader.[82] As in the case of Virgil's manipulation of generic differences, these issues are far from having a merely formalist relevance, and impinge on the widest questions of meaning and our response to the text. The shape of the story or stories within the text reflects the historical and ideological narratives used by the Roman ruling class to legitimize its power. The authority of the epic narrator, and the degrees of knowledge or uncertainty attainable by characters within the narrative, mirror competitions going on in the world outside the text between rival sources of authority and knowledge.

[81] H. Hine, 'Aeneas and the arts (Vergil, *Aeneid* 6.847–50)', in Whitby, Hardie, and Whitby (1987), 173–83.
[82] On the distinction between the story and the way that it is told see S. Chatman, *Story and Discourse* (Ithaca, 1978). Introductory works on narratology: G. Genette, *Narrative Discourse: An Essay in Method* (Ithaca, 1980); M. Bal, *Narratology* (Toronto, 1985). On Virgilian narratology see D. Fowler in Martindale (1997), 259–70.

Beginnings and endings are matters of especial concern for an epic poem, which has to decide where to start and where to stop within the vast span of legendary and historical time that is its legitimate territory. Ovid's hexameter poem the *Metamorphoses* boldly chooses to include the whole of recorded time, 'from the first beginnings of the world down to my own day' (1.3–4). But the *Aeneid*, like the two Homeric epics, opts for a discrete section of a longer story, whether we view that longer story as the whole of the prehistory and history of Rome, of which the *Aeneid* narrates only a small part of the prehistory, or as the story of the poem's hero Aeneas, of which we are told only the segment from his forced departure from Troy to his forcible assertion of his right to settle in Italy by the killing of Turnus.[83] Heinze stressed Virgil's concern to impose on the *Aeneid*, and on its constituent books and episodes, the unity of action (in the sense of a complete action, consisting of an integrated beginning, middle, and end) which Aristotle demanded of the good tragedy and also identified in the *Iliad* and *Odyssey*.[84] Heinze also showed that Virgil is more 'dramatic' than Homer both in the tightness and streamlining of his plotting, and in his creation of surprising and emotional turns of plot. Book 1 begins not with the Sack of Troy, which will be related in flashback by the internal narrator Aeneas in books 2 and 3, but with the sudden violence of the storm unleashed by Juno and calmed by Neptune.

This is a classic example of the *in medias res* epic beginning, but at the same time it sketches out a pattern of opening and closing that determines the movement of the whole poem, and, beyond that, of the whole of Roman history.[85] The Storm is a very literal opening, as the winds rush out when Aeolus opens their prison-house (1.81–3). When Neptune calms the storm he tells the winds that their ruler, Aeolus, should keep them closed up in their prison (1.140–1). This mythological closing is echoed at the end of the speech in which Jupiter calms Venus' distress at the near-annihilation of her son with a preview of the whole

[83] The events of the poem are squeezed into about twenty days, separated by longer or shorter intervals: Heinze (1993), 265–6.

[84] Heinze (1993), 348–69.

[85] The phrase *in medias res* comes from Horace *Ars Poetica* 148 (see Brink ad loc.). On the Storm and its functions as a beginning to the poem see Pöschl (1962), 13–24 (using the musical analogy of an 'overture' to analyse the Storm's introductory presentation of major themes in the epic); Otis (1964), 227–35; R. D. Williams, 'The opening scenes of the *Aeneid*', *PVS* 5 (1965/66), 14–23. See also A. D. Nuttall, *Openings: Narrative Beginnings from the Epic to the Novel* (Oxford, 1992), ch. 1 (focusing mostly on the first eleven lines of the poem). In general on the issues connected with literary beginnings see F. M. Dunn and T. Cole (eds.), *Beginnings in Classical Literature*, YCS 29 (1992); E. W. Said, *Beginnings: Intention and Method* (New York, 1975).

glorious history of his descendants, concluding with a vision of the final closing of the Gates of War under Augustus, imprisoning a personification of *Furor*, roaring in his frustration like the winds in Aeolus' cave (1.293–6; cf. the winds at 1.55–6). The *pax Augusta* is the remoter ending of the story told in the *Aeneid*. Literary openings and closings here enter the world of history, via the particular institution (self-consciously revived by Augustus) of the opening and closing of the gates of the temple of Janus to mark the start and conclusion of war.[86] The rhythm of war and peace that defines the course of Roman history is generalized in the *Aeneid* into a recurrent pattern of the release of violence or madness (*furor*) followed by the painful reimposition of peace and calm, of chaos followed by the restoration of order. The whole of the second half of the poem conforms to this model: the martial frenzy unleashed through the eruption of the Fury Allecto from her Tartarean confinement will only be appeased through the death of Turnus.

The gods who stand, respectively, for chaos and order in the narrative, Juno and Jupiter, are themselves associated with opening and closing.[87] Where Juno keeps on opening up sources of disruption, Jupiter, the god of Fate, strives to impose a closure on the narrative that will guarantee the success of an 'official version' in which Aeneas and his Roman descendants complete their goal of overcoming their enemies and establishing a final settlement.[88] At the end of the *Aeneid* Jupiter strikes a deal with Juno allowing the Trojan settlement in Italy, and then intervenes on earth to frighten off Juturna, whose support for her brother Turnus threatens endlessly to defer the conclusion of the battle. Turnus recognises that it is really Jupiter who is his enemy (12.895); Aeneas completes the plan of Fate with a spear-throw that is compared in a simile to the thunderbolt of Jupiter (12.922–3), followed up with a final sword-thrust.

Finis. But this most conclusive of endings, the death of the hero's enemy, is also an open ending, leaving more stories to be told, more

[86] See Ogilvie on Livy 1.19.1–4; Williams (1968), 426–8. On the *Belli Portae* in the *Aen.* see D. Fowler, 'Opening the gates of war (*Aen.* 7.601–40)', in Stahl (1998), 155–74.
[87] Feeney (1991), 137–8; D. Hershkowitz, *The Madness of Epic: Reading Insanity from Homer to Statius* (Oxford, 1998), ch. 2.
[88] On the closural devices of the *Aen.* see P. R. Hardie, 'Closure in Latin epic', in D. H. Roberts, F. M. Dunn, and D. Fowler (eds.), *Classical Closure* (Princeton, 1997), 139–62; R. N. Mitchell-Boyask, '*Sine fine*: Virgil's masterplot', *AJP* 117 (1996), 289–307. In general on the theoretical issues involved see D. P. Fowler, 'First thoughts on closure: problems and prospects', *MD* 23 (1989), 75–122; id., 'Second thoughts on closure', in D. H. Roberts et al., *Classical Closure*, 3–22. On the death of Turnus see also pp. 99–101 below.

outbreaks of chaos to be reduced to order. (And paradoxically it is an outburst of chaotic emotion that impels Aeneas to deliver the *coup de grâce*.) Since the narrative of the poem stops at a point in the remote past, it is only through a series of repetitions of its plot structure reaching down to Virgil's own day that it can function adequately as a blueprint for the whole of Roman history. The repetitions within the narrative (the unleashing of Allecto in book 7 'repeats' the unleashing of the storm in book 1)[89] must be extrapolated beyond the limits of the narrative to take us in time down to Augustus. Even in the apparently final reconciliation between Jupiter and Juno (12.791–842) allusion to an Ennian Council of the Gods at a later point in mythical time indicates that Juno's hostility towards the Romans will need to be assuaged again in the future.[90] The major prophetic episodes sketch sequences of repetition, of wars (the Speech of Jupiter at 1.254–96; the Shield of Aeneas at 8.626–731), and of generations of Roman heroes (the Speech of Anchises at 6.756–886), which are capped with divine assurances of a triumphant conclusion that the reader may however experience more as pious hopes than as fixed certainties. The Speech of Anchises offers two endings: the universal rule of Augustus (6.791–805), an end to history, and the untimely death of the younger Marcellus (6.860–86), yet another of the many funerals in the poem and one that cheats Augustus' nephew of the triumph that he might have expected. David Quint has shown how the plot of the *Aeneid* is held in tension between two forms of repetition, 'regressive repetition' in the sense of an 'obsessive circular return to a traumatic past', and 'repetition-as-reversal' that allows an element of difference by which the past is mastered.[91] Quint also uses the Renaissance codification of the distinction between epic (as a clearly structured narrative that achieves its goal) and romance (as a narrative of proliferating wanderings or adventures in search of an endlessly deferred goal) to think about the earlier history of the epic tradition.[92]

History is the winners' story, but the *Aeneid*, the story of Roman success, is hospitable to other versions and other points of view. The

---

[89] Allecto and Storm: Otis (1964), 233–4, 328; Pöschl (1962), 71–85; Buchheit (1963), 59–85.

[90] D. C. Feeney, 'The reconciliations of Juno', in Harrison (1990), 339–62.

[91] D. Quint, 'Repetition and ideology in the *Aeneid*', *MD* 24 (1991), 9–54; see also Hardie (1993), 14–18. Quint, like other recent analysts of epic narrative, draws on the psychoanalytic narrative theory of P. Brooks, *Reading for the Plot: Design and Intention in Narrative* (New York, 1985).

[92] Quint (1993), 31–41; see also C. Burrow, *Epic Romance. Homer to Milton* (Oxford, 1993), ch. 2 on Virgil. For reflections on the *Aeneid*'s attempt to arrest the mutability of historical process see P. R. Hardie, 'Augustan poets and the mutability of Rome', in A. Powell (ed.), *Roman Poetry and Propaganda in the Age of Augustus* (Bristol, 1992), 59–82.

divine and human opponents of Aeneas try to write their own stories, viewed as an alternative 'fate' to Jupiter's script, Fate. Juno fosters Carthaginian world-rule, 'if the fates somehow might allow it' (1.17–18); Turnus asserts that he too has his fated duty, to extirpate the criminal race of Trojan wife-snatchers (9.136–7).[93] Even if these alternative scripts are rudely swept away by the juggernaut of Roman Fate, the losers' stories may be told from a point of view that elicits the reader's sympathy.[94] The *Aeneid* shows characters acting in the grip of strong emotions, and also aims at arousing strong emotions in the reader. Heinze identified this as another of the tragic qualities of the poem, seeing a direct connection between the Aristotelian tragic emotions and the astonishment, pity, and fear that the Virgilian narrative arouses.[95] Otis, in his analysis of what he called Virgil's 'subjective style', drew attention to the ways in which the narrative manipulates the reader's feelings by making us empathize and sympathize with the characters.[96] This kind of approach has been given new sharpness and sophistication by the application of modern theoretical approaches to narrative 'focalization', another way of saying the point of view from which an event is seen or experienced.[97] For example, at 4.281 *ardet abire fuga dulcisque relinquere terras* ('he is burning to depart in flight and leave the sweet land'), although it is the narrator who speaks, *dulcis* 'sweet' is said from the point of view of, focalized through, the character of Aeneas, torn between the urge to leave and the attractions of Carthage.

The activity of viewing, and of reacting to and interpreting what is viewed, is inscribed in the text in the device of ecphrasis, the formal description of a work of art that challenges the poet's powers of evoking images through words.[98] On five occasions Aeneas is confronted with

[93] For the idea of conflicting sets of fates see Bailey (1935), 212–13; W. Pötscher, *Vergil und die göttlichen Mächte: Aspekte seiner Weltanschauung* (Hildesheim and New York, 1977), 63–6.

[94] The conflict between 'winners' stories' and 'losers' stories' in epic texts is a central concern of Quint (1993).

[95] Heinze (1993), 370–3.

[96] Otis (1964), ch. 3, 'The subjective style'. Otis, however, drew too sharp a distinction between Virgil's 'subjective' and Homer's 'objective' style; recent narratological analyses of Homer have exploded the idea of a totally impartial and detached Homeric narrator: see I. J. F. De Jong, *Narrators and Focalizers: The Presentation of the Story in the Iliad* (Amsterdam, 1987). Farron (1993) argues that the *Aeneid*'s chief aim is to work on the reader's emotions, rather than to convey messages.

[97] On issues connected with focalization see D. P. Fowler, 'Deviant focalisation in Virgil's *Aeneid*', *PCPS* 36 (1990), 42–63; M. Bonfanti, *Punto di vista e modi della narrazione nell'Eneide* (Pisa, 1985); Conte (1986), 152–4.

[98] Ecphrasis has been the subject of intense theoretical attention in recent years, as a privileged *locus* for the study of the relationship between text and image: see D. Fowler, 'Narrate and describe:

artworks (or something like an artwork) that call for a reaction: (i) the
scenes of the Trojan War in the temple of Juno at Carthage (1.450–
93);[99] (ii) the scenes of Theseus and the Minotaur sculpted by Daedalus
on the temple of Apollo at Cumae (6.14–37);[100] (iii) the Parade of
Heroes in the Underworld (6.756–892; not a work of art as such, but a
ghostly procession of statue-like figures); (iv) the Shield of Aeneas
(8.626–731);[101] (v) the swordbelt of Pallas (described at 10.495–9 at the
moment when Turnus takes it from the body of Pallas, and viewed by
Aeneas with fatal consequences at 12.941–6).[102] The third and fourth of
these are visual embodiments of epic narratives on the later history of
Rome (both the Parade of Heroes and Shield of Aeneas contain Ennian
allusion); Anchises uses the Parade of Heroes to fire Aeneas' nationalist
spirit (6.888–9) in a manner paradigmatic for the effect of the *Aeneid* on
its contemporary readership, whereas with the Shield there is an ironic
gap between the craftsman Vulcan's (and the reader's) knowledge of the
meaning of the scenes (8.627–8) and Aeneas' ignorance thereof (8.730).
The scenes in the temple of Juno and the swordbelt of Pallas both trigger
memories of the past in Aeneas, in the former case of the events
represented in the temple, in the latter of an event with which the
object has been accidentally associated. The Sibyl recalls Aeneas from
his idle contemplation of the scenes on the temple of Apollo to the need
for action in the here and now. In their various ways all these scenes raise
issues of the interpretation and thematic relevance of artworks not just
for the character Aeneas, but for the reader who observes Aeneas
observing. The scene of the Danaids murdering their bridegrooms on
the swordbelt of Pallas has a symbolic relevance to the deaths of both
Pallas and Turnus that operates at a level separate from the logic of
cause and effect within the narrative action. Likewise, for a careful
reader the scene of the labyrinth on the temple of Apollo foreshadows

the problem of ekphrasis', *JRS* 81 (1991), 25–35; A. Laird, 'Sounding out ecphrasis: art and text in
Catullus 64', *JRS* 83 (1993), 18–30; J. Elsner, *Art and Text in Roman Culture* (Cambridge, 1996);
A. Barchiesi in Martindale (1997), 271–81.

[99] R. D. Williams, 'The pictures on Dido's temple (*Aen.* 1.446–93)', *CQ* 10 (1960), 145–51;
D. Clay, 'The archeology of the temple to Juno in Carthage', *CP* 83 (1988), 195–205; A. Barchiesi,
'Rappresentazioni del dolore e interpretazione nell'Eneide', *A&A* 40 (1994), 109–24; M. C. J.
Putnam, 'Dido's murals and Virgilian ekphrasis', *HSCP* forthcoming.

[100] W. Fitzgerald, 'Aeneas, Daedalus, and the labyrinth', *Arethusa* 17 (1984), 51–65;
M. Paschalis, 'The unifying theme of Daedalus' sculptures on the temple of Apollo Cumanus
(*Aen.* 6.20–33)', *Vergilius* 32 (1986), 33–41; Putnam (1995), ch. 4; S. Casali, 'Aeneas and the doors
of the Temple of Apollo', *CJ* 91 (1995), 1–9.

[101] D. West, '*Cernere erat*: the Shield of Aeneas', in Harrison (1990), 295–304; Hardie (1986),
ch. 8; Quint (1993), ch. 1; Gurval (1995), ch. 5.

[102] Conte (1986), 185–95; M. C. J. Putnam, 'Virgil's Danaid ekphrasis', *ICS* 19 (1994), 171–89.

the labyrinthine journey through the Underworld that Aeneas is about to undertake. These imagistic and symbolic connections run not just between the ecphrases and other parts of the text, but between the ecphrases as works of art represented within the text and the work of art that is constituted by the text itself, so that our reading of them reflects on our own activity in reading the *Aeneid*. The Trojan scenes in the Carthaginian temple of Juno are a visual equivalent of the Epic Cycle, of which the *Aeneid* is as it were another instalment: when Aeneas' 'reads' these scenes he does something similar to what we are doing as we read the poem of which this episode is a part.

In this, the first ecphrasis of the poem, Aeneas would seem to be an ideal reader and interpreter, in that as a leading player himself in the Trojan War he knows exactly what is depicted in the scenes. Ironically, he is not thereby automatically best placed to know what is the *meaning* of these scenes in their context.[103] The reader, who has recently witnessed Juno's furious attempt to destroy Aeneas, may suspect that in a temple of Juno the commemoration of the destruction of Troy serves purposes other than the glorification of a brave but doomed race, and pity for *lacrimae rerum*, as Aeneas takes it (1.461–3).

This scene is part of a sustained sequence of episodes in book 1 that explore models of controlling and making sense of narrative structures, in a way that may be taken as programmatic for the joint task of narrator and reader in the poem as a whole.[104] The kinds of generic allusion discussed above (pp. 57-63) are here put to very pointed use: Juno, in her enraged outburst at 1.37–49, takes as model for her desired punishment of Aeneas the model of Minerva's blasting of the impious lesser Ajax, an episode from the cyclic Nostoi that had been dramatized in a tragedy by Accius: this is her first attempt to rescript the narrative outline of the story of Aeneas and his descendants laid out by Jupiter as he unrolls the book of Fate for Venus (1.257–96). As we have seen, that imperious survey provides a model both for the rhythm of events in the rest of the *Aeneid* and in the longer story of Rome. But we may err if we assume easily either that Jupiter is a totally impartial narrator (like the traditional picture of the objective Homeric epic narrator), or that his

---

[103] Foreshadowing and irony are already found in Homer, but intensified in the *Aeneid* through Virgil's use of tragic models: G. E. Duckworth, *Foreshadowing and Suspense in the Epics of Homer, Apollonius and Vergil* (Princeton, 1933); Muecke (n. 40); Quinn (1968), 330–9, 'Tragic irony and insight'; K. J. Reckford, 'Latent tragedy in *Aeneid* VII.1–285', *AJP* 82 (1961), 252–69.

[104] The play of different 'voices' (the 'authorial' and the 'participatory') and of points of view in *Aen.* 1 is the subject of the suggestive article by C. Segal, 'Art and the hero: participation, detachment, and narrative point of view in *Aeneid* 1', *Arethusa* 14 (1981), 67–83.

blueprint will be faithfully followed in the sequel. For example, the simple image of the ending of war and the imprisonment of *Furor* hardly squares with the last scene of the poem, which certainly ends the war in Latium, but leaves us with the final picture of a hero who has not succeeded in bottling up his anger.

We as readers of the speeches of Juno and Jupiter are privy to a level of knowledge about the gods that is inaccessible to the hero of the poem.[105] This ironic disparity between what the hero knows and what the reader and the gods know is brought to a head in the poem's first encounter between a god and a mortal, when Aeneas meets his mother but does not know who she is, because she is in disguise. Aeneas is reduced to making guesses based on the way she looks (327–9), before Venus puts him straight—by deceitfully claiming to be just a typical Carthaginian maiden (335–7). The illusionism of the disguised and deceitful Venus leads naturally to her stagey tragic 'prologue' giving the previous history of Dido. The use of the prologue form suggests a model (that of the tragic heroine) for understanding the story of Dido that is accessible to the reader, but presumably not to Aeneas, who exists many centuries before the birth of Attic tragedy; similarly the reader, but not Aeneas, will be aware that Aeneas' questions to Venus at 327–9 cast himself and his mother in the roles of Odysseus and Nausicaa at *Odyssey* 6.149–52. This charade is ended when Venus reveals her true identity to Aeneas as she departs (402–5). But we cannot always rely on signs from the gods to correct our interpretative errors (and in any case signs from the gods, omens and oracles, can be notoriously tricky to read, as the Trojans discover for example at 3.84–191 in their attempt to obey Apollo's command to search out their 'ancient mother').

Aeneas proceeds to Carthage, where we have already seen him to be a possibly deluded reader of the scenes of the Trojan War. This process of matching new images to old memories continues when Aeneas' gaze is diverted from the striking image of the Amazon queen Penthesilea, last of the scenes in the temple, to his first sighting of the flesh-and-blood queen Dido. Penthesilea, the female ruler that Aeneas knew, is an immediate standard against which to measure the queen that he has never seen;[106] another image of Carthaginian femininity with which to

---

[105] On the divine point of view in the *Aeneid* see E. Block, *The Effects of Divine Manifestation on the Reader's Perspective in Vergil's Aeneid* (New York, 1981).

[106] See R. W. B. Lewis, 'On translating the *Aeneid*', in Commager (1966), 41–52, at 50–2; Williams (1983), 68–9; Conte (1986), 194–5.

match the proudly autonomous Dido will be that of the maiden huntress whom Aeneas (thought he) met in the woods outside the city. The simile at 498–502, the verbal image that together with the artistic image of Penthesilea textually frames the first entrance of Dido, asks to be focalized through the eyes of the viewer within the narrative,[107] Aeneas himself, who sees Dido through a haze of associations that may well incline him to love at first sight (the narrative situation is closely parallel to the typical occasion on which the hero of an ancient novel falls in love at first sight of the heroine). If it is correct to take this hint, then the models by which Aeneas frames his first reaction to the sight of Dido will indeed have momentous consequences for the ensuing narrative. Aeneas' busy matching of real woman with memory images is paralleled by the reader's work in making sense of the literary models alluded to in this scene, for the simile comparing Dido to Diana is closely based on the simile at *Odyssey* 6.102–8 comparing the Phaeacian princess Nausicaa to Artemis. The Homeric story of Odysseus and Nausicaa is one (but just one) of the many literary models with which we the readers, from our memory of earlier literature, will compare and contrast the Dido story in our search to make sense of it.[108] In one way we as readers are superior to the hero in our access to levels of knowledge denied to him, but in another way Aeneas' laborious attempts to make sense of and control the events into which he finds himself thrust are a model for the task of reading and interpretation imposed on the poem's audience.

---

[107] For another example of a simile that may be focalized through one of the characters rather than through the narrator see Williams (1983), 180 on *Aen.* 10.565–70 (is it the Italians who perceive Aeneas as like the monstrous Aegaeon?). The bee simile of the busy Carthaginians at 1.430–6 and the ant simile of the Trojans at 4.402–7 are focalized very literally through the eyes of the characters, respectively Aeneas and Dido, who in each passage are watching the scene from a high vantage point, so that people look small.

[108] For another example of a character in the text undertaking an act of interpretation analogous to that of the reader see J. J. O'Hara, 'Dido as "interpreting character" at *Aeneid* 4.56–66', *Arethusa* 26 (1993), 99–114, developing an argument in O'Hara (1990) that the interpretation of omens and prophecies by characters in the poem bears an analogy to the reading and interpretation of ambiguous works of literature such as the *Aeneid*. The reference to preexisting mythological or narrative models or examples ('exemplarity') on the part of both characters and readers in an allusive narrative such as Virgil's becomes the object of parody in what Conte calls the 'mythomaniac heroes' of Petronius' *Satyricon*, unable to rise above their constant temptation to see the sordid reality of their lives in terms of romantic mythical models: G. B. Conte, *The Hidden Author. An Interpretation of Petronius' Satyricon* (Berkeley, Los Angeles, London, 1996), ch. 1.

Character. Defining the Hero. The Godlike (Herculean) Hero. Epic Women.

The problems faced by Aeneas in establishing the correct frames of reference for the two females that he unexpectedly comes across at Carthage are also paradigmatic for the poem's concern to establish norms of behaviour, patterns of heroism, and the relationship between the individual and the society of which he or she is a part. Dido's eventually tragic instability is an understandable result of the new situation into which this woman has been thrust, formerly a devoted wife, but now a grieving widow who has to take on the role of a queen and lead her people into a new life in exile. Her career closely matches that of the hero Aeneas, who, from being a prince of a junior branch of the Trojan royal family with a good fighting record, is suddenly cast in the role of the leader of the survivors of Troy with a mission not only to establish a new society overseas, but also to lay the foundations for a race destined to world-rule in the distant future, but whose glory he will not live to see. The leader who must define his own role in the service of a new social and nationalist order emerging from the breakdown of a previous order—this is also the challenge facing Octavian/Augustus. The problems that confront Aeneas in his encounters both with other characters who would befriend or oppose him and with his own emotions and desires touch at many points the problems facing a ruler and his society in the far more complex world of late first-century B.C. Rome.

The definition of the hero in the *Aeneid* is also a matter of literary, cultural, and intellectual history. In creating a character[109] Virgil typically starts from a Homeric model, but then superimposes elements selected from the whole of the literary and cultural traditions that separate the age of Augustus from the age of Homer. This almost archaeological stratification of a character has encouraged some to see a linear development in the character of Aeneas, from an old-fashioned Homeric hero motivated by strong individualistic emotion to the socially responsible hero required in Virgil's Rome.[110] But the modern reader

---

[109] The notion of 'creating a character' through the careful layering of diverse models is indebted to J. Griffin's excellent essay 'The creation of characters in the *Aeneid*', in Griffin (1985), 183–97.

[110] The approach of Otis (1964). In general on the character of Aeneas see Camps (1969), ch. 3; Mackie (1988). For differing versions of the 'spiritual development' approach to the character of Aeneas see F. A. Sullivan S. J., 'The spiritual itinerary of Virgil's Aeneas', *AJP* 80 (1959), 150–61

should resist the temptation to expect of an ancient epic the consistent and progressive development of character typical of the nineteenth-century novel.[111] The emotions that Aeneas feels at the very end of the poem (12.945–52) are hard to distinguish from his state of mind at the beginning of the story, when he wakes up to a realization that the Greeks are sacking Troy (2.314–17).

Two further general points are worth making about the relationship between Homeric and Virgilian concepts of the hero. Firstly, there is a fair similarity between the honour code and competitive individualism of the Homeric hero and of the traditional Roman Republican system of aristocratic values (whereas Homeric aristocratic values would have seemed far more anachronistic to a fifth-century Athenian theatre audience). If Aeneas has to rethink his relationship to his past, that past is perhaps better thought of as a time in the very recent past for Virgil's audience rather than as a distant legendary world of heroes.[112] Secondly, it is fallacious to see a simple contrast between an unreflective set of heroic values in Homer and the more complex demands imposed on a proto-Augustan Virgilian hero. The epic hero is always a problem: the *Iliad* and the *Odyssey* already explore issues concerning the relationship of individual and community, the conflict between private emotion and duty, the need to integrate the warrior within the harmonious enclave of marriage and household, just as much as the *Aeneid* does.[113] The *Aeneid* is certainly concerned to judge and revalue standards of heroic behaviour, but in this it is entirely conventional: the history of the epic tradition is the history of the revaluation of the hero.[114]

In looking at the various models from which the character of Aeneas is created, it may be more helpful to think in terms of role-playing than of character-development. The roles are bewilderingly numerous. Aeneas

(the religious hero); T. van Nortwick, *Somewhere I have Never Travelled: The Second Self and the Hero's Journey in Ancient Epic* (New York and Oxford, 1992) (using psychoanalytic models).

[111] In general on the issues of character and selfhood in antiquity see C. B. Pelling (ed.), *Characterization and Individuality in Greek Literature* (Oxford, 1990); C. Gill, *Personality in Greek Epic, Tragedy, and Philosophy. The Self in Dialogue* (Oxford, 1996).

[112] For a comparison of Homeric and Republican values see Thornton (1976), 1–12. The question of anachronistic modes of heroism in the *Aeneid* may be illuminated by recent work on Attic tragedy's exploration of the obsolescence of aristocratic values in a democratic society: see J. P. Vernant, 'The historical moment of tragedy in Greece', in J. P. Vernant and P. Vidal-Naquet, *Myth and Tragedy in Ancient Greece* (New York, 1988), 23–8.

[113] On the problems of the Iliadic hero see esp. J. M. Redfield, *Nature and Culture in the Iliad: The Tragedy of Hector* (Chicago and London, 1975); Gill (n. 111), ch. 2.

[114] Many read the *Odyssey* as implicitly reexamining and criticizing the models of heroism in the *Iliad*: see R. Rutherford, *Homer* (Oxford, 1996), 58–9. For the later tradition see J. M. Steadman, *Milton's Epic Characters* (Chapel Hill, 1968); J. A. Kates, 'The revaluation of the classical heroic in Tasso and Milton', *Comp. Lit.* 26 (1974), 299–317.

plays himself as an Iliadic character,[115] but he must also act out other Iliadic parts, those of a Hector, guarantee of his city's survival, but also of a wrathful and avenging Achilles.[116] His enemies try unsuccessfully to damn him as another Paris (4.215; 7.321, 363–4; 9.136–9). He must also play the part of an Odysseus, both as wanderer and as the slayer of the suitor Turnus in order to win his rightful wife, Lavinia. In his encounter with Dido he also relives some of the experiences of Apollonius of Rhodes' hero, Jason.[117] Other sources are non-literary: later models for leadership include Hellenistic treatises on the good king,[118] and the virtues of the good Roman general.[119] In his anxious concern for the wellbeing of his comrades and dependents he displays the *cura*, responsibility, required of the *princeps*; his notorious taciturnity may reflect the reserved manner of Augustus himself.[120] Virgil is also alert to the intense scrutiny to which the behaviour and morality of the Homeric heroes had been subjected by the various philosophical schools; Odysseus in particular had been held up as the type of the Cynic or Stoic philosopher.[121] The need for Aeneas to submit himself to the dictates of Fate, to endure impassively and to control his emotions, strongly suggests a Stoic framework for viewing his behaviour, and he sometimes speaks like a Stoic,[122] but critics are sharply divided in their judgement as to how far along the path of the Stoic *proficiens* (philo-sophical learner) Aeneas has progressed by the end of the poem.[123]

The Homeric hero is godlike, but always aware of his mortality.[124] The *Aeneid* milks to the full the pathos of mortality, dwelling obsessively

---

[115] Diomedes excuses his refusal to support the Latins with his memory (rather exaggerated!) of Aeneas' prowess in the Iliadic fighting, 11.283 *experto credite.*

[116] See above n. 11.

[117] See Nelis (n. 26); B. E. Levy, 'Homer, Apollonius and the origins of Aeneas', *Vergilius* 7 (1961), 25–9.

[118] Cairns (1989), chs. 2 and 3.

[119] R. G. M. Nisbet, '*Aeneas Imperator*: Roman generalship in an epic context', in Harrison (1990), 378–89.

[120] Feeney, in Harrison (1990), 187–9.

[121] Stanford (1963), chs. 7 and 9; in the *Aeneid* Aeneas has some of the features of this version of Odysseus, whereas the Virgilian Ulysses stands in another tradition of judging Odysseus as the unscrupulous trickster (Stanford (1963), ch. 10). A typical example of this way of reading Homer is Horace *Epistles* 1.2, where the heroes of the *Iliad* are taken as examples of the bad effects of the passions, while Ulixes is 'a useful example of the power of virtue and wisdom' (*Ep.* 1.2.17–18).

[122] E.g. his assurance to the Sibyl at 6.105 that no future ordeal can surprise him, *omnia praecepi atque animo mecum ante peregi* (see Norden and Austin ad loc.).

[122] Aeneas as a Stoic *proficiens*: Heinze (1993), 227; C. M. Bowra, 'Aeneas and the Stoic ideal', *G&R* 3 (1933/34), 8–21; M. W. Edwards, 'The expression of Stoic ideas in the *Aeneid*', *Phoenix* 14 (1960), 151–65; on Aeneas and the Cynic-Stoic ideal of the good king see Cairns (1989), 34–7.

[124] J. Griffin, *Homer on Life and Death* (Oxford, 1980); W. G. Thalmann, *Conventions of Form and Thought in Early Greek Poetry* (Baltimore and London, 1984), index s.v. 'Gods and Men'.

on young warriors cut down in the flower of their youth.[125] Homer
focuses the contrast between the immortality of the gods and the
transience of human existence in a famous scene (*Iliad* 16.431–61) in
which Zeus is dissuaded by Hera from rescuing his mortal son Sarpedon
from death at the hands of Patroclus. Virgil reworks this scene at *Aeneid*
10.464–73, in which Jupiter, remembering his own experience in the
case of Sarpedon, consoles another of his sons, Hercules, to whom the
young Arcadian fighter Pallas has just addressed a futile prayer for
success in his forthcoming duel with Turnus.[126] Hercules had been a
guest-friend of the Arcadians at the time when he rid the site of Rome of
the monster Cacus in a titanic encounter retold to Aeneas by Evander at
8.190–275. This epic narrative within the epic is followed by ritual
hymnic celebration by the Salii of the exploits of Hercules, now a god, at
8.293–302 (301 *decus addite diuis* 'a glory added to the gods').[127]
Hercules is the great example of the suffering hero who transcends
the Homeric barrier between mortal and immortal to become a god. He
does not appear in the main narrative of the *Aeneid*, but his career is a
model for the possibility of converting godlikeness into actual godhead,
a reward that by Virgil's day was held out both to those who achieved
philosophical (Platonic, Stoic) perfection and to the great and bene-
ficent ruler.[128] The Homeric hero often has divine ancestry; the Virgilian
hero elected by Fate both has divine ancestry and will himself be the
ancestor of gods in the future (9.642, Apollo to Ascanius, *dis genite et
geniture deos* 'begotten of gods and begetter of gods'). In his consoling
speech in book 1 Jupiter assures Venus that she will raise her son Aeneas
to heaven (1.259–60; cf. 12.794–5), whither in due course he will be
followed by other great men in Rome's history: Romulus, Julius Caesar,
and eventually Augustus.

---

[125] On the image of death in battle as defloration see D. P. Fowler, 'Vergil on killing virgins', in
Whitby, Hardie, and Whitby (1987), 185–98.

[126] Barchiesi (1984), 16–30.

[127] Aeneas' story is already marked as 'Herculean' by the word *labores* at 1.10, 'labours' inflicted
on him as on Hercules by a persecuting Juno. On the role of the Virgilian Hercules and the model
that he holds up to Aeneas, see G. K. Galinsky, *The Herakles Theme* (Oxford, 1972), 131–52;
Gransden (1976), 17–20; see also J. W. Zarker, 'The Hercules theme in the *Aeneid*', *Vergilius* 18
(1972), 34–48; Feeney (n. 26); id. (1991), 156–61; Hardie (1993), 66–7. Otis, in his cheerfully
optimistic reading of the poem, labels Aeneas a *theios aner* 'divine man' (Otis [1964], 219–22). See
also N. W. De Witt, 'The influence of the saviour sentiment upon Virgil', *TAPA* 54 (1923), 39–50.

[128] In general on ruler-cult see L. R. Taylor, *The Divinity of the Roman Emperor* (Middletown,
1931); S. Weinstock, *Divus Julius* (Oxford, 1971); S. R. F. Price, *Rituals and Power: The Roman
Imperial Cult in Asia Minor* (Cambridge, 1984).

Gender: Epic Women

Epic is a very masculine genre, dealing in narratives of the male activities of quest and conquest. In Homer women are the cause (Helen and Briseis in the *Iliad*) and goal (Penelope in the *Odyssey*) of these male activities, but in the course of the narratives women tend to create obstacles and delays (Calypso and Circe in the *Odyssey*; in *Iliad* 6 Andromache tries to dissuade Hector from returning to the fight). The first two words of the *Aeneid*, *arma uirumque*, immediately strike a very masculine note, reinforced by the fact that in Latin the quality of the hero, *uirtus* 'virtue, courage', literally means 'manliness' (from *uir*).

Like the *Odyssey*, the *Aeneid* is an epic that has as its goal (re)union in marriage. Aeneas' bride-to-be, however, is a strangely passive and enigmatic character who never talks in the poem (although for Oliver Lyne her blush at 12.64–9 speaks volumes).[129] Her actual marriage to Aeneas lies beyond the conclusion of the poem. Other images in the poem of the married state are characterized by loss and death (Priam and Hecuba, 2.506–58; Aeneas and Creusa, 2.735–46, 771–94), or by demonic disruption (the 'wedding' in the cave of Dido and Aeneas, 4.160–72, and its consequences; the crazed Maenadism and eventual suicide of Amata, wife of king Latinus, 7.373–405, 12.593–603);[130] stability is achieved only in a literal (Dido and Sychaeus, 6.472–4) or a figurative afterlife (Andromache and Helenus, 3.294–336).[131] These negative images are related to the fact that Aeneas' divine opponent is the goddess of marriage, Juno, who in her very first intervention in the poem uses her power to perverted ends when she bribes Aeolus to unleash the winds with the sexual lure of a nymph in marriage.

The conflict that motivates the plot of the *Aeneid* is a strongly gendered one.[132] On the divine level it is the opposition of the supreme male god Jupiter and his female consort Juno. Jupiter's sovereign rationality (as it appears at the beginning of the poem) is opposed by the forces of

[129] Lyne (1987), 114–25 [a shorter version of Lyne in McAuslan and Walcot (1990), 157–66]. Cairns (1989), ch. 7 argues unconvincingly that Lavinia's self-effacement itself marks her as the typical maiden of Greek choral lyric.

[130] On Amata see J. W. Zarker, 'Amata. Vergil's other tragic queen', *Vergilius* 15 (1969), 2–24; A. La Penna, 'Amata e Didone', *Maia* 19 (1967), 309–18.

[131] Andromache's marriage in exile to Helenus is a throwback to the Trojan wedded households disrupted by the war; at the same time she is inseparably 'wedded' to the cenotaph of her first husband Hector. There are strong hints that Andromache exists in a kind of shadow land (see n. 64); on the episode see R. E. Grimm, 'Aeneas and Andromache in *Aeneid* 3', *AJP* 88 (1967), 151–62; G. S. West, 'Andromache and Dido', *AJP* 104 (1983), 257–67; Quint (1993), ch. 2.

[132] See now the excellent discussion by E. Oliensis, in Martindale (1997), 303–11.

madness called up by Juno, above all through the agency of Allecto, a she-devil fertile in sowing chaos and discord. The hyper-masculine *furor* of Turnus is the result of possession by the female Fury; extremes seem to meet. Aeneas' other major opponent, Dido, is a real woman, who as a woman scorned turns into a kind of Maenad or Fury. Her tragedy seems to be partly the result of the fact that she is a woman forced to take on a man's responsibilities as the ruler of her people; many features link Dido to the even more monstrous woman in the second half of the poem, the 'Amazon' Camilla, who evokes in equal measure admiration and a fascinated horror, and who succeeds brilliantly for a while in the masculine world of war, before she disastrously reverts from being a warrior to a huntress in her pursuit of the spoils of Chloreus (11.782 *femineo praedae et spoliorum ardebat amore* 'she burned with a *woman's* love of booty and spoils').[133] These images of dangerous women out of their proper place might well remind a Roman audience of the 20s B.C. of that 'horror, the Egyptian wife' (8.688), Cleopatra, who according to Augustan propaganda had threatened the existence of Rome itself.[134]

Before dismissing Virgil simply as a misogynist, or constructing a psychobiographical reading on the basis of hints in the ancient Lives that he was gay,[135] one should consider two female divinities whose role is not merely obstructive or destructive. In Cybele, or the Magna Mater, Virgil found a foreign goddess with a disturbingly orgiastic cult who had been made safe and installed at the centre of Roman religion (her temple was next to Augustus' house on the Palatine). At 9.77–122 the Magna Mater intervenes to save the Trojan ships from being burned by Turnus, by metamorphosing them into nymphs;[136] in a striking simile at 6.784–7 Anchises compares the all-powerful goddess Roma herself to the Magna Mater, mother of the gods.[137] Aeneas' own mother, Venus, is

[133] Camilla: Gransden (1991), 20–5; N. W. DeWitt, 'Vergil's tragedy of maidenhood', *CW* 18 (1924/25), 107–8; W. P. Basson, 'Vergil's Camilla: a paradoxical character', *Acta Classica* 29 (1986), 57–68; G. S. West, 'Chloreus and Camilla', *Vergilius* 31 (1985), 22–9; B. W. Boyd, 'Virgil's Camilla and the traditions of catalogue and ecphrasis (*Aeneid* 7.803–17)', *AJP* 113 (1992), 213–34.

[134] On Roman representations of Cleopatra see M. Wyke, 'Augustan Cleopatras: female power and poetic authority', in A. Powell (ed.), *Roman Poetry and Propaganda in the Age of Augustus* (Bristol, 1992), 98–140.

[135] But the homoeroticism of the *Aeneid* stands in need of further study: for some thoughts see Hardie (1994), 33–4 (on the love of Nisus and Euryalus); Putnam (1995), 27–49 (suggesting a homoerotic charge to the relationship of Aeneas and Pallas).

[136] For further bibliography see Hardie on 9.77–122; add E. L. Harrison, 'The metamorphosis of the ships (*Aeneid* 9.77–122)', *PLLS* 8 (1995), 143–64.

[137] On the Magna Mater in Virgil and Augustan Rome see R. M. Wilhelm, 'Cybele: the Great Mother of Augustan order', *Vergilius* 34 (1988), 77–101; T. P. Wiseman, 'Cybele, Virgil and Augustus', in Woodman and West (1984), 117–28.

another goddess with a double nature, both a disruptive and irrespon-sible divinity of sexual desire, and as *Aeneadum genetrix* the nurturing mother-goddess of the Romans. In the *Aeneid* she disconcertingly appears in both roles, and even combines the two when she acts as sexual temptress to persuade Vulcan (who is at least her lawful husband) to forge a new set of arms for Aeneas at 8.370–406.[138]

Many readers, from at least the time of St Augustine (*Confessions* 1.21) have of course sympathized more with Dido than with Aeneas. In recent years a number of feminist critics have started to look more closely at the ways in which women's voices make themselves heard in the *Aeneid*, finding in them alternative and even oppositional points of view that should not simply be silenced in the epic's celebration of the success of Roman arms and government. The cries of grief in the poem demand a hearing as well as the songs of triumph.[139]

Structure

Recent studies on the narratology of the *Aeneid*, examining such issues as closure and narrative repetition (see pp. 71–4 above), have tended to supersede an earlier fashion for analysis of the structure of the poem in more static terms. An interest in the narrative dynamics of the text has replaced an appreciation of the 'architecture' of the poem; the figures on the well-wrought urn have leapt into an alarmingly unstable state of animation. Yet Virgil's own use of the image of a temple of epic poetry at the beginning of the third *Georgic* invites the reader to contemplate the carefully crafted symmetries of the poem. The *Aeneid* continues the intricate formal patterning of the *Eclogues* and *Georgics*; but in Virgil's epic this Alexandrian *labor* coincides with the elaborate structuring of the narrative that articulates and lends coherence to the vast canvases of the Homeric poems.[140]

[138] Venus in the *Aeneid*: A. Wlosok, *Die Göttin Venus in Vergils Aeneis* (Heidelberg, 1967).

[139] C. G. Perkell, 'On Creusa, Dido, and the quality of victory in Virgil's *Aeneid*', in H. P. Foley (ed.), *Reflections of Women in Antiquity* (New York etc., 1981), 355–77; S. F. Wiltshire, *Public and Private in Vergil's Aeneid* (Amherst, 1989), ch. 2 'Grieving mothers and the costs of attachment'; S. Georgia Nugent, 'Vergil's "voice of the women" in *Aeneid* V', *Arethusa* 25 (1992), 255–92; J. P. Sullivan, 'Dido and the representation of women in Vergil's *Aeneid*', in R. M. Wilhelm and H. Jones (eds.), *The Two Worlds of the Poet: New Perspectives on Vergil* (Detroit, 1992), 64–73.' Books on women in Roman epic are under way by S. Georgia Nugent and A. Keith.

[140] On structural patterns in Homer see e.g. S. L. Schein, *The Mortal Hero: An Introduction to Homer's Iliad* (Berkeley, Los Angeles, London, 1984), 30–3; M. S. Silk, *Homer: The Iliad* (Cambridge, 1987), 37–46; O. Taplin, *Homeric Soundings: The Shaping of the Iliad* (Oxford, 1992); C. W. Macleod, *Homer: Iliad XXIV* (Cambridge, 1982), 16–35.

The most obvious formal feature of the Homeric poems is the use of formulaic repetition, regarded by the oralist school of the earlier part of the twentieth century as simply the result of the mechanics of oral composition, but viewed by recent Homerists more sympathetically as the bearer of poetic significance.[141] No writer in Virgil's day would aim for the degree of repetitiousness of the Homeric poems, but Virgil does achieve a generally Homeric effect by a marked incidence of repetition, of stock epithets (*pius Aeneas*, etc.), formulaic introduction of direct speech, and the like.[142] In many cases verbal repetitions alert the reader to more extensive relationships between their contexts: for example, the phrase *in ualle reducta* 'in a secluded vale' occurs twice, at 6.703 and 8.609, the setting firstly for the souls of the unborn in the Elysian Fields, and secondly for Venus' delivery to Aeneas of his new armour. Both vales, secluded from the main action of the poem, are the stage for major passages of prophecy, the Speech of Anchises and the Shield of Aeneas, passages which reflect each other in many ways. Another example: the phrase *stans celsa in puppi* 'standing on the lofty stern' (the place of the commander in a Roman warship) occurs thrice, at 3.527 of Anchises at the moment when he first catches sight of Italy and sees the omen of the white horses, portending both war and triumphal celebration of peace; at 8.680 of Augustus as he leads the Italians to the victory at Actium that will be celebrated in the triumph that forms the last scene on the Shield; and at 10.261 of Aeneas as he returns to his beleaguered camp to lead the Trojans to victory over the Latins. The formula highlights one of the poem's central themes, that of military struggle and eventual triumph, and its application to the three heroes Anchises, Aeneas, and Augustus highlights the importance of the generational continuity of the Julian *gens* for the successful history of Rome.[143]

Another very pointed repetition is that of the phrase *soluuntur frigore membra* '[his] limbs are loosened in a chill', applied at 1.92 to Aeneas in his panic-stricken despair in the opening storm unleashed by his divine enemy Juno, and at 12.951 to Turnus as his life slips away through the

---

[141] For accounts of Homeric repetition that seek to go beyond the mechanical approach of the oral school see Silk (n. 140), 67, 101–5; A. Kahane, *The Interpretation of Order: A Study in the Poetics of Homeric Repetition* (Oxford, 1994).

[142] On Virgilian repetition see Moskalew (1982); and for a study in an older style see J. Sparrow, *Half-lines and Repetitions in Virgil* (Oxford, 1931); for a case-study see C. P. Segal, 'Vanishing shades: Virgil and Homeric repetitions', *Eranos* 72 (1974), 34–52 (on 2.790–5, 5.738–45, 6.703–6, 12.952).

[143] Moskalew (1982), 136–9; Henry (1989), 115–21; Harrison on 10.261–2. My comments in fact touch only a few of the interconnections triggered by this phrase in the vast echo-chamber of the *Aeneid*, and which through the fire imagery of 8.680–1 and 10.261–2, 270–5 would take us on a tour of the fire imagery of *Aen.* 2 and its interaction with the theme of destruction and rebirth.

stroke of a victorious Aeneas, after Juno has finally agreed to abandon him to his fate. This repetition, at beginning and end of the poem, is part of a much more extensive ring-composition that links the storm scene and the death of Turnus.[144] The application of the phrase to the hero and his arch-enemy creates an inversion: by the end of the poem Aeneas, seen at the beginning in a condition of utter powerlessness, is in total control (of external circumstances, at least, if not of himself). Inversion is a powerful kind of repetition, in which the text alludes to itself but in a relation of opposition (in a manner analogous to the *inter*textual phenomenon of 'opposition in imitation'), and there are many examples in the *Aeneid*. For example, at the beginning of book 9 Juno sends down Iris to urge Turnus into battle (9.1–15); at the end Jupiter sends down Iris to warn off Juno from further aiding Turnus in the fight in the Trojan camp (9.802–5). A complex passage of recapitulatory repetition with ironic inversion is the final meeting of Aeneas with Dido in the Underworld at 6.450–76, that alludes to the whole course of the tragic relationship,[145] from an initial encounter in which one of the pair is less clearly visible than the other (Aeneas wrapped in a cloud at the moment when he first sees Dido in book 1, Dido at 6.452–4 hard to make out in the infernal shadows, like the moon peeping through clouds) to the final flight of one of the pair (Aeneas away from Carthage and towards a new wife in Italy in book 4, Dido away from Aeneas and back to her former husband Sychaeus at 6.472–4). The simile at 6.471 comparing the unresponsive Dido to a rock inverts the simile at 4.441–6 comparing Aeneas in the face of Anna's appeals on Dido's behalf to a firm-rooted oak-tree in an Alpine storm. Inversion also structures the poem's plot as a whole, a tale of a 'world destroyed and world restored'.[146]

On a larger scale, the whole of the *Aeneid* is structured according to a complex and interwoven set of symmetries and contrasts.[147] There is a clear division between the two halves of the poem,[148] the Odyssean wanderings of the first half and the Iliadic war of the second half,

---

[144] On which see Hardie (1986), 177–80. On ring-composition see Moskalew (1982), 116–22.

[145] On this passage see M. von Albrecht, 'Die Kunst der Spiegelung in Vergils Aeneis', *Hermes* 93 (1965), 54–64; see also Hardie (1986), index s.v. 'inversion'.

[146] See P. R. Hardie, *PLLS* 9 (1996), 107–8, 113–14.

[147] Camps (1969), ch. 6 'Principles of structure: continuity and symmetry'; Otis (1964), Appendix 9; Perret (1965), 113–21, 'L'architecture de l'Énéide'; R. Lesueur, *L'Énéide de Virgile: Étude sur la composition rythmique d'une épopée* (Toulouse, 1975), 21–46 contains a useful survey of earlier schemes.

[148] G. E. Duckworth, 'The architecture of the *Aeneid*', *AJP* 77 (1954), 1–15. On the parallels between 1 and 7 see n. 89 above.

marked by the renewed invocation to a Muse at 7.37–45 and by the clear parallelism between Juno's rousing of the storm in book 1 and of Allecto in book 7, and between the deaths of young men (Marcellus and Turnus) that conclude books 6 and 12.[149] Another analysis discerns a tripartite structure,[150] the first four books containing the story of Dido, framing Aeneas' flashback narrative in 2 and 3, the last four concentrating on the battles in the war in Latium and the other main human obstacle to Aeneas' mission, Turnus, while the central four books are characterized by some relaxation of the narrative impetus and by a series of inset narratives, pageants, and spectacles that look both backwards to earlier events (the Games in book 5 on the anniversary of Anchises' death, the first part of Aeneas' journey through the Underworld in book 6, Evander's narrative of Hercules and Cacus in book 8), and forward to later Roman history (the Speech of Anchises, the Shield of Aeneas; the Games in book 5 also contain a variety of foreshadowings), while the Catalogue of Italians provides a survey of the geography and ethnography of primitive Italy.

Structural analysis may also be conducted at the level of the relationship between individual books. As in the *Georgics* there is (at least up to a point) an alternation between even-numbered books, darker and more pathos-charged, and odd-numbered books, lighter and more relaxed; this is most marked in the first half of the poem, where the intensity of books 2, 4 and 6 is punctuated by the generally calmer atmosphere of books 3 and 5.[151] Significant relationships have also been traced between corresponding books in the two halves of the poem, whether that correspondence is sought (a) between the books in their linear sequence (matching 1 with 7, 2 with 8, etc.), or (b), as Otis suggests, according to a concentric arrangement in which (setting aside books 1 and 7 as the corresponding first books of their halves) 2 is matched with

[149] The clarity of this division into halves is complicated by the postponement of the invocation to Erato at the beginning of *Aen.* 7 until after the further narration of the Trojans' journey from Caieta, past the eerie island of Circe, to the mouth of the Tiber: on aspects of Virgil's transitional strategy here see P. R. Hardie, in A. Powell (ed.), *Roman Poetry and Propaganda in the Age of Augustus* (Bristol, 1992), 66–9. In general on Virgil's use of book-divisions see E. L. Harrison, 'The structure of the *Aeneid*: observations on the links between books', *ANRW* II 31.1 (1980), 359–93.
[150] G. E. Duckworth, 'The *Aeneid* as a trilogy', *TAPA* 88 (1957), 17–30; W. A. Camps, 'A note on the structure of the *Aeneid*', *CQ* 4 (1954), 214–15; id., 'A second note on the structure of the *Aeneid*', *CQ* 9 (1959), 53–6, on the central place of the temple/council-chamber of Latinus. There is interesting comparative material in A. Fowler, *Triumphal Forms: Structural Patterns in Elizabethan Poetry* (Cambridge, 1970), on 'triumphal patterns involving significant central points', and the 'numerology of the centre'. Symbolic centres in Virgil: R. F. Thomas, 'Virgil's ecphrastic centrepieces', *HSCP* 87 (1983), 175–84.
[151] Heinze (1993), 363–4; R. S. Conway, 'The architecture of the epic', in *Harvard Lectures on the Vergilian Age* (Cambridge, Mass., 1928), 129–49; Pöschl (1962), 165–73.

12, 3 with 11, and so on.¹⁵² Both schemes if pushed to the limit become
Procrustean, but both yield interesting connections. For example, by the
first scheme 2 is paired with 8, the book on the destruction of Troy with
the book that proleptically tells of the foundation and growth of Rome,
and at the end of each book Aeneas' piety towards family and nation is
symbolized by a tableau in which he shoulders a burden, respectively his
father (2.721–3: the past) and the shield on which are depicted the 'fame
and fate of his descendants' (8.731: the future). By the second scheme 2,
telling of the utter defeat of the Trojans by the Greeks, is paired with 12,
in which Aeneas plays an Achillean role in bringing down Turnus.

Imagery, Allegory, Symbolism

The indefinitely proliferating network of interconnections in the *Aeneid*
that is supported by the structural links discussed in the previous section
is reinforced by Virgil's use of simile, metaphor, and allegory. Imagery
often works to point up structure: Bernard Knox's still classic article on
the imagery of book 2 showed how the structural pattern of destruction
followed by the hope of rebirth is accompanied by recurrences of the
images of serpent and flame: for example the (literal) serpents that kill
the sons of Laocoon near the beginning of the book are echoed and
inverted in the serpent-like flame that licks the head of Aeneas' son at
2.681–4, but which turns out to be an omen of salvation.¹⁵³

The imagery of the *Aeneid* operates at the levels both of small-scale
detail and of whole books and of the poem as a totality; allegory and
symbolism work further to project the meanings of the poem beyond the
narrow confines of the narrative of Aeneas' career on to the larger
historical canvas. At the microscopic level Virgil takes infinite pains with
the traditional epic simile to establish 'multiple correspondences'¹⁵⁴

¹⁵² Otis (1964), 217. Little support has been found for the numerological analysis of G. E.
Duckworth, *Structural Patterns and Proportions in Vergil's Aeneid: A Study in Mathematical
Composition* (Ann Arbor, 1962), according to whom the whole poem is structured on the
Golden Section, and Virgil is a Pythagorean.
¹⁵³ B. M. W. Knox, 'The serpent and the flame: the imagery of the second book of the *Aeneid*',
AJP 71 (1950), 379–400 = Commager (1966), 124–42. Other explorations of the image structure
of the *Aen.* that have worn well include F. L. Newton, 'Recurrent imagery in *Aeneid* 4', *TAPA* 88
(1957), 31–43; B. Fenik, 'Parallelism of theme and imagery in *Aeneid* 2 and 4', *AJP* 80 (1959), 1–
24. For an example of imagistic structures operating over a larger span of the poem see J. W. Hunt,
Forms of Glory. Structure and Sense in Vergil's Aeneid (Carbondale and Edwardsville, 1973), 84–95
on the parallel imagery linking Dido and Turnus, paired structurally as the chief obstacles to Aeneas
in respectively the first four and last four books of the poem.
¹⁵⁴ The term is D. A. West's, in 'Multiple-correspondence similes in the *Aeneid*', in Harrison

between simile and surrounding narrative. So far from being merely ornamental pauses in the narrative, Virgilian similes serve to provide interpretative glosses on the action (whether focalized through the narrator or one of the characters),[155] and even to continue the narrative by other means, as for example the wounded deer simile at 4.69–74.[156]

The wounded deer simile also fits into a much more extensive pattern of imagery that serves both to unify book 4 and to link it with other books. The 'wound of love' has already appeared in the form of a metaphor in the first two lines of book 4; by a typical Virgilian move the figurative wound turns into the literal death-wound inflicted on herself by Dido at the end of the book.[157] The movement between literal and figurative also characterizes the text's dealings with hunting: it is during the literal hunt at 4.129–72 that Dido, whose regal autonomy was illustrated at 1.498–502 in the simile comparing her to the virgin huntress Diana, fully realizes her victimhood in succumbing physically to the consequences of the psychological state of being a 'wounded deer'. The image of the hunt reaches out beyond the Dido story to embrace the scope of the whole poem, from Aeneas' first demonstration of his leadership ability after the catastrophic storm in literally hunting stags to provide food for his men (1.180–94) to the final 'hunting down' of his enemy Turnus in the simile at 12.749–55.[158]

These densely woven imagistic patterns are one of the hallmarks of the Virgilian text, and a full understanding of their importance informs the seminal books by Pöschl (1962) and Putnam (1988).[159] Important precursors in the technique include the intricate image structures of Greek tragedy[160] and the scientific poem of Lucretius, which fuses the resources of literary imagery with a tradition of scientific analogy to

---

(1990), 429–44; id., 'Virgilian multiple-correspondence similes and their antecedents', *Philologus* 114 (1970), 262–75. On similes see also R. A. Hornsby, *Patterns of Action in the Aeneid: An Interpretation of Vergil's Epic Similes* (Iowa City, 1970); R. Rieks, 'Die Gleichnisse Vergils', *ANRW* II 31.2 (1981), 1011–1110; M. Coffey, 'The subject matter of Virgil's similes', *BICS* 8 (1961), 63–75; Lyne (1989), 63–99.

[155] See n. 107.

[156] See Lyne (1989), 77–9; see also index s.vv. 'narrative through imagery'.

[157] J. Ferguson, 'Fire and wound. The imagery of *Aeneid* 4.1 ff.', *PVS* 10 (1970/71), 57–63.

[158] Hunting: J. R. Dunkle, 'The hunter and hunting in the *Aeneid*', *Ramus* 2 (1973), 127–42. Other central images worked out in literal and figurative forms throughout the poem include Knox's flame and serpent, the storm, the mountain (on which see J. H. W. Morwood, 'Aeneas and mount Atlas', *JRS* 75 (1985), 51–9); for other aspects of fire-imagery see P. A. Miller, 'The minotaur within: fire, the labyrinth, and strategies of containment in *Aeneid* 5 and 6', *CP* 90 (1995), 225–40.

[159] For an earlier study of Virgilian symbolism see R. W. Cruttwell, *Virgil's Mind at Work: An Analysis of the Symbolism of the* Aeneid (Oxford, 1946).

[160] P. R. Hardie, 'The *Aeneid* and the *Oresteia*', *PVS* 20 (1991), 29–45, at 31–4.

produce a text that satisfyingly expresses the Epicurean grand unified theory of the universe.[161]

Virgil uses his powers of 'associative integration'[162] not merely to create a sense that everything within the text of the *Aeneid* is part of a tightly unified literary cosmos, but also to forge allegorical or symbolic links between events in the story of Aeneas and the whole of Roman history, and, beyond that, events in the largest framework of mythological history (this way of joining past to present often works in tandem with the use of prophecy or aetiology, discussed above, pp. 63–71). These larger signifying procedures can be viewed as an extension of the smaller-scale figurative devices just discussed; the ancient grammarians defined allegory as a trope, as simply an extended sequence of metaphors.[163] The very first simile in the poem, comparing Neptune calming the storm to a Roman statesman calming a mob (1.148–53), suggests a way of reading the mythological and legendary narrative of the poem as historical allegory.[164] Virgil provides other object-lessons within the poem on how to extend the meanings of the legendary narrative into the wider contexts when he incorporates discrete passages of explicit prophecy into the imagistic pattern of the text. Book 8, with its vision of Augustan Rome during Aeneas' tour of the site of Rome and the potted history of Rome worked on to the Shield of Aeneas by Vulcan, provides good examples. As well as looking forward in time, the book also looks backwards, in the epyllion-like narration by Evander of the earlier struggle on the site of Rome between Hercules and the monster Cacus.[165] The episode is virtually generated out of a drive to construct correspondences with other parts of book 8 and of the rest of the poem: at the end of history as recorded on the Shield of Aeneas this

---

[161] On Lucretian analogy see A. Schiesaro, *Simulacrum et imago: gli argomenti analogici nel De rerum natura* (Pisa, 1990); on the affinities between Virgilian and Lucretian imagistic practice see West (n. 154 [1970]); Hardie (1986), 232–3.

[162] This is the imaginative process discussed in J. Livingston Lowes' study of Samuel Taylor Coleridge, *The Road to Xanadu: A Study in the Ways of the Imagination* (London, 1927); the parallel between Virgil and Livingston Lowes' account of Coleridge has been drawn by several Virgilian critics, e.g. Jackson Knight (1966), 102–3.

[163] Cic. *Or.* 94 *cum fluxerunt continuo plures translationes, alia plane fit oratio; itaque genus hoc Graeci appellant ἀλληγορίαν.* In general on ancient allegory, and Virgilian allegory in particular, see J. Whitman, *Allegory: The Dynamics of an Ancient and Medieval Technique* (Oxford, 1987); F. Buffière, *Les Mythes d'Homère et la pensée grecque* (Paris, 1956); Thornton (1976); A. Wlosok, 'Gemina doctrina: on allegorical interpretation', *PLLS* 5 (1986), 75–84; Hardie (1986), 29–32; Farrell (1991), 257–72. On personification allegory: C. S. Lewis, *The Allegory of Love* (Oxford, 1936); Feeney (1991), s.v. 'personifications'. See also pp. 56–7 above.

[164] On the statesman simile see Pöschl (1962), 20–3; Otis (1964), 229–30; S. J. Harrison, 'Vergil on kingship: the first simile of the *Aeneid*', *PCPS* 34 (1988), 55–9.

[165] Hercules and Cacus: G. K. Galinsky, 'The Hercules-Cacus episode in *Aeneid* VIII', *AJP* 87 (1966), 18–51; Buchheit (1963), 116–33; Hardie (1986), 110–18.

primal struggle between Olympus and the semi-bestial forces of hell will be repeated in the confrontation between the Greco-Roman pantheon and the animal-headed gods of Egypt at Actium (8.698–703). The hymn in praise of Hercules (8.285–305) that follows Evander's narrative alludes to the honour paid to Augustus after Actium of the inclusion of his name, together with other gods, in the *carmen Saliare*.[166] But the Hercules and Cacus story also foreshadows the fight between Aeneas and Turnus, so suggesting yet another connection between the victories of Aeneas and of his descendant Augustus.

This is only to begin unravelling the associations between the Hercules and Cacus story and other legendary and historical events. The connections between the episode and other parts of the *Aeneid* are an invitation to look for connections with events that are not made explicit in the text, but which would be known to the Roman reader. For example, the festival of Hercules at the Ara Maxima that the Arcadians are celebrating took place in historical times on 12th August; Aeneas thus arrives in front of the city-to-be on the eve of the three days, 13–15th August, on which Octavian celebrated his triple triumph in 29 B.C., thus suggesting a further connection between the victories of Hercules over Cacus and of Octavian over Antony and Cleopatra.[167] The narrative that Aeneas hears from the lips of Evander may be regarded as the Ur-epic on a (proto-)Roman saviour hero, and as such as the distant model of the *Aeneid* itself. If we push the analogy, just as the Hercules and Cacus episode functions as a multifaceted reflector of events both within and outside the text, so the *Aeneid* itself might be viewed as a colossal multiple correspondence simile for the whole of Roman history.

That national history is set within the still larger frame of cosmic and mythological history. In the first scene of the poem Aeneas appears to us

[166] See Gransden on 8.285.

[167] Drew (1927), ch. 1; Camps (1969), ch. 10 'Echoes of history'; Binder (1971), a massively detailed study of the historical allusions in book 8. Drew argues for historical allegory in *Aen.* 5 also; for other examples of historical allegory cf. e.g. N. M. Horsfall, '*Turnus ad portas*', *Latomus* 33 (1974), 80–6 (Turnus at 9.47–53 prefigures Hannibal at the gates of Rome); Austin on 2.486 ff. (the sack of Troy probably modelled on the Ennian sack of Alba Longa); A. Bowie (n. 73). On reflections of Cleopatra in that other African queen Dido see Pease (1935), 24–8; Camps (1969), 95–6; on Dido as prefiguring later Carthaginian perfidy see N. M. Horsfall, 'Dido in the light of history', in Harrison (1990), 127–44. The way in which the legendary narrative of the *Aeneid* prefigures later historical events has sometimes been compared to typology, the practice of Biblical interpreters of reading Old Testament events as 'types' of events in the New Testament (e.g. Jonah in the belly of the whale as a type of Christ's descent to Hell); see K. Gransden (1976), 14–20; id., 'Typology, symbolism and allegory in the *Aeneid*', *PVS* 13 (1973/4), 14–27; D. Thompson, 'Allegory and typology in the *Aeneid*', *Arethusa* 3 (1970), 147–53; note the qualifications of Griffin (1985), 184–93.

as a storm-tossed Odysseus, but Hesiodic allusions in the description of
the winds of Aeolus and of the storm itself suggest that the Odyssean
Aeneas is also re-experiencing the far more catastrophic upheavals in the
natural order caused by the primeval struggles between the gods and the
Titans or Giants. The recurrent use of Gigantomachic allusion through-
out the poem aligns the history of Rome and her ancestors with a cosmic
conflict between the forces of chaos and Olympian order.[168] These and
other myths had been subjected by later commentators to a natural-
philosophical allegorization, and as we have already seen (pp. 56–7
above) the *Aeneid* sometimes uses allegory to equivocate between a
mythological and a more scientific view of cosmic processes.[169]

Meaning. Two (and More) Voices. Sources of Authority: Gods and Fate, Rhetoric and Philosophy

> Do I contradict myself?
> Very well then I contradict myself,
> (I am large, I contain multitudes.)
> Walt Whitman *Song of Myself*

The *Aeneid* spreads out its allusive and symbolic tentacles to embrace
the whole of history and the natural universe itself, taking to a logical
conclusion epic's generic drive to be, like its heroes, the greatest and the
best.[170] Yet this totalizing text which seeks to define Rome and its place
in the widest order of things does not, for many readers, succeed in
defining its own meaning and so close off the circle of its own
interpretation. The last fifty years of Virgil criticism have been a
battlefield of competing interpretations of the poem, more often than
not focusing on the reductionist opposition of 'optimist' and 'pessimist',
or, in political terms, Augustan and anti-Augustan readings. These two
kinds of interpretation are sometimes labelled the 'European' and
'Harvard' schools of Virgil criticism, after the places of origin of some
of the leading exponents of each.[171]

---

[168] Gigantomachic allusion: Hardie (1986), chs. 3 and 4; 90–7 on the Storm.
[169] A strong sense of the cosmic aspect of the poem informs the books by Pöschl (1962),
Thornton (1976) (for whom the plot of the poem concerns the 'coherence of the universe'), and
Hardie (1986).
[170] Epic's inherent expansiveness: Hardie (1993), 3–10.
[171] In general on 'European' and 'Harvard' schools of Virgilian criticism see the stimulating
discussion in Johnson (1976), ch. 1; and S. J. Harrison's 'Introduction' to Harrison (1990).
W. Clausen's own reflections on his part in the foundation of the 'Harvard' school (the seminal

The question of authoritative meaning in the *Aeneid* is acute not just because it is a poem that functions as an aetiology for the present-day power of Rome and of Augustus, but because epic was the preeminently authoritative genre in antiquity. Within the epic texts it seems reasonable to seek ultimate authority in the persons of the gods who preside over and participate in the action. The religious authority of epic is great: according to Herodotus 2.53 Homer and Hesiod gave the gods their names, spheres of action, and outward forms. In the Latin epic tradition divine authority and Roman power are already before Virgil inseparably linked, since the supreme god in the Homeric pantheon, Zeus/Jupiter, is also the national god of Rome.[172] On the divine level the plot of the *Aeneid* is the ultimately unsuccessful struggle on the part of Juno to oppose Fate, the 'word' of Jupiter;[173] in contrast to the more generalized notion of fate in Homer as something that delimits the possible activity of the gods and determines the hour of an individual's death, in the *Aeneid* Fate is above all the destiny of the family of Aeneas and of the city of Rome. Jupiter's masterplot, a.k.a. Fate, is laid out in the impressive prophecies at 1.257–96 (Jupiter's speech to Venus), 6.756–86 (the Parade of Heroes in the Underworld), 8.626–728 (the Shield of Aeneas), and 12.830–40 (Jupiter's final speech to Juno).

Yet in recent years critics have questioned the apparently unambiguous certainties revealed in these prophetic passages. O'Hara points out that Jupiter's speech to Venus has the rhetorical goal of assuaging her anxiety, and that it is at best a selective account of the future history of Aeneas and Rome.[174] Furthermore Jupiter is caught in a contradiction when at the beginning of the Council of Gods in book 10 he declares (10.8–9) that he had forbidden the war between Italians and Trojans that had been the first item in his reading from the Book of Fate at 1.263–4.[175] Coming from the god who should represent unswerving

---

article is Clausen [1964a]) are printed at Horsfall (1995), 313–14. Notable examples of the 'European' school include Klingner, Pöschl, Buchheit, Cairns, Galinsky; of the 'Harvard' school Clausen, Adam Parry, Putnam, R. F. Thomas, Boyle, Lyne.

[172] Feeney (1991), 113–14, 140–1. Feeney's chapter 4 is a very stimulating account of the divine machinery of the *Aeneid* working as part of a poetic text. For general introductions to the gods and religion in the *Aeneid* see Camps (1969), ch. 5; Bailey (1935); P. Boyancé, *La Religion de Virgile* (Paris, 1963); Heinze (1993), 235–50; R. Coleman, 'The gods in the *Aeneid*', *G&R* 29 (1982), 143–68; W. Kühn, *Götterszenen bei Vergil* (Heidelberg, 1971). On Fate see Pötscher (n. 93). On the role of Jupiter see A. Wlosok, 'Vergil als Theologe: Iuppiter—pater omnipotens', *Gymn.* 90 (1983), 187–202 = *Res Humanae—Res Divinae: Kleine Schriften* (Heidelberg, 1990), 368–83.

[173] On the etymology of *fatum* from *fari* see O'Hara (1996), 121.

[174] O'Hara (1990), 132–63.

[175] For two very different ways of dealing with this contradiction see Heinze (1993), 278 n. 43 and Lyne (1987), 78–81.

Fate, this unsettling inconsistency raises the possibility that the impress-
ive-sounding and apparently impartial speech with which Jupiter con-
cludes the Council of Gods at 10.104–13 may in fact be as rhetorical in
its way as the splendidly impassioned speeches which Venus and Juno
have just hurled at each other.[176] In the final interview with Juno in
book 12 Jupiter is concerned to soothe injured female pride even more
obviously than is the case with his interview with Venus in book 1, at the
same time as he provides for the conclusive ending of the poem. And
even this apparently final reconciliation was not to be the last occasion
on which Juno had to be brought on side, as any Roman reader of
Ennius would have known.[177]

The Parade of Heroes in book 6 and the Shield of Aeneas in book 8
come with the apparently impeccable authority of, respectively,
Anchises and Vulcan. The triumphalism of the Parade of Heroes is
famously tempered by the mournful coda on the younger Marcellus
(6.860–86), but the main part of the Parade also contains details that
suggest a less than totally positive forecast of the shape of Roman
history.[178] The eschatological setting of the Elysian Fields lures us with
the hope that, with Aeneas, we may be privileged to an overview of
history under the aspect of the eternal verities; hints that Aeneas'
Underworld journey is a kind of initiation into the mysteries reinforce
the sense that here we are admitted to a specially authoritative form of
knowledge.[179] But rather than attaining the certitude of a religious
initiate, Aeneas perhaps has an experience that is merely mysterious.
Was it all just a dream? The hero's passage into and out of the

---

[176] On speeches and rhetoric in the *Aeneid* see Heinze (1993), 314–32; Highet (1972); J. P.
Lynch, 'Laocoön and Sinon: Virgil *Aeneid* 2.40–198', in McAuslan and Walcot (1990), 112–20.
The most searching examination of the place of rhetoric in the *Aeneid* is in D. C. Feeney, 'The
taciturnity of Aeneas', in Harrison (1990), 167–90; Feeney's conclusion that the *Aeneid* is able
comfortably to separate words used rhetorically and words used as a transparent medium for truth
is questioned by P. R. Hardie , 'Fame and defamation in the *Aeneid*: the Council of Latins (*Aen.*
11.225–467)', in Stahl (1998), 243–70.

[177] Feeney (n. 90). On the interview between Jupiter and Juno see also Buchheit (1963), 133–50;
on the (typically Homeric) 'sublime frivolity' of the scene, with its overtones of domestic comedy
see D. West, 'The end and the meaning (*Aen.* 12.791–842)', in Stahl (1998), 303–18.

[178] So D. C. Feeney, 'History and revelation in Vergil's Underworld', *PCPS* 32 (1986), 1–24; for
the contrary view that the Parade of Heroes is 'whole-hearted and successful panegyric' see D. West,
'The pageant of the heroes as panegyric (Virgil, *Aen.* 6.760–886)', in H. D. Jocelyn (ed.), *Tria
Lustra* (Liverpool, 1993), 283–96. On the Parade of Heroes see also R. D. Williams, 'The sixth
book of the *Aeneid*', *G&R* 11 (1964), 48–63; M. von Albrecht, 'Vergils Geschichtsauffassung in der
"Heldenschau"', *WS* 80 (1967), 156–82; N. M. Horsfall, 'The structure and purpose of Vergil's
Parade of Heroes', *Ancient Society* (Macquarie), 12 (1982), 12–18.

[179] Mysteries (see also ch. III n. 87); G. Luck, 'Virgil and the mystery religions', *AJP* 94 (1973),
147–66. In general on Aeneas' journey to the Underworld see J. E. G. Zetzel, '*Romane memento*:
justice and judgment in *Aeneid* 6', *TAPA* 119 (1989), 263–84; R. J. Clark, *Catabasis: Vergil and the
Wisdom-Tradition* (Amsterdam, 1979).

Underworld is expedited by two symbolic objects, whose interpretation is notoriously uncertain, the Golden Bough (6.136–48, 183–211)[180] and the ivory Gate of Sleep (6.893–8).[181] The point may in part be that we delude ourselves if we think that an authoritative reading of the Underworld episode is easily, if at all, possible.

The survey of Roman history on the Shield of Aeneas, all leading to Octavian's victory at Actium and the triple triumph of 29 B.C., seems more straightforward than the complex personalities showcased in the Parade of Heroes, but some have discerned oppositional undertones even here, finding hints of Roman cruelty and failure in the scenes of the punishment of Fufetius Mettus and of the Gauls clambering on to the Capitol, and traces of a sympathy for the defeated in the picture of the defeated Cleopatra fleeing into the embrace of a grieving Nile.[182] The Shield's divine maker Vulcan has an authority little short of that of Jupiter, and he is introduced at 8.627 as *haud uatum ignarus uenturique inscius aeui* 'not ignorant of the prophets or unaware of time to come'. There is a punning ambiguity in *uatum*, which may also be translated as 'poets'; the Shield of Aeneas presents itself as a visual summary of the Latin epic tradition, and of Ennius' *Annals* in particular.[183] Vulcan knows the future history of Rome—because he has read the poets who will chronicle that history. The authority of the Virgilian text is no more or less than that of the other texts on which it draws, and which it completes. Feeney has well shown how the gods in the *Aeneid* cannot be used as an external Archimedean point of reference by which to judge the truth claims of the poem: Jupiter himself cannot escape from the fictive quality of the text.[184] Another sign of the slippery nature of the Virgilian gods, and hence of their authority for the reader, is the debate as to whether, within the fiction of the *Aeneid*, the gods are to be taken as

[180] R. A. Brooks, '*Discolor aura*. Reflections on the golden bough', *AJP* 74 (1953), 260–80 [= Commager (1966), 143–66] (an article often regarded as an important landmark in the 'Harvard' school of interpretation); C. P. Segal, '*Aeternum per saecula nomen.* The Golden Bough and the tragedy of history', *Arion* 4 (1965), 617–57; 5 (1966), 34–72 (using the Golden Bough as a key to the wider antitheses in the *Aeneid* that define the 'tragic fate' of the world); D. A. West, *The Bough and the Gate* (Exeter, 1987); C. Weber, 'The allegory of the Golden Bough', *Vergilius* 41 (1995), 3–34.

[181] See recently R. J. Tarrant, 'Aeneas and the Gates of Sleep', *CP* 77 (1982), 51–5; U. Molyviati-Toptsis, '*Sed falsa ad caelum mittunt insomnia Manes (Aeneid* 6.896)', *AJP* 116 (1995), 639–52.

[182] See Quint (1993), ch. 1; Gurval (1995), ch. 5. In general on the Shield see n. 101.

[183] Vulcan may represent the pretensions of the epic poet to a demiurgic status: P. R. Hardie, 'Cosmological patterns in the *Aeneid*', *PLLS* 5 (1986), 85–97.

[184] Feeney (1991), 151–5; in general on the issues of fictionality see D. C. Feeney, 'Towards an account of the ancient world's concepts of fictive belief' in C. Gill and T. P. Wiseman (eds.), *Lies and Fiction in the Ancient World* (Exeter, 1993), 230–44.

fully real anthropomorphic agents, or as allegories for psychological or natural processes. Does the Fury Allecto really come up from the Underworld to inspire Turnus with battle-lust, or is this just a poetic way of talking about the emergence of dark passions in Turnus' mind?[185]

If the Homeric divine machinery had become difficult to take seriously by Virgil's day, the reader might look for interpretative certainty in a philosophical underpinning of the narrative. The allegorizers had long seen Homer as a source of profound philosophical truths, and Ennius had launched the Latin hexameter epic tradition with a disquisition on Pythagorean philosophy put in the mouth of a phantom Homer.[186] Virgil's own philosophical interests are clear in the *Eclogues* and *Georgics*, and the Life of Donatus reports that at the time of his death he was planning to spend a further three years revising the *Aeneid* and then to devote the rest of his life to philosophy.[187] In the light of all of this, and also of Virgil's continuing fascination with Lucretius' philosophical poem, it would be surprising if Virgil's epic was not strongly coloured by the Hellenistic schools of philosophy. There are certainly traces of Stoic psychology and ethics in the character of Aeneas (see p. 82 above), and the Virgilian conception of Jupiter as mouthpiece of Fate is readily harmonized with the Stoic notion of an all-pervasive providential deity identified with Zeus. At the banquet of Dido, immediately before Aeneas embarks on his own, Odysseus-style, narrative of his previous adventures, we are treated to a performance by the bard Iopas, an exemplary figure of epic's origins, and the song he sings is on astronomy and natural philosophy (1.740–7).[188] The most extended philosophical passage in the poem is the first part of the Speech of Anchises (6.724–5), reworking the speech of the Ennian Homer in an eclectic mixture of Pythagorean, Platonic, and Stoic teachings on the nature of the world and of the soul. But two reflections should warn us against any simple assumption that these are the final truths that the poem has to teach us. Firstly, as is the case with Vulcan's prophetic certitudes, Anchises' philosophical exposition is as much a

---

[185] Feeney (1991), 168–72. Approaches to the gods as psychological allegories: Quinn (1968), 316–20 'Parallel divine and psychological motivation'; Williams (1983), 20–35 'The gods as a trope for human motivation'; Lyne (1987), 66–71 'Working with'.

[186] Skutsch (1985), 147–67.

[187] *Vita Donati* 35.

[188] Hardie (1986), 52–66. On the Song of Iopas see also C. P. Segal, 'The song of Iopas in the *Aeneid*', *Hermes* 99 (1971), 336–49; R. D. Brown, 'The structural function of the Song of Iopas', *HSCP* 93 (1990), 315–34.

tissue of literary allusion as it is a declaration of philosophical allegiance. Secondly, this revelation of divine truths is not the first such vouchsafed to Aeneas by a parent. In book 2, at the climax of the Greek destruction of Troy, Aeneas' mother Venus appears to him in her full divine glory, removes the cloudy veil that normally clogs mortal vision (cf. Anchises' account of the soul enmired in the body at 6.730–4), and reveals to her son the true nature of what is going on (2.589–623). This revealed truth is no philosophical vision of the workings of the universe, but a terrifying apocalypse of the anthropomorphic Homeric gods at work on the destruction of Troy. The contrast with the philosophical revelation offered by Anchises is heightened by the fact that Virgil uses a Homeric model, Athene's removal of the mist from the eyes of Diomedes so that he can distinguish between god and man in the battle (*Iliad* 5.127–32), which had been used as an image of philosophical enlightenment in the Hellenistic period ([Plato] *Alcibiades* II. 150d); Virgil wrenches it back to a mythological world-view. Within the fiction of the *Aeneid* what criterion is available to adjudicate between the competing truth-values of Venus' and Anchises' revelations of a divine order (or disorder)?[189]

Philosophical criteria have been adduced to try to resolve the endlessly contested significance of the last scene in the poem, the death of Turnus. Here the disagreement between the 'optimist' ('European') and the 'pessimist' ('Harvard') schools is at its most intense. The optimists read in the violent death of Turnus the final victory of Fate and *pietas* over the irrational forces that seek to oppose the plan of Jupiter, a foreshadowing of the legitimate vengeance of Octavian against the assassins of his adoptive father, according to an ideology of state revenge that would eventually find monumental expression in the Temple of Mars Ultor that dominated the Forum of Augustus. The pessimists see in Aeneas' enraged killing of a now defenceless Turnus the recrudescence in the hero of the same *furor* that had overmastered him on the night of the Sack of Troy (2.316–17), blinding him to the force of Turnus' appeal to remember his own father Anchises and to pity his, Turnus', aging father Daunus (12.932–6). Crucial to the reader's judgement is our evaluation of this last outburst of the epic emotion *par excellence*, anger, which is where the philosophy comes in. From a Stoic point of view, all violent emotion is undesirable, and Aeneas' act is therefore to be condemned,

---

[189] T. N. Habinek, 'Science and tradition in *Aeneid* 6', *HSCP* 92 (1989), 223–55 discusses the tensions within *Aen.* 6 between scientific cosmology and the traditional exhortations of funeral speeches, and argues that the two discourses are in fact compatible, in line with the Romans' self-defining belief that they were well qualified to unite science and tradition.

but from an Aristotelian or Epicurean point of view anger may be justified in certain circumstances, and a reasonable degree of anger is useful in motivating the warrior. Karl Galinsky has mounted a philosophical defence of the end of the *Aeneid*, particularly in response to the ever more subtle reexaminations of the scene by Michael Putnam, one of the founders of the 'Harvard school'.[190] But those who seek a philosophical solution run the risk of simply exporting the problem of interpreting the end of the *Aeneid* into an unresolved dispute between ancient philosophical schools.

Perhaps the only thing that is clear about the end of the *Aeneid* is that it is a passage of great complexity. Aeneas' last outburst of spontaneous anger is trapped in an intertextual web of literary allusions, legendary and mythological paradigms, and historical, political, and philosophical contexts. It is also a passage that reflects in a bewildering variety of ways on scenes and motifs earlier in the *Aeneid* itself: for example, Aeneas hurling his spear like a thunderbolt or a storm-wind (12.919–25) invites us to see in him a surrogate for the storm-god Jupiter, who uses the violence of the thunderbolt to impose the will of Fate on the world;[191] but Aeneas' refusal to listen to Turnus' appeal to the thought of an aged father puts us in mind of the impious savagery of Neoptolemus, cutting down Polites in front of Priam, who reminds him of the mercy once shown by his father Achilles to himself in the case of another of his sons, Hector (2.526–43).[192] The last scene provocatively blurs the conceptual frameworks by which we had thought to navigate our way through the poem: the opposition between *furor* and a rational *pietas* is confounded by a last infuriated killing, oblivious to Turnus' attempt to exploit *pietas* to a father, that is yet prompted by the reminder of the ties of *pietas* that bind Aeneas to the dead Pallas and *his* father Evander. The opposition between Jupiter's Olympian direction of events in accordance with Fate and Juno's attempts to disrupt Fate with the help of forces from the

[190] G. K. Galinsky, 'The anger of Aeneas', *AJP* 109 (1988), 321–48; id., 'How to be philosophical about the end of the *Aeneid*', *ICS* 19 (1994), 191–201. Putnam's meditations on the end of the poem go back to Putnam (1965), 151–201; his recent collection of essays, Putnam (1995), circles repeatedly around the issues: see esp. chs. 8 and 10. 'Optimist' readers of the end of the poem include Cairns (1989), 82–4; H.-P. Stahl, 'Aeneas—an unheroic hero?', *Arethusa* 14 (1981), 157–86; id., 'The death of Turnus: Augustan Vergil and the political rival', in K. A. Raaflaub and M. Toher (eds.), *Between Republic and Empire. Interpretations of Augustus and his Principate* (Berkeley, Los Angeles, London, 1990), 174–211. The 'pessimists', these days in the majority, include R. Beare, 'Invidious success. Some thoughts on the end of the *Aeneid*', *PVS* 4 (1964/5), 18–30; J. P. Poe, 'Success and failure in the mission of Aeneas', *TAPhA* 96 (1965), 321–36; Johnson (1976), 114–34; Lyne (1987), 85–99, 186–8.

[191] Hardie (1986), 147–54, 177–80.

[192] Barchiesi (1984), 111–18.

Underworld (the giant-like winds in book 1, and the hellish Fury Allecto in book 7) has already been muddied by Jupiter's own use of a *Dira* at 12.843–68 to frighten Turnus and warn off Juturna, and, in completing the plan of Jupiter, Aeneas acts *furiis accensus* (12.946); Virgil's text would not distinguish between a capital and a lower-case *f*: is Aeneas 'ablaze with fury' or 'fired by the Furies'? A mindful and vengeful anger was where the poem started, but there it had fired Juno (1.4, 23–32).[193]

In one respect the final scene provides a satisfying ending to the poem, since it presents in heightened form the competition within the text between different points of view and perspectives. Turnus' dying groan in the last line sounds for many readers as the poem's last protest by the suffering individual against the juggernaut of Roman destiny, as private desires are sacrificed to public mission. Over the last three decades the 'two voices' (public and private) of the *Aeneid*, in Adam Parry's phrase,[194] have proliferated into Oliver Lyne's 'further voices'; the text has become polyphonic or polycentric.[195] Older approaches to the ambiguity of the text,[196] have been supplemented by new approaches to narrative point of view and focalization, to generic play, intertextuality,[197] and to the ideology of texts, all of which have found fertile ground in the *Aeneid*.

---

[193] On Virgil's theological dualism and its confusion see Johnson (1976), 114–34; Hardie (1993), ch. 3; on the parallel between Juno's and Aeneas' anger see Putnam (1995), 4. Attempts to make a sharp distinction between *Dirae* and *Furiae*, or between *furor* and Aeneas' final *furiae* (Cairns [1989], 82–4, criticized by R. F. Thomas, *AJP* 112 [1991], 261) are unpersuasive.

[194] Parry (1963).

[195] Conte (1986), 153.

[196] For a brilliant study of the critical history of ambiguity in Virgil interpretation see C. Martindale, 'Descent into Hell: reading ambiguity, or Virgil and the critics', *PVS* 21 (1993), 111–50; see also C. Perkell, 'Ambiguity and irony: the last resort?', *Helios* 21 (1994), 63–74.

[197] On the effects of allusion in complicating interpretation see R. O. A. M. Lyne, 'Vergil's *Aeneid*: subversion by intertextuality. Catullus 66.39–40 and other examples', *G&R* 41 (1994), 187–204.

V. STYLE, LANGUAGE, METRE

The excitement of the new critical and theoretical approaches applied to Virgil in the last thirty years should not make the reader forget the importance of a close attention to the linguistic and metrical detail of the text for a full appreciation of what Virgil is about. Virgilian ambition manifests itself not just in the extensiveness of the poems' conceptual and allusive scope, but also in a microscopic attention to detail and to the relation of the detail to the wider context. The classic status that his poems immediately achieved was due, as much as to anything, to his perfection of the stylistic and metrical experiments of the previous two centuries of Latin poetry in order to forge a flexible and varied poetic manner, the master and not the slave of both Greek and Latin poetic traditions, responsive to context, and integral to the wider meanings and functions of the poems. For example, in a recent discussion of Virgil's style, O'Hara draws attention to the fact that the ambiguity that has become so central to modern critics' treatments of the meaning and ideology of the poem is generated partly by small-scale indeterminacies of syntax;[1] and I have suggested that stylistic figures such as oxymoron and hypallage contribute to larger structures of paradox in the areas of poetics and ideology.[2] Virgil's liking for stylistic ambiguity and paradox also reminds us that his style is not 'classic' in the sense of a uniformly limpid and serenely balanced manner; his use of language can be difficult and unexpected, often straining at the limits of Latinity. While no later Latin poet can escape the influence of Virgil, it was left to Ovid to perfect 'a poetic *koine*, a stylistic instrument which was freely manageable by writers of lesser genius. The Ovidian manner, as generations of clever English schoolboys have discovered, is imitable; Virgil's is not.'[3]

These days few schoolboys or girls have the chance to make this discovery. On the other hand, the general decrease in that sensitivity to style and usage which comes from prolonged exposure to and practice in a language has been compensated for by the appearance over the last few decades of large-scale English commentaries on most of Virgil. The

---

[1] J. J. O'Hara, in Martindale (1997), 249–51.
[2] P. R. Hardie, 'Virgil: a paradoxical poet?', *PLLS* 9 (1996), 103–21.
[3] E. J. Kenney, 'The style of the *Metamorphoses*', in J. W. Binns (ed.), *Ovid* (London and Boston, 1973), 116–53, at 119.

older discussions of language and style retain their value.[4] Of recent studies one might single out the fascinating pursuit of the significance of linguistic register and imagery by Oliver Lyne (1989), and the remarkable study of various types of repetition in Latin poetry by Jeffrey Wills (1996), a revelation of the wide-ranging implications that can flow from an obsessive scrutiny of stylistic detail. Recent general surveys of the field on a scale larger than that possible here are provided by Horsfall[5] and O'Hara.[6]

In what follows I have tried to provide an object lesson in the incorporation of linguistic, stylistic, and metrical analysis within an overall reading of a particular passage of Virgil. The passage has been chosen more or less at random, but from a book where the rich resources of one of R. D. Williams' commentaries are available. I have tried to show how a close reading of any part of Virgil is rewarded by an attention both to the wider context, which in the case of the *Aeneid* ultimately means the context of the poem as a whole, and to the smallest detail; style cannot be separated from content. Virgil's writing has a symphonic richness: themes and motifs found elsewhere in the poem are repeated and varied, so that any single passage reveals its full meaning and effect only in the light of other parts of the poem, and indeed only after repeated rereadings of the text. Virgil has a strong sense for the structure of his works, but this architectural strength does not override subtle local effects of light and shade (to draw on the terms of yet another art, painting). Not least of the poet's resources is his manipulation of the previous poetic tradition, seen both in the play on the various genres (a good example in this passage is the use of epigrammatic topics in the last two lines), and in allusion to specific authors and texts: in this passage Homer, as one might expect, but also Lucretius are important

---

[4] General treatments: L. R. Palmer, *The Latin Language* (London, 1961), 111–18; L. P. Wilkinson, *Golden Latin Artistry* (Cambridge, 1963); id., 'The language of Virgil and Horace', *CQ* 9 (1959), 181–92; Williams (1968), 722–43; Camps (1969), 61–74. Longer studies: Jackson Knight (1966), 180–281 (highly recommended); Quinn (1968), 350–440; A. Cordier, *Études sur le vocabulaire épique dans l'Énéide* (Paris, 1939). There is a wealth of material (in German) in the stylistic and metrical appendices in Norden (1957). More specialized studies include: R. G. M. Nisbet, 'The style of Virgil's *Eclogues*', *PVS* 20 (1991), 1–14; R. G. Austin, 'Virgilian assonance', *CQ* 23 (1929), 46–55; W. M. Clarke, 'Intentional rhyme in Vergil and Ovid', *TAPA* 103 (1972), 49–77; id., 'Intentional alliteration in Vergil and Ovid', *Latomus* 35 (1976), 276–300. Metre: G. E. Duckworth, *Vergil and Classical Hexameter Poetry: A Study in Metrical Variety* (Ann Arbor, 1969); G. B. Nussbaum, *Vergil's Metre* (Bristol, 1986); S. E. Winbolt, *Latin Hexameter Verse* (London, 1903) was written as an aid for versifiers, but is an excellent handbook for readers of Virgil as well.

[5] Horsfall (1995), ch.5.

[6] J. J. O'Hara in Martindale (1997), 241–58.

presences. Finally it should be stressed that what follows has of course
no claim to be an exhaustive reading of the passage.

Aeneid 5.835–71
Text and Translation

iamque fere mediam caeli Nox umida metam   835
contigerat, placida laxabant membra quiete
sub remis fusi per dura sedilia nautae,
cum leuis aetheriis delapsus Somnus ab astris
aëra dimouit tenebrosum et dispulit umbras,
te, Palinure, petens, tibi somnia tristia portans   840
insonti; puppique deus consedit in alta
Phorbanti similis funditque has ore loquelas:
'Iaside Palinure, ferunt ipsa aequora classem,
aequatae spirant aurae, datur hora quieti.
pone caput fessosque oculos furare labori.   845
ipse ego paulisper pro te tua munera inibo.'
cui uix attollens Palinurus lumina fatur:
'mene salis placidi uultum fluctusque quietos
ignorare iubes? mene huic confidere monstro?
Aenean credam (quid enim?) fallacibus auris   850
et caeli totiens deceptus fraude sereni?'
talia dicta dabat, clauumque adfixus et haerens
nusquam amittebat oculosque sub astra tenebat.
ecce deus ramum Lethaeo rore madentem
uique soporatum Stygia super utraque quassat   855
tempora, cunctantique natantia lumina soluit.
uix primos inopina quies laxauerat artus,
et super incumbens cum puppis parte reuulsa
cumque gubernaclo liquidas proiecit in undas
praecipitem ac socios nequiquam saepe uocantem;   860
ipse uolans tenuis se sustulit ales ad auras.
currit iter tutum non setius aequore classis
promissisque patris Neptuni interrita fertur.
iamque adeo scopulos Sirenum aduecta subibat,
difficilis quondam multorumque ossibus albos   865
(tum rauca adsiduo longe sale saxa sonabant),
cum pater amisso fluitantem errare magistro
sensit, et ipse ratem nocturnis rexit in undis
multa gemens casuque animum concussus amici:
'o nimium caelo et pelago confise sereno,   870
nudus in ignota, Palinure, iacebis harena.'

The dank night was near the mid-point of the sky. The sailors were taking their rest in peace and quiet, stretched out under their oars along the hard benches, when the God of Sleep, parting the dark and misty air, came gliding lightly down from the stars of heaven. He was coming to you, Palinurus, bringing deadly dreams you did not deserve. The god took the shape of Phorbas and sat on the high poop pouring these soft words into the ears of Palinurus: 'Son of Iasius, the sea is carrying the ships along itself. The breeze is gentle and steady. This is an hour for sleep. Put down your head and steal a little time from your labours to rest your tired eyes. I'll take over a short watch for you myself.'

Scarcely lifting his eyes, Palinurus replied: 'Are you asking me to forget what I know about the calm face of the sea and quiet waters? There is a strange power in the sea and I would never rely on it. Winds are liars and believe me, I would never trust them with Aeneas, I who have so often been betrayed by a clear sky.' This was his answer, and he stood by the tiller, gripping it with no intention of letting it go or taking his eyes off the stars. But look! The god takes a branch dripping with the water of Lethe for forgetfulness and the water of Styx for sleep. He shakes it over Palinurus, first one temple, then the other, and for all his struggles it closes his swimming eyes. As soon as this sudden sleep came upon him and his limbs began to relax, the god leaned over him, broke off a part of the poop, tiller and all, and threw him with it into the waves of the sea. Down fell Palinurus, calling again and again on his comrades, but they did not hear. The god then rose on his wings and flew off into the airy breezes, while the ships sped on their way none the worse, sailing safely on in accordance with the promises of Father Neptune.

They were soon coming near the Sirens' rocks, once a difficult coast and white with the bones of drowned men, and at that moment sounding far with the endless grinding of breaker upon rock, when Father Aeneas sensed that he was adrift without a helmsman. In mid-ocean in the dead of night he took control of the ship himself, and grieving to the heart at the loss of his friend, he cried out: 'You trusted too much, Palinurus, to a clear sky and a calm sea, and your body will lie naked on an unknown shore.'

(tr. David West)

These are the closing lines of book 5, a book in which Aeneas, after the wrong turning taken at Carthage in book 4, reasserts his authority and dedication to his family and people with elaborate games in celebration of the anniversary of his father Anchises' death. In these games his own son Iulus/Ascanius has been on display for the first time in an elaborate cavalry exercise, the *lusus Troiae*; the narrator tells us that this institution will continue in Rome down to the present day (5.596–603). Immediately after this glance into the distant future, Juno reenters the narrative to create mayhem, as she attempts to thwart the Trojans' onward journey to Italy by fomenting disaffection among the Trojan women and provoking them to set fire to the ships. The situation is saved by Jupiter himself, who quenches the fire by sending down a violent rainstorm in answer to Aeneas' despairing prayer. Shape and order are then restored to the narrative through the agency of divinely authorized vehicles of fate: the priest Nautes instructs Aeneas to leave behind the fainthearted in Sicily in a new city, Segesta, that will in time be the first Sicilian city to ally itself with the Romans in the First Punic War. Thus is rebellion turned to the constructive purpose of city-founding. Nautes' advice is then confirmed by the ghost of Anchises, who appears to Aeneas in a dream to spur him on his way to Italy, and promises the revelatory interview with himself that will take place in the Elysian Fields in the next book. On the next day Aeneas offers a solemn sacrifice for a safe journey to Italy (772–8). However fair weather will be assured not by ritual, but by a typical piece of epic divine machinery (779–826): Neptune agrees to Venus' request to protect Aeneas against the possibility that Juno might raise another storm like that in book 1, but with the condition that one life must be sacrificed on the journey. Neptune then calms the waves, attended by a majestic and joyful *thiasos* of sea-gods.

Aeneas eagerly gives the order to set sail, but this joyful mood will not last for what remains of the book (with 828 *gaudia pertemptant mentem* 'joy came over [Aeneas'] mind' contrast 869 (Aeneas) *multa gemens*). As a 'minor-key coda' to a book which, after various trials and tribulations, looks optimistically to the future, the death of Palinurus is comparable with the funeral lament for the younger Marcellus that concludes book 6 after the triumphalist parade of future Roman heroes (6.860–86). Marcellus is a kind of sacrifice, a lightning conductor for potential divine envy at the extraordinary achievements of Rome, as Palinurus will turn out to be the one sacrifice stipulated by Neptune in return for the successful passage of the many. But the tonality of the passage is more complex than this. This is one of Virgil's many night-scenes, and it contrasts with the bright daylight (cf. the dawn description at 5.42–3) that floods the games that occupy most of the book; but it is a calm and still night, broken only for a moment by the violence of Palinurus' ejection from the ship at 858–60, and so contrasts with the elemental violence of fire and storm in the episode of the burning of the ships. It is however a deceptive calm, comparable to the beginning of the night that both lulls the Trojans to sleep and provides cover for the Greeks' silent return by sea to Troy in book 2 (250–6). As often in Virgil, literal darkness shades into figurative benightedness. Night is the time of visions both truthful and deceptive; the appearance to Palinurus of Somnus disguised as Phorbas echoes the appearance on the previous night to Aeneas of his father Anchises, a parallelism reinforced by a number of verbal similarities. The language of 721–3:

et Nox atra polum bigis subuecta tenebat.
uisa dehinc caelo facies delapsa parentis
Anchisae subito talis effundere uoces.

And black Night driving upward in her chariot possessed the sky. Then the shape of my father Anchises appeared, gliding down from the sky, and of a sudden poured forth the following words.

is echoed in the description of Night in 835–6, the descent of Somnus in 838, and the introduction of Somnus' speech in 842; the formulaic phrase *Nox umida* occurs at both 738 and 835 in the context of a reference to the midpoint of the night. Palinurus may be duped into believing that this is Phorbas, but he cannot be deceived in his helmsman's understanding of the untrustworthy ways of the sea, and must be rendered literally sightless and mindless in sleep.

At 867–8 Aeneas perceives that the ship is without a helmsman, and himself then 'governs' (868 *rexit*) the ship; by hinting at the common image of the king at the helm of the ship of state this action recapitulates what has been a major theme of book 5, Aeneas' assertion of his role as a good king (he has already replaced Anchises as father-figure for the Trojans; here he replaces Palinurus as helmsman of the fleet); it is ironic that, for all his vigilant clear-sightedness, Aeneas then misinterprets the evidence in concluding that Palinurus paid the price for an over-confidence of which the reader knows that he is not guilty (870 *confise* pointedly echoes 849 *confidere*). So, in the last scene of a book in which the hero seems to have made real progress in self-confidence and knowledge of what the future holds, Aeneas is in a situation much like that at the beginning of the book, certain of the direction in which he is travelling (5.1–2), but only darkly able to make sense of an unexpected event, the appearance of flames rising above the walls of Carthage (3–7; both Dido and Palinurus will give Aeneas a more accurate account of their fate in the next book). If the *Aeneid* tells of the progress of a hero towards his destiny, it is a painfully slow progress, marked by frequent backsliding.

This ring-composition extends further; at the beginning of the book Aeneas' and the Trojans' attempt to make sense of what they see is immediately followed by an episode involving Palinurus (8–34), just as at the end the death of Palinurus is followed by Aeneas' reflections on what he perceives.[7] Ring-composition is a strong way of marking

[7] See Heinze (1993), 357.

closure in a book; this passage functions as an ending in other ways, but at the same time leaves doors open for the continuation of the narrative in the next book. We have here a self-contained little episode, an encounter between a mortal and a god which is decisively concluded first by loss of consciousness, and then, as it appears, death by drowning. As Alessandro Barchiesi has shown, Aeneas' comment in the last two lines faithfully reproduces the topics of funerary epigrams for those drowned at sea (the excessive confidence of those who entrust themselves to the sea, the thought of the body lying naked on a strange shore);[8] this is an epitaph to round off a life and a book. A metrical detail perhaps also signals that this is an ending, for 871 has the rare feature of a trochaic caesura in both fourth and fifth feet, usually avoided 'because of the feeling that the line ending is anticipated' (Williams on 5.52); this is a line that knows that it will end a book, and is just a little too eager to get there.

But this is not in fact the end of the story, for it will be retold by the ghost of Palinurus himself in the Underworld at 6.337–83, although notoriously what is offered in the first person to Aeneas as the whole truth and nothing but the truth contains a number of contradictions with what the narrator tells us here in book 5.[9] And while this episode is a version, at least, of an ending to the story of Palinurus, for Aeneas and the other Trojans it is a transitional passage, part of the continuing journey from Sicily to Cumae. Its transitional nature is made clearer still by the postponement of the two lines describing the arrival of the fleet in Italy until the beginning of the next book (according to Servius the result of an editorial decision by Varius and Tucca); not only that, but we have to wait until the first three words of book 6 for the formal marker of the end of Aeneas' utterance ('thus he spoke, weeping'). The stages in the story of the death of Palinurus (the interventions respectively of Somnus and of Aeneas) are marked by the two occurrences of *iamque* (*adeo*)

---

[8] A. Barchiesi, 'Palinuro e Caieta. Due "epigrammi" virgiliani (*Aen.* V 870 sg.; VII 1–4)', *Maia* 31 (1979), 3–11. Barchiesi also shows that the 'epigram' at the end of book 5 is balanced by the 'epigram' on another Trojan lost on the journey, Caieta, at 7.1–4; fittingly these two funerary epigrams frame book 6, the 'book of the dead'; Barchiesi also points to the contrast between the 'unknown sand' on which Aeneas imagines Palinurus' body, and the name given by Caieta to 'our shores' at 7.1–2; after the revelations of book 6 the Trojans' bewildered wandering over strange seas and lands has been replaced by a fuller knowledge of their destined home in Italy. Palinurus will himself give his name to an Italian landmark (6.381).

[9] For the details see Williams (1960), pp. xxv–xxviii; the usual solution has been to argue that we have two versions which Virgil would have reconciled in the final revision of the poem. For alternative approaches see F. E. Brenk, '*Unum pro multis caput*: myth, history, and symbolic imagery in Vergil's Palinurus incident', *Latomus* 43 (1984), 776–801 at 776 n. 3.

followed by inverted *cum* (a favourite Virgilian usage)[10] at 835–8 and 864–7, but these temporal markers also plot the continuing progress of the Trojans' course on into the next book.

As a piece of epic machinery the action of Somnus combines two famous Iliadic models, in a typical Virgilian conflation of separate Homeric passages:[11] firstly the sending by Zeus to the sleeping Agamemnon of a 'destructive dream' (οὖλος Ὄνειρος: cf. 5.840 *somnia tristia*) disguised as Nestor at *Iliad* 2.1–34; and secondly Hera's use of *Hypnos*, Sleep, in order to send Zeus to sleep at *Iliad* 14.231–91. The Homeric Sleep is the brother of Death, and Virgil's sinister Somnus brings death as well as sleep to Palinurus. That the 'dew of Lethe' dripping from his branch at 854 brings the oblivion of death is made clear in the following words *uique soporatum Stygia*: the phrase can be read as an elegant variation on *Lethaeo rore madentem*, a typical example of Virgilian 'theme and variation'[12] (there is another example in this passage at 839 *aëra dimouit tenebrosum et dispulit umbras*), but *Stygia* makes it unequivocal that this is the sleep of death, a draught from the river of death, the Styx.

Virgil develops the Homeric models in other ways. 835–7 are both a marker of time and also an elliptical example of the '*nox erat* topos', 'it was night and all were asleep; but x did not sleep'.[13] In this passage instead of the reader being told in so many words that Palinurus alone of the sailors was not asleep, Somnus descends to ensure that he too becomes one of the sleepers; the point is reinforced by the echo of 836 *placida laxabant membra quiete* (the other sailors) in 857 *quies laxauerat artus* (Palinurus). The language of 835–7 already suggests the temptation to sleep: the hour of the night is defined firstly by an astronomical specification, with pronounced sound effects in the hypnotic alliteration and assonance of *mediam . . . umida metam*, and secondly by a

[10] See Williams on 5.84–5; on Virgil's use of *iamque adeo* 'at this very moment' (here contrasted with 835 *iamque fere* 'at approximately this time') see Austin on 2.567.

[11] On the models see H. R. Steiner, *Der Traum in der Aeneis* (Bern, 1952), 78–85; Virgil also draws on the death of Menelaus' helmsman Phrontis, killed by Apollo's darts, at *Od.* 3.278–83, and the death of Elpenor, who falls asleep on a roof and on waking plunges to his death, at *Od.* 10.552–60. Within the *Aeneid* Somnus' two-stage assault on Palinurus, attempting first persuasion in the disguise of a mortal, and then resorting to violence, is closely paralleled in the manner of Allecto's assault on Turnus at 7.415–59. The precipitation of Palinurus from his post at 858–60 has a closer parallel within book 5 in the ejection of the helmsman Menoetes by the impatient Gyas in the ship-race at 172–82, a comic episode replayed as tragedy in the death of Palinurus, the first of a number of occasions in the *Aeneid* on which the thrills and spills of the games are echoed in the life and death struggles of the real business of the poem: see Putnam (1988), 75–6 (ibid., 93–104 for a lengthy discussion of the death of Palinurus).

[12] Henry (1873–92), index s.vv. 'Theme and Variation'. Henry goes so far as to describe this as 'the most pleasing peculiarity of the style of Virgil'.

[13] See Pease on 4.522–7 (the most famous example in the *Aeneid*).

description of the effect of the hour on mortals. The epithet *dura* of *sedilia* is focalized through the sailors: soft and gentle sleep offers temporary respite from the hard labour of rowing. Modern readers should beware of an overly subjective interpretation of Virgilian sound effects, but this passage contains some clear examples: Palinurus nods off at 856 *cunctantique natantia lumina soluit*, with its repeated sounds, coincidence of ictus and accent, and absence of a strong caesura to hold up the irresistible power of sleep; there are similar effects at *Geo.* 4.496 *conditque natantia lumina somnus* (Eurydice), and *Aen.* 2.9 *suadentque cadentia sidera somnos*. Very different are the harsh sounds of 866, conveying the incessant breaking of waves on rocks, with the particular feature of the triple alliteration (of *s*) at the end of the line, possibly a survival from the Saturnian metre of early Latin poetry.[14] The harsh sound of the sea also contrasts with the sounds that used to be heard in this place, the irresistibly sweet song of the Sirens, who killed themselves after Odysseus had successfully passed by them.

In 840 the pathos of Sleep's lethal attack on his victim is expressed through the use of apostrophe, the device (going back to Homer) whereby the 'objective' narrator descends from his aloof pedestal to address directly a character in the action, often at moments of heightened emotion. The effect here is increased by the repetition *te ... tibi ...*, and by the like-sounding *petens* and *portans* at the caesura and the end of the line; Sleep comes on remorselessly. This is also a line of five dactyls, after which the spondaic *insonti* that begins the next line, followed by a strong pause, falls with great emphasis.[15] Palinurus is an innocent scapegoat.

The brief exchange of speeches between Somnus and Palinurus is carefully composed and finely characterized. Each is given four lines, but of sharply contrasting tone. Somnus begins by courteously addressing Palinurus by name and patronym, followed by a tricolon, three parallel clauses that reinforce their message with incantatory echoic effects in *aequora ... | aequatae ... aurae, ... hora quieti*. Commentators disagree as to the exact meaning of *aequatae*: 'blowing evenly', or 'filling the sails evenly'. Perhaps the exact sense is not important; what matters is the general evenness of the winds and their effect, and the word was perhaps suggested to Virgil by the preceding *aequora*, a poetic word for 'sea', but here in a context that activates its full sense of 'the level surface' of the calm sea. Likewise the general import of the clause *datur*

[14] See Austin on 4.29.
[15] See Winbolt (n. 4), 21–5 on 'Pause after $1\frac{1}{2}$ feet'.

hora quieti is clear, but its precise meaning is ambiguous.[16] Somnus draws the conclusion from his observations on the weather and the hour in two measured sentences each occupying one line, the first ordering Palinurus to 'steal his tired eyes from his toil', with a bold metaphor in *furare* and an emphatic repetition of ending (homoeoteleuton) in *fessosque oculos* (the juxtaposition of case-endings of the same sound is usually avoided except for particular effects: note also 840 *somnia tristia*),[17] while the second sentence calmly states Somnus' offer to take Palinurus' place. Somnus' soothing invitation also conceals a sinister ambiguity, for *pone caput* 'lay down your head' could also be understood as 'yield up your life' (remember Neptune's words at 815 *unum pro multis dabitur caput* 'one life will be given for many').[18] Palinurus replies in a very different tone with three indignant rhetorical questions, with enjambment in 849 and 851. The first two questions are given urgency by the anaphora of *mene ..? mene ..?* (it is with *mene ..?* that the angry Juno makes her first entry in the poem at 1.37); the second group of two lines is taken up with the third question, beginning emphatically with *Aenean*; Palinurus' indignation is roused by the thought that *he* could be negligent in the service of his leader *Aeneas* (cf. also Palinurus' protestation at 6.351–4). He refers to the sea as a *monstrum*, a favourite Virgilian word for a supernatural agent of evil; Nettleship's suggestion that *monstro* here means 'sign', 'the sign (a fallacious one) being the present calm of the sea', is also attractive, given the interest shown in the rest of this passage in interpreting the evidence of one's senses. The parenthetic *(quid enim?)* is vigorously colloquial (cf. e.g. Horace *Satires* 1.1.7); the only other example of the collocation in the *Aeneid* is at 12.798, in the course of a blunt address by Jupiter to Juno. Palinurus' determination is reaffirmed in the ensuing narrative in the doublet *adfixus et haerens* and in the internal rhyme in 853 . . . *amittebat . . . tenebat* (the so-called 'leonine rhyme', found also in Palinurus' own account of his devotion to his post at 6.350 *cui datus haerebam custos cursusque regebam* 'its appointed guardian I stuck to my post and guided the ship's course').

By comparison with the Homeric personifications of Dream and Sleep, who have a solid presence equal to that of the Olympian gods with whom they interact, the status and appearance of Virgil's Somnus

[16] Henry suggests three possibilities: '(1) "the hour is given (you) for rest"; (2) "the hour is sacred to rest"; (3) "the hour is being given (by others) to rest", *i.e.,* everyone is asleep.'
[17] On homoeoteleuton see Williams on 5.845; Norden on 6.638 ff.
[18] The ambiguity is noted by Putnam (1988), 97. See *OLD* s.vv. *caput* 4 'The life of a person'; *pono* 10b 'to yield up (life)'.

are shadowy and imprecise. He 'lightly glides' down from the stars (838), 'parting the dark air' (like a curtain?) in a manner that is difficult precisely to visualize. In 861 *ales* points to the frequent representation of Sleep as winged (as on the famous red-figure *crater* by Euxitheos and Euphronios showing Sleep and Death carrying the body of Sarpedon), but this is far from Homer's detailed description of Hypnos' trans-formation into a bird of a named species perched on a fir-tree (*Il.* 14.289–91). Somnus hovers between being a fully-fledged per-sonification, and a figure of speech or a psychological allegory. He appears shortly after a conventional use of the image of the chariot of Night in an indication of time (835–6); it is as if he is generated out of the traditional linguistic resources of epic. In addressing this per-sonification Palinurus slips himself into the language of personification to describe the treacherous sea, with its smiling face, but really a *monstrum*. Ironically he should beware of the trickery not of the sea, but of s/Sleep.

How should we read the interview with Sleep? As a fully realized example of divine machinery, or as an allegory of Palinurus' own mental processes? Is he really wide awake up until the moment that Somnus shakes his dewy bough over him, or is his consciousness slipping from the start, and is the whole interview with 'Phorbas' the delusion of a half-waking state? Is Palinurus really trying to persuade *himself* that he is not going to fall asleep? This uncertainty is sharply focused in the uncertainty that commentators have about 847 *cui uix attollens Palinurus lumina fatur*, of which Servius remarks 'either because he does not remove his eyes from watching the stars (cf. 853), or because he is already weighed down by the presence of the god, which is the better interpretation'.[19] Williams agrees that the second reading 'certainly gives a natural meaning: but the other is much more appropriate to the context. Palinurus' indignant reply, with . . . its wakeful-sounding movement, gives a most marked contrast to the persuasive and sleepy tones which Somnus had used to him.' But perhaps we should stress 'wakeful-*sounding*'; it is at least worth noting that Ovid, one of Virgil's most acute readers, reuses 847 in his own extended description of Somnus at *Metamorphoses* 11.618–19 *tardaque deus grauitate iacentes | uix oculos tollens iterumque*

---

[19] For further discussion of the line see H. Offermann, 'Vergil, *Aeneis* 5.847 und die Pali-nurusepisode', *Hermes* 99 (1971), 164–73, arguing that *uix attollens . . . lumina* is to be taken of Palinurus' struggle against sleep, pointing among other things to *Aen.* 4.688–9 *illa grauis oculos conata attollere rursus | deficit* (Dido's struggle against death).

iterumque relabens . . .[20] Like Palinurus and Aeneas, the reader also is called upon to make sense of the signs (the words on the page) in front of us, and there is more than one way of doing that.

I want to end by peeling off yet another of the layers that Virgil wraps round an episode based ultimately on Homeric models. Both the moral choice (vigilant toil over easeful sleep) and the intellectual choice (how to judge appearances correctly) are accompanied by a number of Lucretian echoes, that give a light philosophical colouring to the whole episode. *placida quiete* in 836 is a Lucretian collocation (*De rerum natura* 1.463), here contrasted with the *labor* (845) to which Palinurus is committed. On a large scale the *Aeneid* tells of the need for the hero Aeneas to continue with his labours in the face of recurrent temptations to find an easy way out; on the smaller scale compare Nisus' rejection in book 9 of *placida quies* in favour of an active career in a speech that contains other philosophical colouring.[21] The clause introducing the speech of Somnus at 842, *funditque has ore loquelas* echoes Lucretius' prayer at *De rerum natura* 1.39–40 *suauis ex ore loquelas* | *funde* ('pour sweet words from your mouth'), addressed to a Venus who has the power to reduce the active Mars to an amorous languor, and who at the very beginning of the poem is introduced as the goddess who brings calm weather.[22] The terms in which Palinurus questions the reliability of the calm weather announced by Somnus are themselves Lucretian: with the language of 848–51 compare *De rerum natura* 2.559 *subdola cum ridet placidi pellacia ponti* ('when the deceitful seductiveness of the calm sea smiles'), and 5.1004–5 *nec poterat quemquam placidi pellacia ponti* | *subdola pellicere in fraudem ridentibus undis* ('nor could the deceitful seductiveness of the calm sea lure anyone into danger with its smiling waves'). Finally Aeneas' realization that the ship is drifting aimlessly is also expressed in Lucretian language: with 867 *fluitantem errare* compare *De rerum natura* 3.1052 *atque animi incerto fluitans errore uagaris* ('you drift, floating on the aimless wanderings of your mind'). Lucretius is talking of mental error and, as often, using maritime imagery; as we have seen there is irony in the fact that Aeneas is able

---

[20] This is not Ovid's only imitation of our passage: the weighty *superincumbens* (a Virgilian coinage, unless it is to be taken as two words *super incumbens*) is humorously used at *Met.* 15.21–2 *hunc superincumbens pressum grauitate soporis* | *clauiger adloquitur*, where Myscelos, already weighed down by sleep, is further oppressed by the incubus of the heavyweight Hercules. There may be a further joke in *clauiger* 'club-bearing' (*claua*); the adjective could also mean 'tiller-bearing' (*clauus*), and Palinurus goes down still clinging to the tiller of his ship (852 *clauum* = 859 *gubernaclo*).

[21] See Hardie on 9.184–5, 187, 190.

[22] *De rer. nat.* 1.6 *te fugiunt uenti, te nubila caeli* may be echoed in the description of Neptune's calming of the weather at *Aen.* 5.821 *fugiunt uasto aethere nimbi.*

to steer the ship, but is adrift in his interpretation of the fate of Palinurus. It would be wrong to describe this passage as philosophical in any rigorous sense, but one result of the allusive complexity of Virgil's poetry is that we are simultaneously offered different ways for thinking about the actions represented; we can either content ourselves with the traditional divine machinery of Homeric fictions, or we can handle the episode within a frame of Hellenistic allegory and psychology of the kind found in Lucretius.

BIBLIOGRAPHICAL NOTE

Commentaries

There are now large-scale modern commentaries in English on all of Virgil except *Aen.* 12. *Eclogues*: Coleman (1977) may still give more help to the reader trying to make sense of these mysterious poems than Clausen (1994), which contains much choice learning. *Georgics*: the two recent commentaries nicely complement each other: Thomas (1988) is especially good on the poetics and Alexandrian allusivity of the poem; Mynors (1990) displays a countryman's expertise in the agricultural technicalities and contains a wealth of other valuable material. *Aeneid* 1: Austin (1971); *Aen.* 2: Austin (1964); *Aen.* 3: Williams (1962); *Aen.* 4: Austin (1955); *Aen.* 5: Williams (1960); *Aen.* 6: Austin (1977); *Aen.* 7 and 8: Fordyce (1977); *Aen.* 8: Gransden (1976), Eden (1975); *Aen.* 9: Hardie (1994); *Aen.* 10: Harrison (1991); *Aen.* 11: Gransden (1991). Pease (1935) on *Aeneid* 4 is a colossal assemblage of material; Norden (1957) on *Aeneid* 6 is one of the classics of commentary writing. On a smaller scale R. D. Williams' commentaries on *Ecl.* and *Geo.* (1979) and *Aen.* (1973) are very user-friendly; the older two-volume commentary on *Aen.* by T. E. Page (1894, 1900) is still valuable.

Translations

Dryden's *Aeneid*, like Pope's *Iliad*, is a classic of English poetry in its own right. Virgil has set his later translators a hard challenge. All three poems are translated in verse that keeps quite close to the Latin by C. Day Lewis (Oxford, 1966; repr. 1983, with an introduction and notes by R. O. A. M. Lyne). For the *Eclogues* there is a close verse translation with notes by A. J. Boyle (Melbourne, 1976), and a stylish Penguin translation by G. Lee (Harmondsworth, 1984). For the *Georgics* there is a good Penguin verse translation by L. P. Wilkinson (Harmondsworth, 1982); and also a verse translation by R. Wells (Manchester, 1982). There are modern verse translations of the *Aeneid* by R. Fitzgerald (first published in 1984), and A. Mandelbaum (first published in 1971). The older Penguin translation by W. Jackson Knight has been replaced with that by D. West (1991), which is honest in making no pretension to reproduce the poetry of the *Aeneid* and scrupulous in its fidelity to the meaning of the Latin.

Bibliographies and other aids

Of great use are the *Aufstieg und Niedergang* bibliographies, on the *Eclogues* by W. W. Briggs for the years 1927–1977, in *ANRW* II 31.2 (1981), 1267–1357; on the *Georgics* by W. Suerbaum, for the years 1875–1975, in *ANRW* II 31.1 (1980), 395–499, and for the *Aeneid* by Suerbaum for the years 1875–1975, ibid., 3–358. The journal of the American Vergil Society, *Vergilius*, publishes annual annotated bibliographies, and there are also annual listings in *L'Année Philologique*. The *Enciclopedia Virgiliana* (6 vols, Rome, 1984–91) is an enormous and beautifully produced treasure-house for those with any Italian. Horsfall (1995) is a useful handbook, self-consciously characterized by an older style of scholarship; Martindale (1997) contains essays, many with a theoretical element, on a wide range of topics. Collections of important articles are edited by Commager (1966) and Harrison (1990). Concordance: H. H. Warwick, *A Vergil Concordance* (Minneapolis, 1975); for the more technologically minded the Packard Humanities Institute CD ROM Data Base of Latin literature allows computer searches of the text of Virgil.

SELECT BIBLIOGRAPHY

This aims to include only the most important works; items listed here are referred to in the notes by author and date.

Alpers, P. (1979): *The Singer of the Eclogues: A Study of Virgilian Pastoral* (Berkeley, Los Angeles, London).

Anderson, W. S. (1969): *The Art of the Aeneid* (Englewood Cliffs, New Jersey).

Austin, R. G. (1955): *P. Vergili Maronis Aeneidos Liber Quartus* (Oxford).

—— (1964): *P. Vergili Maronis Aeneidos Liber Secundus* (Oxford).

—— (1971): *P. Vergili Maronis Aeneidos Liber Primus* (Oxford).

—— (1977): *P. Vergili Maronis Aeneidos Liber Sextus* (Oxford).

Bailey, C. (1935): *Religion in Virgil* (Oxford).

Barchiesi, A. (1984): *La Traccia del Modello: Effetti Omerici nella Narrazione Virgiliana* (Pisa).

Berg, W. (1974): *Early Virgil* (London).

Binder, G. (1971): *Aeneas und Augustus: Interpretationen zum 8. Buch der Aeneis* (Meisenheim).

Boyle, A. J., ed. (1975): *Ancient Pastoral. Ramus Essays on Greek and Roman Pastoral Poetry* (Berwick, Victoria).

—— (1979): *Virgil's Ascraean Song: Ramus Essays on the Georgics* (Berwick, Victoria).

—— (1986): *The Chaonian Dove: Studies in the Eclogues, Georgics, and Aeneid of Virgil* (Leiden).

Briggs, W. W. (1980): *Narrative and Simile from the Georgics in the Aeneid* (Leiden).

Brown, E. L. (1963): *Numeri Vergiliani: Studies in Eclogues and Georgics* (Brussels).

Buchheit, V. (1963): *Vergil über die Sendung Roms: Untersuchungen zum Bellum Punicum und zur Aeneis* (Heidelberg).

—— (1972): *Der Anspruch des Dichters in Vergils Georgika: Dichtertum und Heilsweg* (Darmstadt).

Cairns, F. (1972): *Generic Composition in Greek and Roman Poetry* (Edinburgh).

—— (1989): *Virgil's Augustan Epic* (Cambridge).

Camps, W. A. (1969): *An Introduction to Virgil's Aeneid* (Oxford).

Clausen, W. (1964a): 'An interpretation of the *Aeneid*', *HSCP* 68.139–47 = Commager (1966), 75–88.

—— (1964b): 'Callimachus and Latin Poetry', *GRBS* 5.181–96.

—— (1987): *Virgil's Aeneid and the Tradition of Hellenistic Poetry* (Berkeley, Los Angeles, London).

—— (1994): *Virgil: Eclogues* (Oxford).

Coleiro (1979): *An Introduction to Vergil's Bucolics with a Critical Edition of the Text* (Amsterdam).

Coleman, R. (1977): *Vergil: Eclogues* (Cambridge).

Commager, S., ed. (1966): *Virgil: A Collection of Critical Essays* (Englewood Cliffs, NJ).

Comparetti, D. (1895): *Vergil in the Middle Ages*, tr. E. F. M. Benecke (London and New York).

Conte, G. B. (1986): *The Rhetoric of Imitation: Genre and Poetic Memory in Virgil and Other Latin Poets* (Ithaca and London).

Dahlmann, H. (1954): 'Der Bienenstaat in Vergils Georgica', *Abh. der Mainzer Akad. der Wiss.* (Geistesklasse no. 10), 547–62 = *Kleine Schriften* (Hildesheim, 1970), 181–96.

Desport, M. (1952): *L'Incantation virgilienne: Virgile et Orphée* (Bordeaux).

Drew, D. L. (1927): *The Allegory of the Aeneid* (Oxford).

DuQuesnay, I. M. Le M. (1976/77): 'Virgil's fifth *Eclogue*: the song of Mopsus and the new Daphnis', *PVS* 16.18–41.

—— (1977): 'Vergil's fourth *Eclogue*', *Papers of the Liverpool Latin Seminar 1976*, 25–99.

—— (1979): 'From Polyphemus to Corydon: Virgil, *Eclogue* 2 and the *Idylls* of Theocritus', in West and Woodman (1979), 35–69.

—— (1981): 'Vergil's First *Eclogue*', *Papers of the Liverpool Latin Seminar*, 3.29–182.

Eden, P. T. (1975): *A Commentary on Virgil Aeneid VIII* (Leiden).

Farrell, J. (1991): *Vergil's Georgics and the Traditions of Ancient Epic: The Art of Allusion in Literary History* (New York and Oxford).

Farron, S. (1993): *Vergil's Aeneid: A Poem of Grief and Love* (Leiden, New York, and Cologne).

Feeney, D. C. (1991): *The Gods in Epic* (Oxford).

Galinsky, G. K. (1969): *Aeneas, Sicily, and Rome* (Princeton).

—— (1996) *Augustan Culture: An Interpretive Introduction* (Princeton).

Goldberg, S. M. (1995): *Epic in Republican Rome* (New York and Oxford).

Goldhill, S. D. (1991): *The Poet's Voice* (Cambridge).

Gransden, K. W. (1976): *Virgil Aeneid Book VIII* (Cambridge).

——(1984): *Virgil's Iliad: An Essay on Epic Narrative* (Cambridge).

—— (1991): *Virgil Aeneid Book XI* (Cambridge).

Griffin, J. (1985): *Latin Poets and Roman Life* (London).

Gurval, R. A. (1995): *Actium and Augustus: The Politics and Emotions of Civil War* (Ann Arbor).

Hardie, P. R. (1986): *Virgil's Aeneid: Cosmos and Imperium* (Oxford).

—— (1993): *The Epic Successors of Virgil: A Study in the Dynamics of a Tradition* (Cambridge).

—— (1994): *Virgil Aeneid Book IX* (Cambridge).

Harrison, S. J. (1991): *Vergil Aeneid 10* (Oxford).

—— ed. (1990): *Oxford Readings in Vergil's Aeneid* (Oxford and New York).

Heinze, R. (1993): *Virgil's Epic Technique*, tr. H. and D. Harvey and F. Robertson (Bristol).

Henry, E. (1989): *The Vigour of Prophecy: A Study of Virgil's Aeneid* (Bristol).

Henry, J. (1873–92): *Aeneidea, or Critical, Exegetical, and Aesthetical Remarks on the Aeneid*, 4 vols. (London, Dublin, Edinburgh, Meissen).

Highet, G. (1972): *The Speeches in Vergil's Aeneid* (Princeton).

Hinds, S. (1987): *The Metamorphosis of Persephone: Ovid and the Self-conscious Muse* (Cambridge).

Horsfall, N., ed. (1995): *A Companion to the Study of Virgil* (Leiden, New York, Cologne).

Jackson Knight, W. F. (1966): *Roman Vergil*, 3rd edn (Harmondsworth).

Johnson, W. R. (1976): *Darkness Visible: A Study of Vergil's Aeneid* (Berkeley, Los Angeles, London).

Johnston, P. A. (1980): *Vergil's Agricultural Golden Age: A Study of the Georgics* (Leiden).

Kenney, E. J. and Clausen, W., eds. (1982): *Cambridge History of Classical Literature*, vol. 2, *Latin Literature* (Cambridge).

Klingner, F. (1963): *Virgils Georgica: Über das Landleben* (Zurich). (1967): *Virgil: Bucolica, Georgica, Aeneis* (Zurich and Stuttgart).

Knauer, G. N. (1964a): *Die Aeneis und Homer* (Göttingen).

—— (1964b): 'Vergil's *Aeneid* and Homer', *GRBS* 5.61–84 = Harrison (1990), 390–412.

Knox, B. M. W. (1950): 'The serpent and the flame: the imagery of the second book of the *Aeneid*, *AJP* 71.379–400 = Commager (1966), 124–42.

Leach, E. W. (1974): *Vergil's Eclogues: Landscapes of Experience* (Ithaca).

Lee, M. O. (1996): *Virgil as Orpheus: A Study of the Georgics* (Albany).

Lyne, R. O. A. M. (1987): *Further Voices in Vergil's Aeneid* (Oxford).

—— (1989): *Words and the Poet: Characteristic Techniques of Style in Vergil's Aeneid* (Oxford).

McAuslan, I. and Walcot, P., eds. (1990): *Virgil (Greece and Rome Studies)* (Oxford).

Mackie, C. J. (1988): *The Characterisation of Aeneas* (Edinburgh).

Martindale, C., ed. (1997): *The Cambridge Companion to Virgil* (Cambridge).

Miles, G. B. (1980): *Virgil's Georgics: A New Interpretation* (Berkeley, Los Angeles, London).

Moskalew, W. (1982): *Formular Language and Poetic Design in the Aeneid* (Leiden).

Mynors, R. A. B. (1990): *Virgil: Georgics* (Oxford).

Norden, E. (1957): *P. Vergilius Maro: Aeneis Buch VI*, 4th edn (Darmstadt).

O'Hara, J. J. (1990): *Death and the Optimistic Prophecy in Vergil's Aeneid* (Princeton).

—— (1996): *True Names: Vergil and the Alexandrian Tradition of Etymological Wordplay* (Ann Arbor).

Otis, B. (1964): *Virgil: A Study in Civilized Poetry* (Oxford).

Page, T. E. (1894, 1900): *The Aeneid*, 2 vols. (London).

Parry, A. (1963): 'The two voices of Virgil's *Aeneid*', *Arion* 2.66–80 = Commager (1966), 107–23.

Pease, A. S. (1935): *Publi Vergilii Maronis Aeneidos Liber Quartus* (Cambridge, Mass.).

Perkell, C. (1989): *The Poet's Truth: A Study of the Poet in Virgil's Georgics* (Berkeley, Los Angeles, London).

Perret, J. (1965): *Virgile*, rev. edn. (Paris).

Pöschl, V. (1962): *Virgil's Poetic Art*, tr. M. Seligson (Michigan).

Putnam, M. C. J. (1970): *Virgil's Pastoral Art: Studies in the Eclogues* (Princeton).

—— (1979): *Virgil's Poem of the Earth: Studies in the Georgics* (Princeton).

—— (1988): *The Poetry of the Aeneid*, 2nd edn. (1st edn. 1965) (Ithaca and London).

—— (1995): *Virgil's Aeneid: Interpretation and Influence* (Chapel Hill and London).

Quinn, K. (1968): *Virgil's Aeneid: A Critical Description* (London).

Quint, D. (1993): *Epic and Empire: Politics and Generic Form from Virgil to Milton* (Princeton).

Rose, H. J. (1942): *The Eclogues of Virgil* (Berkeley and Los Angeles).

Rosenmeyer, T. G. (1969): *The Green Cabinet: Theocritus and the European Pastoral Lyric* (Berkeley and Los Angeles).

Ross, D. O. (1975): *Backgrounds to Augustan Poetry: Gallus, Elegy, and Rome* (Cambridge).

—— (1987): *Virgil's Elements: Physics and Poetry in the Georgics* (Princeton).

Schlunk, R. R. (1974): *The Homeric Scholia and the Aeneid: A Study of the Influence of Ancient Literary Criticism on Vergil* (Ann Arbor).

Schmidt, E. A. (1972): *Poetische Reflexion. Vergils Bukolik* (Munich).

Segal, C. P. (1981): *Poetry and Myth in Ancient Pastoral: Essays on Theocritus and Virgil* (Princeton).

Sellar, W. Y. (1877): *The Roman Poets of the Augustan Age: Virgil* (Oxford).

Skutsch, O. (1985): *The Annals of Q. Ennius* (Oxford).

Stahl, H.-P. (1998): *Vergil's Aeneid: Augustan Epic and Political Context* (London).

Stanford, W. B. (1963): *The Ulysses Theme*, 2nd edn. (Oxford).

Syme, R. (1939): *The Roman Revolution* (Oxford).

Thomas, R. F. (1982): *Lands and Peoples in Roman Poetry: The Ethnographical Tradition* (Cambridge).

—— (1988): *Virgil: Georgics*, 2 vols (Cambridge).

Thornton, A. (1976): *The Living Universe: Gods and Men in Virgil's Aeneid* (Leiden).

Toohey, P. (1996): *Epic Lessons. An Introduction to Ancient Didactic Poetry* (London and New York).

van Sickle, J. (1978): *The Design of Virgil's Bucolics* (Rome).

Weinstock, S. (1971): *Divus Julius* (Oxford).

West, D. and Woodman, T., eds. (1979): *Creative Imitation and Latin Literature* (Cambridge).

Whitby, M., Hardie, P. R., and Whitby, M., eds. (1987): *Homo Viator: Classical Essays for John Bramble* (Bristol).

White, P. (1993): *Promised Verse: Poets in the Society of Augustan Rome* (Cambridge, Mass. and London).

Wigodsky, M. (1972): *Vergil and Early Latin Poetry* (Wiesbaden).

Wilkinson, L. P. (1969): *The Georgics of Virgil: A Critical Survey* (Cambridge).

Williams, G. (1968): *Tradition and Originality in Roman Poetry* (Oxford).

—— (1983): *Technique and Ideas in the Aeneid* (New Haven and London).

Williams, R. D. (1960): *P. Vergili Maronis Aeneidos Liber Quintus* (Oxford).

—— (1962): *P. Vergili Maronis Aeneidos Liber Tertius* (Oxford).

—— (1973): *The Aeneid of Virgil*, 2 vols. (London).

—— (1979): *Virgil: The Eclogues and Georgics* (New York).

Wills, J. (1996): *Repetition in Latin Poetry: Figures of Allusion* (Oxford).

Woodman, T. and West, D., eds. (1974): *Quality and Pleasure in Latin Poetry* (Cambridge).

Woodman, T. and West, D., eds. (1984): *Poetry and Politics in the Age of Augustus* (Cambridge).

Wright, J. R. G. (1983): 'Virgil's pastoral programme. Theocritus, Callimachus and *Eclogue* I', *PCPS* 29.107–60.

Zanker, P. (1988): *The Power of Images in the Age of Augustus*, tr. A. Shapiro (Ann Arbor).

ABOUT THE AUTHOR

Philip Hardie is a University Lecturer in Classics at Cambridge University, and a Fellow of New Hall. He is the author of *Virgil's Aeneid: Cosmos and Imperium* (Oxford, 1986); *The Epic Successors of Virgil* (Cambridge, 1993); *Virgil Aeneid Book IX* (Cambridge, 1994); and of various articles on Greek and Latin literature.

INDEX

Achilles, 56, 70
acrostics, 43
Aeneas, 80–2, 107
Aeneid: and the 'subjective style', 75; book-divisions in, 89 n. 149; dramatic qualities of, 72, 75; gendering of, 84–6; 'voices of', 77, 101
aetiology, 29 n. 7, 44, 60, 63–5
Alexandrianism, 8, 10, 16, 23, 29, 55
Allecto, 61, 62 n. 45, 73, 74 n. 89
allegory, 19–20, 31 n. 12, 38 n. 45, 42, 56–7, 92–3, 98, 111–12
alliteration, 103 n. 4, 109–10
allusion, 8, 17, 43, 55–7, 101 n. 197
Amata, 84
ambiguity, 51–2, 101 n. 196, 102
Andromache, 84
antiquarianism, 64–5
Apollonius of Rhodes, 15, 59–60, 82 n. 117
apostrophe, 110
Ara Pacis, 3
Aratus, 32
Arcadia, 25, 61
Aristotle, 32, 72
Ascanius, 68
Augustus (see also Octavian), 65–6, 69, 80, 82

basilikos logos, 8 n. 13, 20–1
biographical criticism, 2, 19, 33
Bion, 10
bugonia, 38

Callimachus, 16, 17 n. 46, 23 n. 60, 32, 40, 49, 59–60
Calvus, 15
Camilla, 85
Cato the Elder, 34
Catullus, 13, 21, 45, 58–9
characterization, 80–2
Cicero, 32, 34
Circe, 89 n. 149
civil war, 38, 48
Cleopatra, 85, 93
closure, 73 n. 88
Columella, 32, 33 n. 23
cosmic themes, 11, 14, 35, 93–4
cultural histories, 11, 38–9, 69–71
cyclic epic, 54 n. 4, 77

decorum, 56
didactic, 28–32, 43; addressee, 28 n. 1

Dido, 61–2, 78–9, 80, 85, 91
'divine man', 12, 20–2, 31, 36, 83
'double allusion', 41
dualism, 101 n. 193

echo, 11 n. 23
Eclogues: and realism, 9; chronology of, 24–5; dramatic quality of, 9, 26–7; landscapes of, 25 n. 69; names in, 7; title of, 5 n. 1
ecphrasis, 7, 75–7
elegy, 13–14, 46, 61
Empedocles, 31
Ennius, 41, 53–4, 63, 97
epic and romance, 74
Epicureanism, 12, 22
epyllion, 45
Eratosthenes, 32
ethnography, 35, 38, 70
etymology, 43, 66
exile, 66

farming, 29 n. 4, 33–4
Fate, 73, 75, 77, 95–6
'focalization', 75, 79 n. 107
foreshadowing, 77 n. 103
Forum of Augustus, 68 n. 68, 99
framing devices, 26, 45
funerary epigram, 108
furor, 63, 73, 78, 85, 99–101

Gallus, 13–16, 45–6
generational continuity, 37, 67–9
genre, 6, 14, 42–3, 57–63; hierarchy of genres, 1, 28, 61 n. 37
gens Iulia, 64
Georgics: and epic, 40–2; date of, 35
gigantomachy, 94
Golden Age, 21, 30, 39, 52, 69
Golden Bough, 97

'Harvard' and 'European' schools of criticism, 50–2, 94, 99–100
Heinze, Richard, 1 n. 1
Hellenization of Rome, 70–1
Hercules, 83
Herodotus, 95
heroes, mortality of, 82–3
heroism, 81
Hesiod, 20, 29–30, 36–7
Homer, 42, 46, 53–7, 81, 87

homoeoteleuton, 111
homoeroticism, 85 n. 135

imagery, hunting, 91; literal and figurative, 91; military, of farming, 34 n. 31, 36
imitation, see allusion
in medias res, 72
'interpreting characters', 79 n. 108
inversion, 88, 90
Iopas, 98
irony, 76–8

Janus, gates of, 73
Julius Caesar, 5, 22, 35, 68
Juno, 62, 73, 84
Jupiter, 72–3, 95–6

kingship, 82
ktistic epic, 64

Lavinia, 84
love and sex, 12, 31, 37, 47, 91
Lucretius, 10–12, 14, 22, 30–1, 41, 44, 49, 51–2, 54, 91–2, 113–14

Maecenas, 35–6
Magna Mater, 85
Marcellus, 69, 106
metamorphosis, 44
Milton, 10, 63 n. 45
mysteries, 47, 96

narratology, 71 n. 82
neoterics, 10, 15, 46
Nicander, 29
night scenes, 106–7
nox erat topos, 109
numerology, 24 n. 63, 49 n. 96, 90 n. 152

Octavian (see also Augustus), 1, 19, 24, 28, 31, 35–6, 47–8, 93
Odysseus (Ulysses), 22, 70, 82
Orpheus, 11, 18 n. 49, 45–8
otium, 12–13, 22, 43
Ovid, 15, 22 n. 59, 58, 72, 112–13

Palatine temple of Apollo, 36
Pallas, swordbelt of, 76
paradox, 51, 58 n. 20, 102
Parthenius, 15
pastoral, definitions of, 4–10; in *Aeneid*, 60–1; in *Georgics*, 42–3; song-contests, 16–18

patronage, 2
Penthesilea, 78–9
Philitas, 10, 43
philosophy (see also Epicureanism, Stoicism), 52, 54, 98–100
pietas, 100
Pindar, 41
poetic genealogies, 14–16, 39–41, 53
poetic initiation, 7, 13 n. 33, 14, 17
poetry books, 23
Pollio, 10, 20 24 n. 65
polyphony, 26, 52, 101
'proems in the middle', 15, 40
propaganda, 2
Propertius, 54

recusatio, 16, 40
religion, 47, 65, 95
repetition, 74, 103; formulaic, 87–8
rhetoric, 95, 96 n. 176
riddles, 18, 21
ring-composition, 88, 107–8
Rota Virgilii, 1 n. 1
ruler-cult, 83 n. 128

sacrifice, 52
saviour figure, see 'divine man'
Servius, 13, 45
ship of state, 107
Silius Italicus, 57 n. 16
similes, 61, 90–1
Stoicism, 52, 82, 98, 99

'theme and variation', 109 n. 12
Theocritus, 6–9, 60
Theophrastus, 32
theoxeny, 60
tragedy, 46, 62–3, 78, 91; Roman, 63
Trojan origins of Rome, 64, 70
Turnus, 63 n. 46
typology, 93 n. 167

Ulysses, see Odysseus

Varro, 32, 64 n. 52, 66
uates, 18, 29, 97
Venus, 85–6
Virgil, as universal poet, 57; life of, 1–2, 19, 98
Vulcan, 97

writing in the pastoral world, 17 n. 46

INDEX OF CHIEF PASSAGES DISCUSSED

Eclogues **1**: 1, 26–7; **2**: 8 n. 10, 10 n. 22; **3**: 9 n. 17, 11 n. 24, 16 n. 44, 18 n. 50; **4**: 20–1; **5**: 7, 17, 21–2; **6**: 14–16; **7**: 16, 19 n. 51; **8**: 9, 24 n. 65; **9**: 17–18; **10**: 13–14

Georgics **1**: 29–30; (1–42): 36 n. 36; (118–59): 30; (145–6): 51; (169–75): 36 n. 39; (351–463): 32 n. 18; (466–514): 35 n. 33
2 (136–76): 34 n. 30; (458–540): 31 n. 14
3 (1–48): 40–1; (242–83): 31 n. 16; (322–38): 32 n. 19; (478–566): 31 n. 15
4 (116–48): 43; (315–558): 44–8; (559–66): 48 n. 89

Aeneid **1** (1–11): 55 n. 7, 65; (33): 63; (34–296): 72–3, 77, 93–4; (148–53): 92; (314–68): 62, 78; (498–502): 62 n. 41, 79
2: 67–8, 69; (589–623): 99

3 (97–8): 56; (294–355): 67, 84 n. 131
4: 61–2
5: 68; (835–71): 104–14
6 (14–37): 76 n. 100; (450–76): 88; (679–892): 53–4, 74, 98–9; (692–3): 58; (756–892): 96; (847–53): 71; (893–8): 97
7 (37): 59; (601–40): 73; (641–817): 65
8: 60, 65, 66–7, 92–3; (184–305): 83, 92; (314–36): 69–70; (626–731); 76 n. 101, 97
9 (77–122): 85 n. 136; (176–449): 69 n. 72; (598–620): 70
10 (1–117): 95–6; (163–214): 65 n. 59; (464–73): 83
11 (225–467): 96 n. 176
12 (791–842): 74, 96; (919–52): 73, 99–101

New Surveys in the Classics

Regular subscribers to the journal *Greece and Rome* receive a volume in the New Surveys in the Classics series as part of their subscription. The following volumes are also available to purchase as books.

Volume 36 *Roman Oratory* (ISBN 0521687225)
Volume 35 *The Second Sophistic* (ISBN 0198568819)
Volume 33 *Reception Studies* (ISBN 0198528655)
Volume 32 *The Invention of Prose* (ISBN 0198525234)
Volume 31 *Greek Historians* (ISBN 019922501X)
Volume 30 *Roman Religion* (ISBN 0199224331)
Volume 29 *Greek Science* (ISBN 0199223955)
Volume 28 *Virgil* (ISBN 0199223424)
Volume 27 *Latin Historians* (ISBN 0199222932)
Volume 26 *Homer* (ISBN 0199222096)
Volume 25 *Greek Thought* (ISBN 0199220743)
Volume 24 *Greek Religion* (ISBN 0199220735)

LaVergne, TN USA
09 October 2010

200023LV00003B/1/P